FINANCING YOUR NEW OR GROWING BUSINESS

How to Find and Raise Capital for Your Venture

RALPH ALTEROWITZ
AND JON ZONDERMAN

EP
Entrepreneur Press

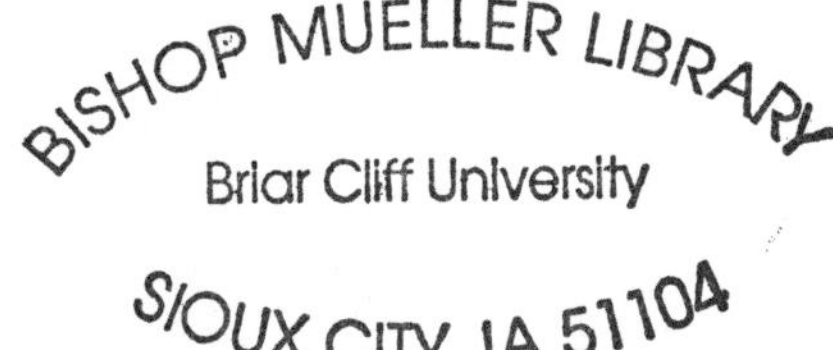

Editorial Director: Jere Calmes
Cover Design: Beth Hanson-Winter
Composition and Production: Eliot House Productions

Library of Congress Cataloging-in-Publication
Alterowitz, Ralph.
Financing your new or growing business: how to find and get venture capital/Ralph Alterowitz and Jon Zonderman.
p. cm. (Entrepreneur mentor series)
ISBN 1-891984-53-3
1. Venture capital—United States. 2. New business enterprises—United States—Finance. 3. Business enterprises—United States—Finance. I. Zonderman, Jon. II. Title. III. Series.
HG4963.A38 2002
658.15'224—dc21 2002020547

Printed in Canada

09 08 07 06 05 04 03 02 10 9 8 7 6 5 4 3 2

Table of Contents

INTRODUCTION
The Never-Ending Quest for Capital

Most entrepreneurs who start a business think the venture is going to make them rich. A few say they are primarily interested in seeing their ideas or visions become a reality, but they still want to build a lucrative, successful business.

This eternal optimism is spawned by America's unique blend of democracy and capitalism. America has the most robust and open flow of capital in the world, allowing almost anyone who would like to start a business to find the cash to do so.

But the reality of entrepreneurship, including the often difficult tasks of accessing capital, often dampens dreams. The hard truth is that half of all new businesses created each year go out of business in the first four years. They succumb to competition, lack of a viable market, inability to take a technology past the prototype stage, or a lack of capital. Many close simply because the entrepreneur runs out of energy to maintain the business; after all, operating a small company is all-consuming, a 24/7 way of life.

Sometimes, if the company is good at what it does and gets lucky, it will be bought by a larger company that has the deep pockets to take the products or processes to the next level.

The majority of companies that make it past infancy into corporate adolescence do so without engaging in a public stock offering. Their stock remains closely held. Sometimes this is by design; other times it's because no investor has been willing to help the entrepreneur realize the vision.

Only a few entrepreneurs—perhaps one in 5,000 or 10,000—will ever get rich from the initial public offering of their company's stock.

Small Business Capital Needs

According to federal government data, there are approximately 7.4 million small businesses (those with fewer than 500 employees) in the United States. Almost 80 percent of them have ten or fewer employees. Small businesses account for about 99 percent of all businesses in the United States, employ about 54 percent of workers, and generate about 52 percent of the country's gross domestic product (GDP).

Most new jobs in the United States are created by businesses with under 500 employees.

Most new jobs in the United States are created by businesses with under 500 employees. In 2000 and 2001, even as large companies were shedding workers, the nation's unemployment rate did not skyrocket because smaller companies were soaking up much of the talent being let go.

Where's the Money?

Every new company needs money to get started, whether it's $5,000 to launch a home-based crafts business, $500,000 to open a new restaurant, or $5 million to take a bit of technology developed at a university laboratory to the first stage of commercial development.

The business press likes to focus on the last of these three kinds of companies, because technology and innovation are sexy, and innovation combined with the need for money attracts the most serious investors—professional venture capitalists—interested in nurturing such companies.

But again, the truth is far different than the dream. The vast majority of new-business owners, like owners of small companies in general, will never meet a professional venture capitalist interested in their company. Most entrepreneurs have to look for less glamorous solutions for their capital needs. In order for owners of new, small, or growing companies to raise capital, they need to engage in a long process of understanding who they are, what their company is, what their capital needs are, and what the best solutions to these needs are.

This book is about venture funding in the real world, the world beyond the snazzy offices on Sand Hill Road, the world where mom and dad and the guy who sells supplies to you on credit are your venture capitalists, the world that most entrepreneurs really inhabit.

> In order for owners of new, small, or growing companies to raise capital, they need to engage in a long process of understanding who they are, what their company does, what their capital needs are, and what the best solutions to these needs are.

Venture Capital Climate

During the first three months of 2000, venture capital (VC) companies were pouring an enormous amount of money into start-up and early-stage ventures, a trend that had been building since about 1997. Most of the beneficiaries of this wild VC spending spree were dotcom companies, those taking advantage of the revolution in computer-to-computer communications brought about by the Internet and the World Wide Web.

These companies leveraged their intellectual capital in information technology and focused on capturing and manipulating information, and on creating computerized trading markets for goods and services, often in an effort to sell more cheaply than traditional intermediaries in the distribution system. For a while, they grew wildly and achieved astronomical stock-market valuations when they became publicly traded companies.

VC firms, eager to get in on the ground floor of "the next Amazon.com," abandoned their tradition of waiting to invest until there was a viable product. It seemed that anyone with a new company whose name ended in ".com" was guaranteed millions of dollars in start-up investment, where three years earlier he would have

VC Payout

According to Venture Economics and the National Venture Capital Association, the heyday for VC firms cashing out of investments lasted exactly one year, from the fourth quarter of 1999 to the third quarter of 2000.

In the third quarter of 1999, VC firms distributed $3.7 billion from sales of entrepreneurial companies to other companies or IPOs to limited partner investors in the form of cash and publicly traded stock. In the fourth quarter, that figure nearly tripled to over $10.6 billion.

The peak came in the first quarter of 2000, when the payout was $18.7 billion. By the fourth quarter, the payout had shrunk to $6.8 billion, and by the second quarter of 2001 it was barely $2.1 billion.

been passing the hat among friends and family for seed capital.

The dotcom bubble began to deflate in March 2000, and by the spring of 2001 less than half as much money was being invested in such companies as during early 2000. That trend continued as public-stock investors continued to punish dotcom companies, killing some and crippling many more. The market for initial public offerings (IPOs) of common stock essentially dried up for much of 2001. VC firms took enormous sums out of IPOs from late 1999 to the middle of 2000, but then reality set in (see sidebar above).

Venture capitalists did not simply drop their interest in businesses because of the poor outlook. They were increasingly forced to hold available funds as reserves to shore up weak companies in which they had made earlier investments. This gave them less money to invest in new companies. In addition, they moved away from funding start-ups because of the added risks. VCs were also often putting much more of their time into working closely with these companies.

They were also forced to spend time trying to extract value from these companies by selling them to other companies (often competitors) that were looking to purchase technology, even if they lost money in the transactions.

Now that the dotcom bubble has burst, entrepreneurs looking for early-stage capital are again turning to friends, family, and angel investors for their first funding, just as they did in the 1980s and early 1990s.

Now that the dotcom bubble has burst, entrepreneurs looking for early-stage capital are again turning to friends, family, and angel investors for their first funding, just as they did in the 1980s and early 1990s.

In 1999, one particular company was oversubscribed for first-round equity financing from friends and family. Rather than raise as much as it could at that time, the company took the advice of its financial advisor and raised only as much as it had originally hoped to. The advisors and founders thought they had enough money, and since it had been so easy to raise the capital they were convinced they could always raise more if necessary.

But in late 2000, when the company went back to the friends and family capital market, it could only raise one-third of the amount it needed. The investing climate had dramatically changed, and the venture capitalists' cupboards were bare.

The World After 9/11

While the terrorist attacks against the United States in September 2001 did not directly affect the venture capital climate *per se*, they did change the psychological climate throughout the business world. From large corporations to small businesses, executives and business owners—like other Americans—have rethought the priorities in their lives. The pace of life for many is different. The balance between office, home, and community has shifted.

How exactly this will play out for the next generation of those seeking funding for businesses based on new ideas is not known. By the end of 2001 VC investing was beginning to pick up, and VCs were successfully raising funds from wealthy investors and institutions.

The annual MoneyTree survey conducted by PricewaterhousCoopers, Venture Economics, and the National Association of Venture Capitalists found that VC firms invested $7.1 billion in the fourth quarter of 2001, the first quarter-over-quarter increase after five successive quarter-over-quarter declines that had taken VC investments down from their record of $26.3 billion in the second quarter of 2000.

To be sure, in 2002 VCs and angels are less exuberant than they were three or four years earlier, but they are still eager to invest in high-quality business concepts that have the potential to reach large markets and change the way people go about their lives.

The bursting of the dotcom bubble began the country's descent into its first recession in a decade, and the events of September 11 magnified and solidified that economic downturn. In all recessions, borrowing becomes more difficult, especially for companies and individuals without a solid track record. While interest rates in general came down sharply through 2001, banks, finance companies, leasing companies, and others have today returned to the fundamentals of credit in the loans they make, which makes bootstrap funding (discussed in the fourth section of this book) all the more difficult yet all the more important.

In short, for those whose frame of reference for financing new and growing businesses is the period from 1995 to 2000, today is a new era.

How This Book Is Organized

This book is structured to provide you with a wide spectrum of financing opportunities for a new or growing business. They are all, to one degree or another, sources of "venture" capital or "risk" capital in that they provide

Where are Entrepreneurs Going?

In its 20th annual Small Business Survey, conducted in early 2002, Dun and Bradstreet found that the dotcom meltdown had forced entrepreneurs to change how they funded their new businesses. Far more business start-ups were funded using various forms of borrowing in 2001 than in 2000.

In 2001, 15 percent more entrepreneurs used trade credit to fund their start-up than in the previous year; 11 percent more borrowed using company credit cards and 5 percent more borrowed using personal credit cards; 10 percent more took out personal bank loans and 9 percent more used commercial bank loans; 3 percent more borrowed from family or friends; and 2 percent more used their business's accounts receivable as collateral.

Also, 16 percent more entrepreneurs used money from their own savings to start their companies in 2001 than did so in 2000.

capital for risky, entrepreneurial ventures. The book moves from the most glamorous options—equity investments by professional investors, semiprofessional angels, and amateur friends and family investors—to the least glamorous option—bootstrap financing through equity loans on your house, loans against accounts receivable, and even credit-card financing.

> The ultimate goal of most entrepreneurs is—and should be—to create a large business.

Entrepreneurship and the financing that allows it to occur is cyclical, like every other aspect of our dynamic economy. In periods where professional VC firms are hunkering down, entrepreneurs might have sought VC financing in times of easier financing need to reach out more to angels, and those who in better times would have attracted attention from angels must look to friends and family and bootstrap financing (see sidebar above).

The book begins with a discussion of the universe of private investors who will invest with you in exchange for equity (a portion of ownership) in your venture. While it is true that most entrepreneurs rely overwhelmingly on debt (borrowing) to raise capital, most successful entrepreneurial businesses outgrow their ability to expand through internally generated capital and debt. They simply must broaden the pool of investors willing to risk their capital. Many entrepreneurs also round up some equity investments from friends and family, then use that money to leverage further borrowing and investment.

The ultimate goal of most entrepreneurs is—and should be—to create a large business. Entrepreneurial businesses are like sharks in that they need to keep moving (i.e., growing) or eventually they will die. Any business person seeking to create and grow a large business should seek to eventually sell stock to the public (although it must be said that more than a few of the country's largest and most successful companies are still privately owned) or sell the company to a larger, publicly traded company.

Section I of this book, chapters 1 to 12, discusses the progression of equity investors whom entrepreneurs turn to as they seek to raise ever larger sums of money for their ventures. It covers friends and family, angels—sophisticated individual investors who invest in new ventures—and professionally managed VC funds. It describes each type of investor's traits, how to find them, and what kind of relationship they usually wish to have with the venture.

The last chapter in Section I covers the various forms of investment agreements; private placements through individual term sheets or private placement memorandums, direct public offerings, reverse mergers, and full-fledged IPOs.

Section II, chapters 13 to 19, describes the range of business partners who might be willing and able to help finance your company, either through taking an equity position, extending trade debt, or engaging in an alliance or licensing agreement.

Section III, chapters 20 to 22, focuses on funding you can receive from various government agencies.

Section IV, chapters 23 to 28, presents the many bootstrap financing techniques, from using your personal credit cards to selling the company's accounts receivable.

Finally, Section V, chapters 29 to 33, talks about the ins and outs of negotiating with potential investors and lenders, and how to "do the deal."

At some point in your search for capital you will be asked to invest the time, energy, and possibly money necessary to prepare a detailed business plan. While this book does not include a discussion of writing a business plan, there are literally dozens of books available on that subject.

We have also created a set of tools, forms, and exhibits that you can download from www.venturetechcorp.com.

Interested in downloading the tools, forms, and reference materials found in this book so you can modify them for your personal use?

Visit

www.venturetechcorp.com

On this site you may also

- submit a question for online answer
- view other people's questions and the answers provided
- view additional material of interest to entrepreneurs
- link to other sites for entrepreneurs
- provide your own "war stories" about raising capital

SECTION I

▲ ▲ ▲

EQUITY INVESTORS

CHAPTER

1

THE ENTREPRENEUR PROFILE AND GAME PLAN FOR RAISING CAPITAL

KNOW YOUR FINANCING NEEDS

There are many ways to raise money for your start-up or young business. Some are more productive than others. The key to raising capital is understanding who you are, what your company is, and the positive and negative attributes of all the individuals and institutions that provide capital.

Too often, entrepreneurs approach almost anyone they think has money as a potential investor and continue to pursue anyone who gives them the slightest bit of encouragement. Those who have been through the capital-raising effort know that most of these apparent opportunities are dead ends.

Hunting for money to fund your business must be thought of in cold, calculating terms. Preparing pitches and traveling to meet "potential investors" who have little to offer is a waste of time and money. The longer you try to raise capital through different channels, the more shopworn your business proposal becomes and the more your venture takes on the reputation of one that can't raise funds.

Most entrepreneurs do not think in an organized way about raising capital. But, they should. To create a game plan, you need to crystallize your attributes and those of your company, and target investors who have an affinity with one or more of those attributes. By defining yourself and your company you will be able to segment the investor universe and spend your time, money, and energy pitching to investors who have the highest probability of a payoff.

You can start by using the *Entrepreneur Profile* (Appendix A) to develop your capital-raising strategy. Again, by knowing yourself better you will be able to target potential investors for your venture. The entrepreneur profile addresses many of the same issues you need to discuss in your company's business plan, but focuses more on you and your venture as an extension of you, rather than on you as the company manager.

The profile has nine questions, each of which demands some level of analysis.

1. Who are you as an entrepreneur?
2. In what geographic area do you want to start your venture?
3. What type of business are you in?
4. What and where is your market?
5. What round of financing are you seeking?
6. How much money do you need?
7. What do you need the money for?
8. How quickly do you need the money?
9. Are you looking for debt or equity capital?

Take an activist, evangelical approach to raising capital; target high-probability and high-success sources of capital.

Who Are You as an Entrepreneur?

When looking for capital, who you are can be as important as what you wish to do with the money. Most money is raised through networks. Closely examining your demographic particulars can help you determine if there are specific people or institutions who might want to help with your capital-raising efforts.

As crass as it may seem, your ethnic and other personal demographic characteristics can help you secure financing. Take advantage of any particular trait you have that can help you get the cash you need for your vision to become a reality. This is worth doing regardless of your philosophical point of view about universalism versus ethnic, religious, or racial particularism.

For instance, you may see yourself as an entrepreneur, not as a "woman entrepreneur." But you'd be smart to capitalize (pun definitely intended) on your gender. There are an increasing number of angel investor networks, as well as federal and state programs, that target women entrepreneurs for loans and equity investments. These are discussed throughout the book in the context of particular capital-raising techniques.

It is also worth looking into special programs if you are African American, Hispanic, or Asian. The Small Business Administration (SBA), for example, works to funnel capital to minority businesses. Government agencies also often set aside a portion of all contracts or subcontracts on public projects for minority- or women-owned small businesses.

> As crass as it may seem, your ethnic and other personal demographic characteristics can help you secure financing.

In addition to these formal programs, there are informal networks that focus their investment efforts on particular groups of entrepreneurs. Some groups specialize in funneling private investment dollars to entrepreneurs who graduated from the same college, university, or business school. The Asian immigrant community has long utilized informal networks in which individuals put a particular amount of money into a common fund each month. Every three or four months the fund is loaned out at low or no interest for a period of time—or simply given as seed capital—to a network member to start a new business.

Investor groups also form around other affinities, such as executives in a particular industry or full-time angel investors from a specific geographic area.

What Geographic Area Do You Want to Work In?

All states and some counties and municipalities have programs designed to attract businesses. These may include tax incentives, such as state corporate income tax credits or a local property-tax phase in (where the personal property tax begins very low, and gradually increases until it reaches its full level); low-interest loans; or access to community development block grant (CDBG) or other federal funding that is distributed locally.

In addition, many investor organizations only invest in businesses that are local, statewide, or regional. Locating in an area with an abundance of other small or start-up companies provides you with the advantage of a critical mass of entrepreneurial spirit, as well as a group of professional service providers used to dealing with entrepreneurs.

All states and some counties and municipalities have programs designed to attract businesses.

Business Type

Will your venture produce goods? Will it provide services? Will it engage in research and development, and possibly the marketing of custom devices, systems, or processes?

It is important to articulate the exact nature of your business, especially one that is highly technical. This enables you to search for venture capitalists who know and understand the technology. It can also help you determine if you are a candidate for other capital-raising strategies, such as licensing the technology or entering into a joint venture or technology partnership, joint marketing arrangement, or other form of strategic alliance.

Since the mid-1980s, professional VC firms have become increasingly specialized. Many focus their investments on a single area of technology, such as drug delivery systems or photo-optics. They also understand how difficult and expensive it is to take a sophisticated new technology to market and often try to fund companies that have at least begun to explore the myriad of strategic options they can engage in with larger companies with more marketing resouces.

Market

Understanding your market can lead you to new sources of funding. For instance, in the mid-1990s, a group of entrepreneurs was working on a new cardiac screening device. In the course of traveling through eastern Europe, they discovered some knowledge about the high incidence of cardiac problems there. Back in the United States, they approached a foundation focused on developing solutions to problems in eastern Europe and won major funding to test the new technology in that part of the world.

Finance Round

Venture financing is described as happening in "rounds." The first round of financing from sources outside the entrepreneur's own pocket is usually called "seed" funding. Some entrepreneurs are able to put up enough money themselves to cover the seed round, while others actually need money for the "preseed" round.

Preseed and seed funding usually cover office, workshop, and/or laboratory space for the first 6 to 12 months of operation, as well as salaries for a couple of staff. Part of the entrepreneur's seed investment is often working for no pay for the first few months, or even the first year.

After the seed round, there are usually one to four rounds of private equity investment, with each round being a larger infusion of capital. Then, if the company is still growing, has actual products and revenues, and has not become a target for a purchase by another company, the investors usually consider an initial public offering of stock.

There are only a few courses that deal with raising capital for a start-up. So create your own. Find a VC professional who will spend time with you helping you understand his or her process and criteria for making an investment.

How Much Money Do You Need?

The amount of money you need helps determine the kind of capital you go after. For instance, if you need \$100,000 or even \$500,000, don't target your sights on professionally managed VC funds; they generally don't make investments that small. The exception might be smaller regional funds or federally sponsored Small

Business Investment Companies (SBICs), discussed in chapter 20. On the other hand, if you need more than $1 million, you are outside the range of any of the SBA's loan programs.

Most investments of under $1 million come from individual angel investors or from pooling smaller investments made by friends and family members.

Part of the entrepreneur's seed investment is often working for no pay for the first few months, or even the first year.

What Do You Need the Money For?

Are you raising money to support research and development (R&D), buy equipment, hire personnel, develop prototypes, or begin product marketing? Investors often provide funds for specific uses, and some shy away from particular uses. For instance, "general operating expenses" doesn't tell a potential investor much about how you will use his funds. If you are looking for R&D funding, you might consider one of the many federal programs that provide low-interest loans or outright grants, such as the Small Business Innovation Research (SBIR) program. Also, consider government programs that require your technology and award contracts for its development. How long is the money expected to last; and will it be enough to reach important milestones?

Debt or Equity

The most important question for an entrepreneur looking to raise capital is whether to take on debt (borrow money) or sell equity to outside investors (have investors put up money that does not have to be paid back in exchange for a percentage of the ownership interest in the company).

The SBA's Office of Advocacy reported that in 1995 small businesses raised 93 percent of their capital needs through simple forms of debt and 7 percent through equity. In contrast, large companies (those with more than 500 employees) raised 83 percent of their capital needs through sales of securities (both equity in the form of stock and debt in the form of bonds) and only 17 percent through traditional debt such as bank loans, commercial mortgages, finance company debt, and trade debt.

Many entrepreneurs take on $100,000 or more of personal debt to start their businesses and put as much as half of their net worth on the line. Almost 90 percent of entrepreneurs start their businesses with their own personal assets. Many also rely on the personal assets of friends, family, and cofounders.

It is not uncommon for company founders to take out second mortgages or refinance their homes, to take personal loans pledging other assets as collateral, to borrow against retirement funds, and max out one or more personal credit cards.

Some equity investors initially provide funding in what is known as a debt-to-equity swap. This is a loan that converts to a predetermined equity ownership position as performance milestones are reached. For instance, an angel investor might agree to make a $500,000 loan to your company, at the prime rate plus 10 percent interest per year. Four milestones are set, and at each milestone, $125,000 of the loan, plus any accumulated interest, is converted into 5 percent of the company's stock.

If some or all of the milestones are never reached, the entrepreneur must pay back the portion of the initial loan, with interest, that was not converted into equity.

You have to analyze a lot of trade-offs to determine whether you want to go with debt financing or equity financing. In either case, your financier will have some level of control over your ability to make business decisions and maneuver your company. Whoever provides the funding will, to some degree, become a partner in your business and management decisions. While an equity investor has direct input into your decision making

Assess your entrepreneurial assets. Set up feedback sessions with your banker, attorney, accountant, etc. After you have described yourself and your venture, have them behave as potential investors and ask questions. Do the same with someone from your local Small Business Development Center.

Many entrepreneurs take on $100,000 or more of personal debt to start their businesses and put as much as half of their net worth on the line.

(usually by controlling seats on your board of directors), a lender doesn't have that level of control.

How Quickly Do You Need the Money?

If you need money quickly, it will probably be easier to get debt financing than an infusion of equity since negotiating the specifics of a sale of equity can take a long time. Some banks make loan decisions relatively quickly, but if you don't have collateral you may not secure a loan, and if you do, the interest rate can be onerous.

There are a number of ways to raise money quickly, ranging from borrowing from a family member or friend to selling your accounts receivable at a discount.

Chapter Key Points

- There are many ways to raise money for a start-up or growing business.
- An entrepreneur needs a game plan for raising money.
- Understanding yourself as an entrepreneur is important to raising money successfully.
- There are nine key questions to ask about yourself and your business when developing a money-raising game plan.
- You must be willing to put your own financial resources at risk in order to get investments or loans from others.

CHAPTER

2

THE EQUITY-INVESTOR UNIVERSE

DIFFERENT INVESTORS MEET YOUR DIFFERENT NEEDS

Unless you are incredibly wealthy, it is nearly impossible to grow a large company using only your own capital and loan proceeds. Most businesses that grow large enough to become publicly owned have to find private equity financing at some point in their growth cycle.

To be sure, if you are going to start a business, you must invest some money in it. Any professional investor in private equity deals will want an entrepreneur to have some of their own money at risk—commonly referred to as "skin in the game."

If you have the free cash to invest, so much the better. But you may have to borrow in order to start your business. This doubles the risk. Finding a way to get cash to put up for your entrepreneurial venture is often referred to as "bootstrap financing."

Equity Investors

For growth financing that is beyond your own means, you will generally turn to one of four classes of equity investors:

1. Friends and family members
2. Wealthy angels investors
3. Professional VC firms
4. Investors in business development companies (BDCs) and other venture-oriented mutual funds.

To fully understand the differences among these various investors, it is also important to know the life cycle of a new venture and its need for cash. This chapter describes the various types of equity investors, which are discussed in detail in later chapters, then puts them each in the context of the venture life cycle.

Remember, all of these investors want an equity position in your company. That means that in order for you to get access to their money, you will have to sell a piece of the company to them. This is an important point. Think back to how you answered the questions in the entrepreneur profile. As you go out and search for capital, be mindful of the trade-offs involved in raising capital and maintaining operating and ownership control of your company. (In reality, professional venture capitalists and even angel investors usually structure a deal in a complex fashion in which they take a special class of stock that gives them special rights in the event your company fails. They convert this "preferred" stock to common stock over time.

Friends and Family

By far the largest pool of outside investors in new and young companies are the founder's family and close friends. This is especially true for entrepreneurs who do not have dreams of IPO grandeur but aim to establish companies that will always be privately held.

Friends and family members are the easiest investors to find, approach, and persuade to invest.

Friends and family members are the easiest investors to find, approach, and persuade to invest. They often invest on the entrepreneur's conviction about the venture, rather than on a rigorous analysis of a business plan.

That is not to say that friends and family cannot be a powerful source or early-stage financing for entrepreneurs who wish their companies to get big and want to stay out of the clutches of the large VC firms. (See chapters 3 through 5 for more on friends and family.)

Angels

Entrepreneurs also turn to angels for seed funding (seed funding is usually for amounts under $500,000).

Angels are wealthy individuals who invests in companies even though they have little or no personal relationship with the entrepreneur before making the deal. Angels are semiprofessional venture capitalists. They generally invest on their own, although they may team up in informal groups to fund a particular venture.

Some angels are entrepreneurs themselves, people who have started, operated, and then cashed out of lucrative businesses. They may use their investment as a way to nurture a new company and mentor an aspiring entrepreneur, without having to live the new venture day-to-day.

It's harder to estimate the exact size of the angel community than it is the VC community, since VC firms have some level of regulatory paperwork they have to do. But estimates are that each year angels put as much money into new and growing businesses as venture capitalists do.

For 1999, each group invested between $30 and $40 billion. In the years leading up to 1999, angels probably invested more than VCs; 1999 was during the peak of the dotcom-bubble years, when many VCs were investing gargantuan sums in rank start-up companies. During 2000 and 2001, as the dotcom bubble was imploding, both VC and angel investments in new companies declined. At the same time, VCs put much of their capital into companies they had already invested in in an effort to salvage some of those investments. This left start-up businesses to go to angels, as they had in the years leading up to the dotcom frenzy.

At any time, there are about a half million angels actively looking to put money into entrepreneurial businesses, out of between two and three million angels who have made an investment at some point. Angels invest in some 50,000 deals a year, about ten times as many invest-

Angels are wealthy individuals who invests in companies even though they have little or no personal relationship with the entrepreneur before making the deal.

ments as the funds operated by VC firms. Eighty percent or more of angel investments are made in start-up or seed-stage deals. (See chapters 6 through 8 for more on angels.)

Professional Venture Capitalists

Professional venture capitalists are the managers of VC funds. A VC fund is a pool of money raised from a small number of wealthy individuals and institutions such as pension funds, universities, or foundations. The fund is closed, meaning that once the desired amount of money is raised, no more investors can get into it. The fund has a finite lifetime, at which point the value of the fund is disbursed to the investors.

VC funds are usually established as limited partnerships, with the passive investors being limited partners and the professional managers being general partners. The professional managers collect an annual fee for conducting the fund's business. They usually own a portion of the fund as well, and share in its gains or losses just like the passive investors.

A VC fund is a pool of money raised from a small number of wealthy individuals and institutions such as pension funds, universities, or foundations.

A VC firm may operate a number of funds, opening a new one to a new group of investors as soon as the previous one has been fully subscribed. Funds are typically $50 to $500 million per fund, although some funds are getting close to a billion today. Each fund maintains a managable portfolio of investments to monitor and to cash out of when it comes time to disburse proceeds to investors. It is going to be interesting to see if VC funds become smaller again now, after the dotcom crash and the market gyrations that accompanied the terrorist attacks of September 11, 2001.

Over a period of time—usually two to four years—the fund's managing partners invest the pool of money in a number of new or young and growing companies. In exchange for the cash the VC fund invests, it receives equity in the company (a portion of the company's stock). (See chapter 12 for more on how the typical VC deal is structured.) Many VC firms also take seats on the company's board of directors.

The VC firm's goal is to make the most money possible for its investors. VC funds try to achieve cumulative annual returns of 25 to 30 percent, although they usually do not pay out on an annual basis but rather when the fund is dissolved. In order to do this, the fund's managers try to invest in companies that will eventually have their stock publicly traded through an initial public offering (IPO) or that will be sold to a publicly traded corporation.

The VC firm's goal is to make the most money possible for its investors.

In reality, very few companies that receive VC funding actually engage in an IPO. Some are sold to companies that are already publicly traded—which is almost as good. Others remain modest privately held companies, in which case the venture capitalists usually sell their positions back to the entrepreneurs. Still others close their doors.

Companies that are destined to attempt an IPO often go through three, four, or even five rounds of private financing before that is accomplished. The majority of VC firms do not provide start-up and seed-stage funding, which is usually $100,000 to $500,000.

According to PricewaterhouseCoopers' Money Tree Survey, of the $36 billion invested by VC firms in 1999, about $1 billion—less than 3 percent—was start-up and seed funding. VC funds are far more likely to make investments of $2 to $10 million in a company that has used seed funding to prove its concept, create a product, and even generate a few early sales. In all, VC firms invest in *fewer than 5,000* deals each year.

Professional venture capitalists generally don't invest in start-up companies because of the higher degree of risk. In addition, the amount of due diligence work involved is the same for a $500,000 investment as for a $5 million investment, and the rewards are not as great.

Venture-Oriented Mutual Fund Investors

Investing in a VC fund used to be for the very rich only. The Securities and Exchange Commission (SEC) only allows VC firms to market their closed funds to "sophisticated investors," who the SEC defines as those with over $1 million in individual (not family) net worth or over $200,000 per year in income. And many VC funds insist on a minimum investment of $1 million, $2 million, or even $5 million for a spot in one of their funds.

> *By the time you finish defining yourself and your business, you will find that you may never need to deal with a VC firm. This will enable you to spend your time and money most effectively seeking capital from more appropriate sources.*

But smaller investors are now able to invest in private placements and diversify their holdings without having to go through the work involved in making a private deal as an angel. They do this through investing in one of the kinds of funds that make VC investments.

One such fund is a business development company, a closed-end mutual fund that has a fixed number of shares and trades like a stock on a stock exchange.

Another vehicle is a so-called private equity fund of funds. These are mutual funds that the SEC allows to have a maximum of 500 investors. Minimum investments are between $250,000 and $1 million. These funds then spread their pool of money among firms that specialize in a number of investment vehicles, including venture capital and leveraged buyouts of public companies.

Still a third vehicle is to find a traditional mutual fund that has begun dabbling in private venture investments. The SEC allows mutual funds to hold up to 15 percent of their investments in positions that are not liquid—meaning they do not trade on an exchange. A number of specialized funds, mostly technology funds, have begun either putting money into VC funds or making VC-type investments in individual companies.

The Life Cycle of a New Business Venture

Starting from ground zero, there is a natural progression of funding sources you look to when trying to raise capital. These are shown in figure 2-1.

First there is you. Then there are your family and close friends. Next come the angels. Finally, there are VC professionals. As you track along this continuum from left to right, it's important to understand a few things.

First, the more "professional" the potential investor, the more objective the analysis of your prospective venture will be.

Second, your cost of capital increases as you move along the funding food chain.

Third, your preparation costs increase as you move farther up the funding food chain. These variables are shown in figure 2-2.

FIGURE 2-1 Progression of Funding Sources for a New or Young Business

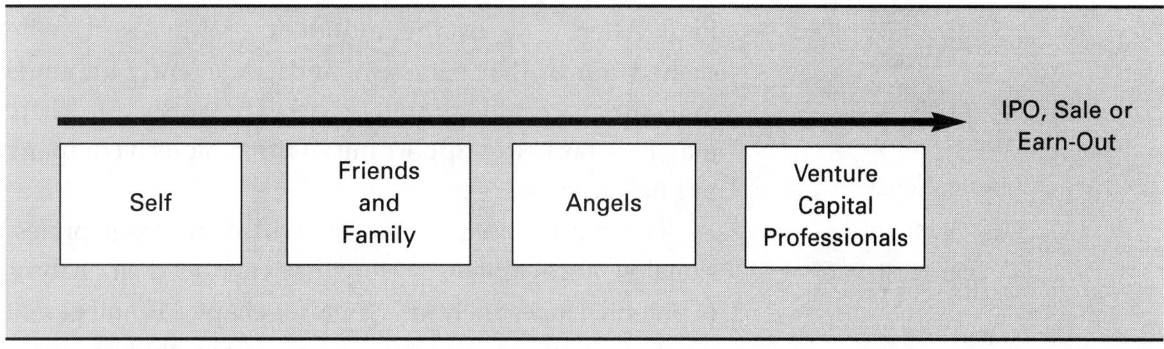

FIGURE 2-2 Progression of Funding Sources and Characteristics of Funding Decisions

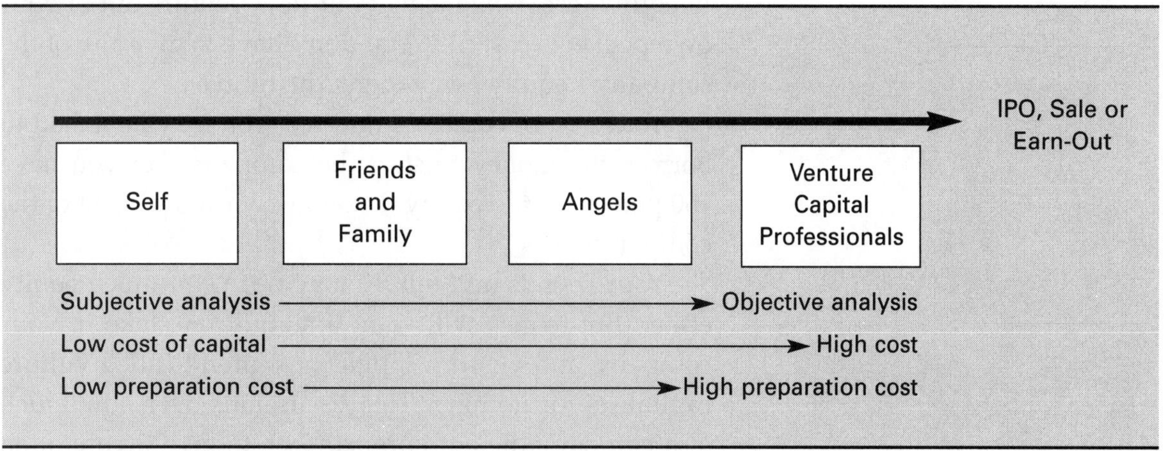

Subjective to Objective Analysis

Your analysis of your venture is purely subjective. If you didn't believe in your business concept, you wouldn't invest your time money in it. But that doesn't mean your idea will make a successful business. Your friends and family can't be expected to be objective either. Their relationship to you taints their ability to objectively analyze the merits of your idea.

Angels are theoretically objective. But even they are in a position where their personal preferences (the kind of business they had been in previously, etc.) and their psychological makeup, draw them toward certain kinds of investments over other kinds. For instance, Paul Allen, one of the founders of Microsoft, who cashed out of that company and is currently an angel investor, naturally gravitates toward software. There may be a far better opportunity with a biotech company but he's a software guy.

The most objective analysis will come from a professional venture capitalist.

The most objective analysis will come from professional venture capitalists. How they conduct their analysis of potential investments is a topic for chapter 11 and part of the discussion of what venture capitalists want from you.

Equity Cost of Capital

In equity terms, financing your new venture out of your own pocket is cost free. You don't have to give any of the company's equity away to get the funds.

Your cost of capital is not free. You may have had to borrow the money to start the company. But you have 100 percent of the equity (i.e., you own 100 percent of the company).

Your friends and family may not want much equity either. But angels will want a significant stake in your company, and venture capital pros aren't called vulture capitalists for nothing. The discussions over how much of a company the entrepreneur has to give up are often the most knotty in the relationship between funders and entrepreneurs.

It's also important to remember that if you give away too much equity too early, there may not be enough left over to get the last round of funding necessary to take the company to the final stage before going public.

That's why it is so important to think about the end of the funding process before taking the first step. As you plot your company's first five years, try to match the staging of equity investments to the milestones you hope to reach. Each milestone reached successfully should reduce your cost of raising more equity capital.

Angels are theoretically objective.

Preparation Costs

The third variable in equity sales by entrepreneurs to investors is the preparation costs involved. Again, you don't need any contract with yourself, so your preparation costs for getting equity from your own pocket are little beyond those of incorporating and setting up a set of business accounting books.

As you seek investments from outsiders, however, there can be significant costs in legal fees to draw up the appropriate documentation for the investments. Depending on what route you choose—unregulated agreements with individuals or regulated agreements with a limited number of investors who are solicited—you will need to have prepared either individual term sheets, an investment memorandum (known as a private placement memorandum), or a prospectus. The cost of negotiating terms can go into the thousands of dollars (lawyers are expensive). But this is a fraction of the cost of preparing an IPO, which can be up to 10 percent of the amount being raised in legal and investment banking fees (most of which goes to the investment bank that underwrites the offering).

Investor "Fit"

Whomever you select as an investor, that person or a person representing that company, will be with you for a long time. When looking for investors, you need to go through a screening process, just as you would if you were hiring a key employee. A key investor may merely wish to touch base every week or two, or may be on the phone with you constantly, and in the office two or three times a week, haranguing you over every little matter.

When looking for investors, you need to go through a screening process, just as you would if you were hiring a key employee.

If your initial impression of a potential investor is that you can't work with that person, don't take the money. You should not be willing to take capital from someone who will be nothing but grief in the future.

In addition to getting a sense of personal fit, it is important to determine what an investor can contribute to your company in addition to providing capital. Does the investor have contacts with suppliers, marketing support, a network of others who might provide future financing, or some other important capability? If you can't determine this before the person invests, there is little likelihood you will find out later.

The "Fit" Analysis

Before accepting an investment, do a fit analysis of the investor. This enables you to select investors who are most compatible with you and your business. The fit analysis has four elements, which are:

1. The potential investor must be compatible with the nature of the business. This means being familiar with the business model and the technological universe the business is working in (i.e., a potential investor with a background in computer hardware may not be the best fit for an e-business company that focuses on distribution of health care products).
2. The potential investor must be capable of, and enjoy, executing in the desired position. When

speaking with investors who would like some involvement in the company's operations, look for people who fill gaps in the current management or operating structure.

3. You should be able to interact with the investor in a manner that is not totally focused on business. If you can't have dinner with the potential investor and talk about your family and hobbies, find someone else. You will be working 18-hour days but should still be able to disengage for a few moments.
4. The potential investor must be able to get along with the senior management and operating staff. If this person is going to be an integral part of the organization, she has to be able to talk with others besides you.

Start with efforts that are easy to win. They help season you through experience. When you succeed your confidence increases.

The bottom line is that a potential investor has to become a part of the team, in a capacity that is consistent with the business functioning well. In one business, an entrepreneur needed capital, and the one person who was willing to invest would not budge from having a 50 percent vote in major decisions.

The investor was a full-time professional in another company in a completely unrelated field and was not involved in the entrepreneurial company's day-to-day operations. Yet he persisted in overriding the entrepreneur's judgment in critical business decisions. The company eventually bogged down and was unable to find future capital investments.

You should never allow yourself to be handcuffed with oppressive stipulations made by investors. Such stipulations are more frequently problems with angel investors and friends and family than with professional venture capitalists.

The bottom line is that a potential investor has to become a part of the team, in a capacity that is consistent with the business functioning well.

Some of these issues are intangibles—like karma—of a personal relationship. Others are issues to be negotiated

Entrepreneur Self Test

Your business plan and capital-raising pitch will be judged on eight major elements. Judge each on a 1 to 10 basis (10 being highest). If your plan and pitch doesn't garner an eight or better on at least five criteria, you will have trouble attracting financing.

1. *Management.* For most professional venture capitalists, and many angels, the three most important elements of a prospective investment are management, management, and management. Is your management team the strongest it can be?
2. *Innovation.* What is your new business's claim to fame? Is it new technology, a breakthrough in quality or production process, or a marketing innovation?
3. *Market potential.* Is your market big? Is it easily defined? Is it unserved or underserved?
4. *Expansion potential.* Does your innovation have potential to go beyond its immediate market? Can it be incorporated into many products, services, or processes?
5. *Financial projections.* Can your business generate $100 million in revenues annually within five years? Are your projections credible given the market and expansion potential?
6. *Impact.* Does your business have a substantive and easily quantifiable impact on a particular locality or region? This is especially important if you seek funding from angel networks or VC firms that specialize in making regional or local investments.
7. *Ability to raise capital.* No investor wants to think he is the only one willing to bet on your business. The more people competing to invest, the more you will be able to raise.
8. *Skin in the game.* How much of your own capital is at risk? How much are you willing to put at risk to get an angel or VC firm to invest?

during the formalization of the business relationship. (See chapters 29 and 30 on the specific sections of a private investment agreement, and chapter 31 on negotiating.)

Chapter Key Points

- There are four classes of equity investors: friends and family, wealthy angel investors, professional VC firms, and investors in business development companies and venture-oriented mutual funds.
- Friends and family are usually the easiest investors to find and to convince to invest in your company.
- Angels are often entrepreneurs themselves and can be extremely helpful in ways other than simply providing investment capital.
- Professional venture capitalists make investments specifically to earn a high rate of return—25 to 30 percent annually for the life of the investment.
- Investor "fit" is an important concept. If you cannot work with a potential investor, you should not accept capital from that person.

CHAPTER

3

WHO ARE FRIENDS AND FAMILY?

NEVER LOSE THE TRUST OF THOSE CLOSE TO YOU

Once they've generated all the capital they can through personal savings, many entrepreneurs turn to friends and family to raise money for their businesses.

The term "friends and family" actually has two meanings. One is literal, and the other is a legal term with a specific definition.

The literal meaning of friends is people with whom you have a close relationship, based on an enjoyment of each other's company and personal attributes. The literal meaning of family is those people related to you by birth or marriage.

The legal meaning of friends and family, however, is embodied in the federal securities laws. It is a term used to define a relationship between a person looking to raise capital and someone willing to invest capital.

Those who fit the legal definition of "friends and family" may be offered an opportunity to make a private investment in your company without you having to go through the rigorous process of registering the sale of equity securities with either federal or state securities regulators. Securities regulations are discussed in more detail in chapter 12.

Three Ways to Get Capital from Friends and Family

There are three ways you can raise capital from friends and family. Each way has unique advantages, yet all the methods share the same potential disadvantages. The three ways are:

1. Loan
2. Gift
3. Equity sale

Loan

Nothing says you can't accept a loan from a friend or family member. In fact, family members probably loan as much money to their entrepreneur relatives as banks do.

A loan from a family member or friend has at least three advantages over a commercial loan. First, the lender rarely asks for any collateral on the loan. It is purely a personal loan. Second, the loan can be made quickly. You can have a discussion with your Uncle Mike one morning and deposit a check in your company's account that afternoon. Third, many loans from friends or family members are written at a below-market interest rate. As long as the interest is equal to what the lender would receive on a comparable bank deposit, the reduced interest is a legitimate gift. (See the sidebar on reduced-interest gifts, page 29).

One resource everyone has is their address book. Use yours.

Gift

Gift taxes, if any are due, are paid by the person making a gift. Any individual is allowed to give a gift of up to $10,000 per year to any other individual without incurring a gift tax. That means that your parents, for instance, could give you a gift of $20,000 ($10,000 from each) to help jump-start your business. In fact, they could give you gifts of $20,000 on December 24th and another $20,000 two weeks later without incurring a gift tax.

Or, they could write you a loan where your annual interest payment is under $20,000. Each year, after your company pays the interest on the loan, they could turn around and give you back the interest amount as a gift for that year (you do have to write the check for the interest, for tax and accounting records). If they wrote you a three-year loan with a 9 percent interest rate, they could loan you almost $200,000, and all the interest you paid annually could come back to you as a gift. (In order for them to return the interest to you as a gift, they need to set the interest rate at what a bank would charge for a comparable loan. Or, they could reduce the interest rate, and consider the reduced rate as the gift, as discussed in the sidebar on page 29.)

The gift tax (a federal tax) is tightly intertwined with the federal estate tax, and a person can choose to make gifts totaling the amount of the federal estate tax exemption while he or she is alive without incurring a gift tax (however, in this case the estate tax exemption would have been waived). Such gifts can be made over and above the annual $10,000 tax-free threshold.

One way of presenting your business opportunity to friends and family is to give them an alternative (e.g. would you prefer to invest in my company or give me a loan?). This bounds the person's thinking so he or she is more likely to say yes to providing you with capital in some way.

That means that a person could give a total of $1 million in tax-free gifts in 2002, increasing to $3 million in tax-free gifts in 2009, as the federal estate-tax exemption increases. Currently, the gift tax is slated to remain in some form even after the estate tax is repealed in 2010. With these tax-law changes enacted in 2001, the timing of such large gifts must be well thought out. Careful planning among the giver, the recipient, and their respective tax advisers is important.

Equity

Friends and family are also frequently called on to become equity investors early in a company's life.

You can usually receive equity money quickly from friends and family. They already have a relationship with you and therefore may not look critically at your business plan. This also means that you will usually get favorable valuation terms for the business (i.e., friends and family won't ask for as large a stake in your business as angels or professional venture capitalists would).

Mixing Business with Friends and Family

The disadvantages of turning to friends and family for capital have to do with the potential for disturbing the current relationships among you. Because the investment is so clearly being made in you as a friend or relative and not completely on the virtues of your business plan (although there may be many), there can be emotional distractions in the course of growing the business.

These distractions can cause business or personal conflicts. Regardless of whether the capital was contributed as a loan, a gift, or an equity investment, someone who is close to you may feel he or she has more of a right to have a say in the way you run your business. If the business goes sour, there may be recriminations. If angels or professional venture capitalists who invest later negotiate favorable conditions, early friends-and-family investors may feel that you did not protect their interests adequately.

The disadvantages of turning to friends and family for capital have to do with the potential for disturbing the current relationships among you.

Create a Business Relationship

To minimize the potential for confusion and future problems in your relationship with a friends-and-family source of capital, it is imperative that you use a business approach in dealing with such an investor. This approach goes beyond defining and committing to writing the terms of your financial agreement. It means that you work with any friend or family investor and treat that person as you would a purely business contact.

Many entrepreneurs immediately think: "I can't do that, I've known Mike for years," or "It will turn Aunt Sadie off if I do that." But you need to change both your mindset and the mindset of your friend or family investor.

When money comes into play, the relationship will change, whether you want it to or not. By being explicit at the outset that the business aspect of the relationship is separate, you are able to move the relationship in a positive direction, rather than simply reacting to harsh feelings later.

> Successful interactions with friends and relatives who invest in your business demand that you lay the groundwork.

Successful interactions with friends and relatives who invest in your business demand that you lay the groundwork. The first step is to tell any prospective investor that this matter is separate from the other aspects of your current relationship. For you it is important that the potential investor consider the investment on its merits. You want him or her to judge you as a potential entrepreneur on those qualities, not simply on your current relationship.

Of course, we all know friends and family members won't be able to completely ignore their prior relationship with you. And that's okay; as you'll see in the chapters about angel investors, many of them are willing to invest in entrepreneurial companies for reasons that are not purely financial (i.e., to help their local or regional economy, invest in alumni from their university, or to foster entrepreneurship among women or minorities). If someone wants to give you "an extra five points" or a "gold star" for being a friend or a family member that's OK. But the fact of your friendship or kinship should not be the sole basis for the investment decision.

You should set up a meeting with the potential investor, just as you would with any other investor to present and discuss the investment opportunity. Prepare for that meeting by analyzing the friend or family member investor as you would any third-party investor. Consider the kinds of business-related conversations you have had with the person, the person's level of financial and investing sophistication, and other factors. Make the presentation simple and straightforward.

The meeting should be held when it is convenient for the prospect. Make it separate from any nonbusiness event, such as a family dinner, and dress in appropriate business attire. If the prospective investor works outside the home, try to meet during a work day when it is convenient (i.e., early morning, lunch, or immediately after work) at the prospect's place of business, and dress appropriately to that person's work (i.e., business casual if that person owns a small retail business or manages a production plant; suit and tie for men, or suit, pantsuit, or skirt and blouse for women if the prospect is a corporate executive or professional).

Prepare appropriate documents for the friend or family prospect to review, including a business plan or

A Gift of Reduced Interest

Friends and family members can combine a loan to an entrepreneur with a gift. They can do this by writing a loan at a reduced interest rate. The low interest rate is, in effect, a gift.

Banks earn income by taking deposits and paying interest on them, then loaning out the money at a higher rate of interest. The difference between the interest the bank pays on deposits and the interest it charges on loans is called the "spread." As long as the person making the loan charges interest equal to the amount he or she would earn on a bank deposit of the same size and duration, reduced interest is a legitimate gift.

For example, your sister could lend you $100,000 for a period of three years. As long as she sets the interest rate equal to or above what her money would earn if placed in a three-year certificate of deposit (CD) (about 4 percent in early 2002), it is a legitimate gift.

In contrast, if you could get a bank to write you an unsecured loan for three years in early 2002, the interest rate would probably be the Prime Rate plus 4 to 6 percent, or between 8.5 and 10.5 percent.

That's a difference between paying your sister $4,000 in interest and paying the bank between $8,500 and $10,500—over $4,000 in savings. Even if your sister asked for a little above the bank CD rate to compensate for the risk, she still would charge you less than a bank would.

prospectus and basic agreements and term sheet (term sheets are discussed in chapter 12). For example, if the prospect has said she might be interested in making a loan, you should come to the meeting with a written loan agreement that states the loan amount, interest rate, repayment terms, and the lender's rights should you not fulfill your obligations. Terms should be negotiated, just as with any other lender.

As you speak with friends, family, and angels, it is a good idea to determine their particular backgrounds and affiliations, and leverage them into opportunities to meet others.

A relative may decide to give you money as a gift. This does not lessen your responsibility to conduct yourself as a business person and have the same type of meeting you would with a potential friend or family lender or equity investor, at which you make your presentation and state your business case. Should the gift materialize, write a formal thank-you letter that restates what you are using the money for (people who give gifts often like to know what they helped buy).

If you are receiving an equity capital infusion, create a term sheet just as you would for an angel investor with whom you have no previous relationship. During the meeting, the terms will be discussed and possibly negotiated. The term sheet should state clearly such things as the equity investor's rights in terms of the company's operations and the investor's level of involvement, which may include a position on the board of directors or an advisory committee.

A key part of the meeting should be the discussion of risk. Be clear that there is no guarantee the investor will get his or her money back, let alone a return on the investment. Before accepting money on any terms from a friend or family member, explain as clearly as possible, both verbally and in writing in the documentation you provide, the level of risk to their investor's capital that exists from the investments in your business. Make sure your benefactor has the financial ability to put this money at risk. This risk should be made clear again before signing and perhaps even a third time.

Friends and family are a valuable and vital source of funding for entrepreneurs, yet they are often underrated. Entrepreneurs do not tend to address this universe of potential financial support methodically. They think of several people and approach them willy-nilly. Without an organized approach, two things are likely to happen.

> Friends and family are a valuable and vital source of funding for entrepreneurs.

1. Many potential friends-and-family investors are never identified, and therefore not considered and approached. The next chapter outlines a methodology for identifying and approaching such investors.
2. Friends and relatives become alienated, and relationships become strained or even ruptured, either because an individual was not invited to participate or felt that he or she was not warned adequately of the risks of participation. Many friends and family members (especially relatives) will say that "you don't need to go through the whole song and dance for me." However, they will respect you for acting like a business person and appreciate your treating them as a serious, sophisticated investor and not just like dear, old Uncle Mike.

Chapter Key Points

- Friends and family can be a valuable source of capital for an entrepreneur.
- Prospective friends and family investors should be treated in a businesslike manner, as you would any other investor.
- Prospective friends and family investors need special attention when it comes to discussions of business risk. They may say they don't need to hear it, but they do.
- Friends and family can often utilize gifts and estate-tax exemptions that angel investors or venture capitalists could not or would not use to structure deals that are advantageous to both them and you.
- When working with friends and family investors, you will often create the terms under which the transaction will take place. Be fair.

CHAPTER

4

FINDING FRIENDS AND FAMILY

EFFECTIVE NETWORKING IS THE KEY

The concept of "finding" friends and family may seem odd. Friends and family are "just there."

But when conducting a search for capital for your entrepreneurial business, it is important to separate the friends and family who are "just there" from those who may be legitimate sources of loans, gifts, or equity infusions for your company.

We sometimes use the analogy of net fishing, or "trawling," to create an image of the search for capital. You cast your net into the water, then as you move your boat (company) forward, you catch a number of fish. When you haul the net aboard, you realize that many of the fish you've caught are not the ones you were after (not appropriate investors).

As any commercial fisherman will tell you, the key to having a successful fishing trip is not necessarily the size of the net you use, but where you fish. You don't really know how large your fishing ground is for friends and family until you organize them into lists of potential targets. Later, when you go fishing for angel investors and professional venture capitalists, you will use bigger nets.

It's All About Relationships

Look at the relationships and networks in your daily life. These can be called "membership" networks. They include social clubs, religious groups, fraternal organizations, local chapters of business and technical groups, and trade associations. There is also a host of school-related groups, including alumni associations, faculty relationships, or college fraternities.

In planning the campaign to raise money from friends and family, it's easiest to think about who you know by separating them into groups. These groups can be labeled and sorted by your areas of activity or interest. For example, you may have friends among your co-workers, neighbors, fellow religious congregants, and college alumni. The same approach can be used to identify your relatives. Some people you know may be placed in more than one category. You may consider some people friends even though you interact infrequently.

> In planning the campaign to raise money from friends and family, it's easiest to think about who you know by separating them into groups.

One convenient way to organize your universe of friends and family is by creating a matrix. Along the side (the y axis) list all of your affiliations through which you might have contacts. Across the top (the x axis) list how frequently you have contact with these people. This matrix is shown in figure 4-1.

Figure 4-1 is a worksheet for use in identifying the individuals in your friends-and-family network. You can personalize this matrix by adding subcategories where necessary. For instance, under alumni, you may have contacts from high school, college, and graduate or professional school whom you want to separate. Or, under religious, perhaps you have contacts in your own congregation, as well as through a noncongregational group you participate in, such as a state or regional denominational organization or a community interfaith organization.

After you have created this matrix, reshuffle it into four charts, each one containing a list of people with whom you have contact at different intervals (we use at least once a week, at least once a month, once every three or four months, and less frequently).

As you create your list of contacts, you can also determine if any of those people provide you with "second order" or "once removed" contacts, fitting into the

FIGURE 4-1 Friends and Family Network

Name	Affiliation or Activity	Frequency of Contact			
		Weekly	Monthly	3-4 Months	Less Frequent
	Academic				
	Alumni				
	Arts				
	Theater				
	Symphony				
	Other				
	Civic/Community				
	PTA				
	YMCA/JCC				
	Other				
	Ethnic				
	Family				
	Aunts/Uncles				
	Cousins				
	Parents				
	Siblings				
	Neighbors				
	Local Politics				
	Professional Assns.				
	Religious				
	Service Providers				
	Lawyer				
	Doctor				
	Other				
	Retail				
	Car maintenance				
	Dry cleaner				
	Hair				
	Restaurants				
	Social				
	Book club				
	Cooking/Dining				
	Dancing				
	Other				
	Sports/Athletics				
	Golf				
	Gym				
	Racquet sports				
	Running/Walking				
	Swimming				
	Other				
	Work				

acquaintance category. They can be listed in a different color or on a different chart, with a reference to the intermediary. For instance, your sister-in-law's uncle Harry, whom you have only met once (at your brother's wedding) might be a good person to approach. He knows your brother and sister-in-law well enough, since he sees them every Christmas at your sister-in-law's folks, so he will at least recognize your name. You can even ask your brother or sister-in-law to give him a "heads-up" that you are going to call, or you can send him some documentation and follow that up with a call.

An intensive effort aimed at either those who you know through a particular activity or those you have the most frequent contact with can reap substantial rewards in terms of prospective financial backers. Try to gather a little background information on each person you identify as a potential prospect. This will help you tailor your approach and draft your script for the initial discussion.

The downside of having a large number of friends and family who all know each other is that if one person is turned off by your presentation, it could spark dissatisfaction among a large group.

Friends and Family Presentations

There are a couple of advantages to having a large group of potential friends-and-family investors.

First, you can use the presentations you give these people as practice sessions or "dry runs" to hone your skills for when you try to acquire capital from more "professional" sources, such as angels and venture capitalists.

Second, because you can be less formal, it is possible to do a small group presentation for people with whom you have the same affinity relationship (e.g., a group of first cousins or the Wednesday night cooking club).

The downside of having a large number of friends and family who all know each other is that if one person is turned off by your presentation, it could spark dissatisfaction among a large group.

You can minimize the chances of this happening in a couple of ways.

1. Before you take your presentation to potential investors, "road test" it with some people you don't expect will be investors and whom you trust to give you honest, constructive feedback.
2. Work your presentations to friends and family among a widely dispersed group. Don't simply go through all of your contacts from work, then all those from churches, then all those from the book club. Choose one member of each affinity group from whom you think you have the best chance of attracting an investment.

Remember also that these people are close to you and want you to succeed. Take their criticism as constructive and not as a personal attack. At the end of every meeting, even if the person expresses no interest in exploring the idea further, ask if he or she knows of anyone who you should approach or who might be able to help you further refine your business plan and/or revenue model.

Someone, whose friend Jack knows a lot about the industry in which you are trying to start or grow a business, might be willing to invest later if Jack says your idea is good. It's even better if Jack invests or comes on board as a consultant or advisory board member. Whenever someone agrees to become an investor, ask that person if you may use his or her name as a reference for other potential investors, or if he or she would be willing to speak with other potential investors about making an investment.

Whenever someone agrees to become an investor, ask that person if you may use his or her name as a reference for other potential investors, or if he or she would be willing to speak with other potential investors about making an investment.

Friends and Family Capital

Raising money through friends and family is the cheapest way to get capital. Terms of any agreement are usually more favorable than with angels or professional venture capitalists; negotiations are less time-consuming; and there are no commission costs for intermediaries. It is definitely worthwhile to expend the necessary time and energy to do a professional job with your presentations and discussions and thereby increase your possibility of success.

Also, if the people who you gather into your friends and family net are not able or willing to back you, chances are at least a few of them have access to angels.

Chapter Key Points

- When looking for friends-and-family investors, cast a wide net.
- Categorize your friends and family by your affiliations and relationships.
- Use a matrix to define relationships. Determine how frequently you have contact with the people on your lists, and which people can provide you with "once-removed" contacts as well.
- Use friends and family as a training ground to develop and fine-tune your pitch for later use with angels and venture capitalists.
- Always end a meeting by asking if the person you have spoken to knows of anyone who might be interested in meeting with you as a potential investor.

CHAPTER

5

WHAT DO FRIENDS AND FAMILY WANT FROM YOU?

TREAT FRIENDS AND FAMILY IN AN ARMS-LENGTH FASHION

"Whatever you give me is OK."

"I know you'll be fair."

"I trust you."

You may hear any one of these comments, a variation of one, or possibly even all three, from a family member or friend when you begin discussing the equity share you will give in exchange for an investment in your company.

Family members and close friends invest in your company because they like you, think you're bright, or want to give "one of their own" a helping hand. Although some may see an opportunity to get in on the ground floor of something that could be big, return on their investment is not the primary motivation for investing in your company. This is true even for your family or friends who may also invest in other companies as arms-length angels.

Generally friends or family will accept your documentation for the friends-and-family stock offering, which is known as a private placement memorandum (PPM) as presented without much question. A PPM is a simple version of the full prospectus that must be issued with a public sale of stock. A PPM or a stock prospectus states the cost per share to the investor as well as the rights the investor has as a stockholder. The PPM also includes disclosure about the company's current financial state, its plan for the future, and a statement of the risks involved in the investment.

If you are going to sell stock to a number of friends and family members, each prospective investor must be given the same offer, and the offer must be exempt from registration with the federal Securities and Exchange Commission (SEC). A lawyer must draft the PPM and it must be marketed to investors in such a way that it falls into one of the exemptions for stock offerings under securities laws. This will be discussed in more detail in chapter 12.

Some friends and family will not want to bother reading disclosure documents and may even say they do not need or want a formal agreement. It's up to you to make sure they do read the disclosure and understand the risks involved in investing in your company. It's your obligation to see that there is a formal written agreement, and that it has been created, signed, and notarized to make it legal and binding.

Some friends and family will not want to bother reading disclosure documents, and may even say they do not need or want a formal agreement.

Differences in Motivation

Let's look at the differences in motivation between family members and friends who invest in your company.

Family

Family members usually want to help, and they want to see someone in their family succeed. In most cases, entrepreneurs come to family members with an investment opportunity; family members don't often approach entrepreneurs looking for a way to invest their money. Family members expect that their entrepreneur relative will give them as good a deal—or possible a better deal—than they would give an unrelated investor. Of course, this is not possibly, since friends and family who are approached in the same time frame about investing must be allowed to do so under the terms of the same private placement memorandum.

Most relatives will accept the terms offered. Their thinking is that the entrepreneur would not take advantage of them. The basis for their investment is trust and family loyalty.

The entire deal can usually be closed in a few phone calls or over a meal. A formal presentation is rarely needed, although it's a good idea to request that you make one. There are two reasons to give your family members a presentation. First, it helps them understand the risks involved in the investment. Second, it's good to practice in front of a friendly audience; their questions, including the silly, naive ones they ask because they feel close to you, often point to holes in your presentation or even in your business plan.

Friends

Friends are more likely to treat an investment in your company as an arms-length transaction. They may want an attorney or business counsel to review your documentation and provide advice. You do have a relationship of trust with them, but unless they are your closest friends, they will probably use the old Reagan-administration adage about nuclear weapons, "Trust but verify."

Friends are more likely to treat an investment in your company as an arms-length transaction.

Terms

Friends and family most often help fund a business that is either a rank start-up or very close to that stage. You may have done some work and spent some money on equipment and/or business services, but your business probably has little if any real value.

In all likelihood you have no prototype of your product (you may have drawings or specifications); no clear marketplace defined; and no prospective customers. So how do your price your shares? How do you determine what percentage of the equity in your company a friend or family should get for an investment of, say, $10,000 or $25,000 dollars.

Closing a loan or sale of equity with a family member usually takes two to four weeks; for a friend it can take two to eight weeks.

Any valuation benchmark you set will be arbitrary. Get advice from an accountant or attorney who has worked with small businesses that have received outside financing. They can help value the business realistically so you do not give away too large an equity stake or constrain your ability to make business decisions.

Before taking on your first outside investors, it is important to establish milestones the company has to reach in order to achieve higher valuations for future sales of equity. One common approach is to structure the PPM as a debt-equity arrangement, with the debt at a high interest rate and the investor having an option to convert the debt to equity during a finite period. For instance, an interest-only $25,000 loan could be written for a three-year term, with an interest rate of 15 percent ($3,750) annually, with the interest deferred for two years and the entire principal due after three years.

At any time during the three years, the lender could convert the loan to equity and refund all interest payments previously made. This allows the lender to decide over a period of time if he or she feels the company has long-term viability and wants to become an equity owner.

Closing a loan or sale of equity with a family member usually takes two to four weeks; for a friend it can take two to eight weeks. This is a lot less time than it takes to close a similar arrangement with an angel or a professional VC.

Approaching Friends and Family

Approaching friends and family should not be done casually. You need to treat them with the same care, concern, consideration, and attention you would any other potential investor.

Have a prospectus of your business (a business plan or a summary, minus the marketing hype) and a PPM

After All, What Are Friends For?

In the early 1960s, a recent medical school graduate wanted to start his own pharmaceutical company. He asked a group of classmates to invest $5,000 each in his venture. Some of his investors had to borrow money from their own families to make the investment. But he was bright, a good scientist, and they trusted him to be a good businessman.

After some years of struggling, his company became successful enough to be purchased by a publicly traded drug company. Those who stuck with the investment were rewarded with common stock in the major company. Through the 1970s and 1980s, this company became increasingly successful, and the stock split a number of times.

A series of mergers and acquisitions in the 1980s and 1990s left investors who held their stock with holdings in ever larger and more successful companies. In 1999, the company in which the small drug company then sat was bought by a global drug company based in Europe in which stock traded on that country's market was not allowed to be owned by individual foreigners. The last of the initial investors were forced to cash out of their position, for well over $2 million each.

ready. This is especially important with friends and family, many of whom would not be considered "sophisticated investors" under SEC rules. Sophisticated investors can be expected to cut through the usual hype and understand a business plan and perform enough due diligence to understand all of the business risks involved. Friends and family, given their relationship with you and level of trust, will not always do that.

Documentation must be consistent with the securities regulations in the state in which the PPM is being offered (so-called blue sky laws). If you are pitching your offer to people in different states, your lawyer needs to check the PPM against each state's regulations.

A statement of risks must be included in your offering memorandum. Each investor, including friends and family, must be given an accredited investor form to complete. If you don't have such forms when an investor hands you a check, that money should be placed in escrow until you get the form signed by the investor. In addition, each investor has 60 days in which to request a return of his or her investment.

In some instances, your legal counsel may decide that all money raised must be held in escrow until you reach your fundraising goal for that particular round of financing. You may structure your memorandum as such an "all or nothing" round of financing or leave out this clause and be free to use money as it is raised, regardless of how much is ultimately raised.

Each investor, including friends and family, must be given an accredited investor form to complete.

Guidelines

When it comes to business, your relationship with friends or family needs to be different than it is for backyard barbecues. If a friend or family member wishes to invest in your company, the transaction must be treated in a businesslike way. Your future relationship, not only with the investor but with all of his or her peers, is at stake. Try to follow these five guidelines:

1. From the first discussion about a possible investment, make it clear to the potential investor that this a business relationship, not merely an extension of the family relationship. Your relatives and some friends will tell you that is not necessary; tell them it is. Blame it on your lawyer if necessary. Tell your potential family or friend investor that your attorney said unless investments are handled strictly as business, you can get in trouble down the line.
2. Provide a potential family or friend investor with all of the same documentation you would provide an arms-length angel or a professional venture

capitalist. Ideally, you should give the person a full verbal presentation that sets forth the vision for the company and the particulars of the investment.

They may not read the documents now, or they may just browse them, but they will have them for future reference. And who knows, they may show them to someone they know who is an angel, who might want to get in on your next round of financing.

Make sure all agreements are in writing.

3. Make sure all agreements are in writing. Again, many family members and some friends will suggest that written agreements are not necessary among people with a relationship of trust. Untrue. Written agreements are always necessary; in a relationship of trust they can be completed quickly, and neither party needs to spend a lot of time or legal energy trying to create an unfair advantage through the agreement. But there should be a written document that sets out the parameters of the business relationship. Again, when all else fails, blame your lawyer.
4. Tell the potential investor to exercise the same caution and due diligence he or she would exercise if making an arms-length arrangement. Encourage the investor to talk to his or her attorney and/or accountant before committing to the investment. Some people will change their minds during the course of these discussions, and assure them up front that if they do change their minds about the investment, the personal relationship will not be harmed.
5. Find out if the investor wants to be involved in the company's operations, and if so, how. Everyone has expectations. Many angel investors want an active role in the company. So do many friends and family.

With friends-and-family investors, you need to be especially careful about matching your expectations of an investor's role with theirs. Never allow any role they take in the company's operations to jeopardize the non-business aspects of your relationship.

Put their expectations in perspective, and ask them to do the same. They may not want to hear you say you do not want a family-member investor looking over your shoulder all the time, but they need to hear it. If you can't come to terms about the role the investor wants to play, you may have to say "thank you, but no thank you" to the investment.

Chapter Key Points

- Family have different motivations for investing than friends.
- Friends and family usually invest in the newest companies, which have the largest business risks.
- Some friends, and more commonly family, will not even want to read your private placement memorandum. Make sure they do.
- Closing a friends-and-family investment is usually much quicker than closing an investment with an angel or a VC.
- From your first contact with a potential friend or family investor, the discussions should be businesslike, and agreements should be made in writing.

CHAPTER

6

WHO ARE ANGELS?

HEAVEN-SENT CASH CAN JUMP-START YOUR BUSINESS

Most people think that angels, or angel investors, are wealthy individuals willing and able to put capital at risk in other people's ventures. The term "wealthy" may be a misnomer, however. "Capital at risk" can be any amount, as low as $1,000 in some instances.

Don't think of angels in terms of the amount of money they are willing to invest in a venture; think of them in terms of their relationship to the entrepreneur. Angel investors have a less personal relationship with the entrepreneur than do friends and family but may be closer than professional venture capitalists.

For instance, one group of entrepreneurs needed $500,000 to take a new medical device to the prototype stage. They were professionals in the field in which the device would be used. Through a combination of friends, family, professional contacts, and others they raised the entire sum through investments of $5,000 or $10,000 per investor.

The investors who were "once removed" from the entrepreneurs—friends of friends, or professional acquaintances of their professional acquaintances—meet the definition of angels. This is not the typical story you read about angel investors. It is far less glamorous than the one about the entrepreneur who cashed out his company's stock and began backing other entrepreneurs at $250,000 per investment, or the retired corporate executive who started an angels club that makes investments of at least

$500,000 in each company and has three or four members who also act as company advisors and board members (these guys certainly do exist).

Remember the analogy from chapter 2, about "trawling" for capital by casting a net? While that net was only large enough to "catch" investors from among your personal relationships (friends and family) searching for angel investors requires a larger net. Such a net can catch investors from a much larger pool of prospects.

All evidence that angels will be more important in the future than they were during the go-go dotcom years of the late 1990s. With VCs funding fewer new companies and providing less funding in each investment, more early-stage investing is going to fall onto the shoulders of angels.

All evidence that angels will be more important in the future than they were during the go-go dotcom years of the late 1990s.

Many angel prospects are brought close enough to be caught in your net because they have personal or professional relationships with individuals you know, such as your lawyer, accountant, or banker. Others can be drawn in because they have some affinity for you as an entrepreneur; for instance, you live in the same metropolitan area, you attended the same college or graduate school, or your business is in an industry in which the angel has worked or is currently working.

Not all angel investors are alike. They are scattered throughout society. Angels may exist among your relatives, friends, business associates, advisors, and social acquaintances. Remember, the line between the angel and the friends and family investor can sometimes be blurry.

To you, the angels among these people fall within the realm of friends and family, because you know them personally and are able to reach them without intervention. To other entrepreneurs they are angels. In the same way, you may find angels among other entrepreneurs' friends and family.

Remember the movie *Six Degrees of Separation*? The angel investor community is somewhat akin to the

A Real Angel

Ed, a vice president of business development and contracts for a medium-size aerospace company, received settlement from an injury claim when he was 48. His salary, and that of his wife, was enough for the family to live on, so Ed decided to use his windfall as risk capital.

A few months later, a business associate suggested that he and Ed co-invest in a start-up company that manufactures industrial products. Each man invested $50,000. They set 15 percent as their target annual rate of return, compounded, and agreed that the exit strategy should be a sale to a larger company within five years.

Since making that investment in 1997, Ed has tried to make one angel investment each year. He hopes to invest $40,000 to $50,000 in each deal but once invested $100,000 in a company he found especially promising. He often co-invests with one or two other angels, especially in very risky ventures in which he wishes to invest a smaller sum.

Ed only considers deals that come from quality referrals, have a unique product advantage, have an entrepreneur who has made a significant cash investment, and where he can achieve "personal satisfaction" knowing that his investment did some good for the entrepreneur. He prefers to invest in businesses that he understands, and where he can help the entrepreneur by providing business contacts and marketing leads.

characters in that movie—everyone is connected to someone who is connected to someone else. Your task is to find out how you can use your contacts to bridge those degrees of separation and get to investors. The next chapter will include more on how to go about finding angels.

Angels as Informal Investors

Angels are often referred to—especially by academics who study them—as "informal investors." In 1981, William Wetzel, a professor at the University of New Hampshire's business school, and his colleagues began studying informal investors throughout New England. Their groundbreaking research in understanding the

> As informal investors, angels rely on methods of operation that are less formal than those of professional venture capitalists.

pool of capital represented by informal investors helped define the key differences between angels and professional venture capitalists.

During the mid- and late 1980s, capital from informal investors helped fuel the wave of East Coast technology. Professional venture capitalists across the country were beginning to pull back from investing after getting burned by failures during the early 1980s. They were also responding to changes in tax rates that occurred during the Reagan presidency (i.e., by drastically reducing the top rate of income tax, venture capital lost some of its allure as a tax shelter.)

As informal investors, angels rely on methods of operation that are less formal than those of professional venture capitalists. While they still want their risk-capital investments to be successful and generate an above-average return on investment, they don't always focus exclusively on the bottom line when deciding where to make an investment.

Angel Demographics

Many angels are entrepreneurs themselves, and veterans of the business world in one way or another. Although the informal investor population is highly diverse, it is possible to create a recognizable profile of an angel. A number of academic studies have tried to do this through large mail surveys but obtained the typical low direct-mail return rate.

Interviews conducted through the University of Maryland business school proved more successful. Over a four-year period during the early 1990s, an instructor and co-author of this book, along with several students, interviewed dozens of angel investors from the mid-Atlantic region, one of the most active angel communities in America. The study showed that the four most important demographic aspects of angels are:

- occupation
- education
- age
- gender and race

Occupation

The largest percentage, 25 percent, of angels worked in finance, either as financial managers, accountants, or nearly full-time investors. An additional 20 percent were involved more generally in "business" and another 20 percent in engineering and technical occupations.

The other 35 percent were spread among a wide spectrum of occupations, including medicine, manufacturing, building, biotech, real estate, and teaching.

Angels manage a portfolio of their own personal investments.

Education

About 40 percent of interviewees had at least a bachelor's degree (twice the national rate at the time the survey was taken). Approximately one third of the total sample had a master's degree or higher, and a number had professional degrees or certification. Very few in the sample had not completed high school.

Age

Survey respondents averaged about 45 years of age, which was consistent with most other studies.

Gender and Race

Fewer than 20 percent of angels in this study, as in others, were minorities or women.

Unlike VC managers, who manage a portfolio of investments for passive limited-partner investors, angels manage a portfolio of their own personal investments. They therefore have a set of motivations that are somewhat different than professional VC managers.

Although some angels inherited the money they use for risk-capital investing, the majority use money they accumulated from their own earnings over time.

Angels get into venture investing in a variety of ways, from being asked to partner with someone in a small business to answering a newspaper classified advertisement seeking investors. Their knowledge of how to analyze an investment opportunity is often rudimentary and they tend to be self-taught. They often view any investment opportunity through the particular situation that brought them to risk-capital investing.

Angels are usually more receptive than professionally managed VC funds to investing early in start-up and young businesses. This may have something to do with the size of the investment they are willing and/or able to make, as well as with the fact that professional venture capitalists have shied away from such investments because the risk/reward balance is notoriously difficult to quantify, or the risk/reward may be unacceptable.

Another characteristic of angel investors is that they are sometimes willing to accept a smaller financial return on their investment in order to obtain some nonfinancial return.

Many angels are willing—and even desire—to contribute directly to the venture's welfare by taking on one or more roles, including hands-on participation in management. Those angels who take on a management role—either paid, unpaid, or as a condition of their investment—are often called "value-added investors." This is discussed in more detail in chapter 8.

Another characteristic of angel investors is that they are sometimes willing to accept a smaller financial return on their investment in order to obtain some nonfinancial return. Such a return might simply be the ability to support young entrepreneurs in their geographic region, or minority or women entrepreneurs. It might also mean an opportunity to contribute to the development of a socially useful technology. Studies throughout the 1980s by Wetzel and his colleagues, as well as research and anecdotal evidence since then, have shown this to be a key aspect of angels' reasons for backing particular companies. This is also discussed in more detail in chapter 8.

This willingness of angels to direct their money toward particular kinds of companies or entrepreneurs makes them an essential part of the community of risk-capital investors. Entrepreneurs should look closely at this segment of the community when analyzing opportunities to raise capital for a new or growing business.

Angels as Risk-Capital Investors

Angels occupy an important position on the spectrum of capital providers for entrepreneurial businesses. In addition to providing more early-stage capital for young and growing companies than most entrepreneurs can gather from friends and family, angels also act as a leading indicator of a company's potential viability and a "stamp of approval" for venture capitalists.

Steve Brotman, founder and general partner of Silicon Alley Venture Partners in New York, told the magazine Alleycat News in May 2001 that "having an angel investor can enhance a company's value even beyond cash and contacts. [Venture capitalists] tend to see an angel as a sign—a benchmark—that the start-up under review might be worth more than a casual glance."

"Having an angel investor can enhance a company's value even beyond cash and contacts. [Venture capitalists] tend to see an angel as a sign—a benchmark—that the start-up under review might be worth more than a casual glance."
—STEVE BROTMAN, ALLEYCAT NEWS, MAY 2001

Commercial banks and other large lenders rarely if ever lend funds to companies with few assets, with no salable product, or a small customer base. And few professional venture capitalists invest in such "concept businesses" either (the dotcom frenzy of 1998 to 2000 notwithstanding).

Friends and family members, credit cards and second mortgages are often used to get a company started. However, this funding is rarely enough to sustain the business for the months or even years it can take to create and market a product, or bring an invention through the necessary rigorous commercial development process.

Angels provide a capital bridge to support an entrepreneurial business while it moves from the high-risk, still speculative phase to a lower-risk, more substantive status that can attract professional venture capital.

Angel investors at the dawn of the 21st century are generally willing to invest larger amounts of money than friends or family. They represent a pool of more sophisticated investors, what might be called "semi-professional" venture capitalists who fill the niche for substantive capital infusions into "in-between" entrepreneurial efforts.

Dealing with an Angel

Angel investors at the dawn of the 21st century are generally willing to invest larger amounts of money than friends or family.

Working with an angel can sometimes be difficult. Although today they more frequently work in tandem with other angels or even professionally managed VC funds, they often invest individually and demand unique terms for their investments. Angels can be as insistent as venture capitalists on a well thought-out exit strategy. They also tend to be tough negotiators, requiring a large portion of equity, management control, or both in order get them to come on board. These issues will be discussed in more detail in chapter 8, "What Do Angels Want From You?"

Where Do Angels Come From?

The concept of an angel investor is about 100 years old and was born on Broadway. Angels were first described as wealthy theatergoers solicited by playwrights who needed money to bring their plays to the stage or to keep their failing theatrical productions afloat. These generous last-minute financial benefactors were like angels who descended from heaven and brought a worthy piece of art out of obscurity to the audience of theatergoers.

Over the years, that system became more professional. Today theatrical production companies and individual producers regularly spin their Rolodex in order to round up funding from corporations and wealthy individuals to finance a play.

Risk capital has long been raised from wealthy individual investors for other business ventures as well. The great fortunes of the 19th century robber barons were built when private investors put their wealth at risk in mining, railroads, and other ventures. In the 20th century, the capital markets became more professional and liquid with the growth of regional and national stock exchanges, and institutional investors grew more prominent. Individual financial backers of entrepreneurial efforts faded somewhat into the background.

Risk capital has long been raised from wealthy individual investors for other business ventures as well.

In the first part of the 20th century, corporate investment in technological innovation was consolidated in a few enormous laboratories. These included IBM's Watson Laboratory in New York; Bell Labs in New Jersey, which remained with AT&T after its divestiture into a long-distance company and seven local "Baby Bell" operating companies and is now part of Lucent Technology and Xerox's Palo Alto Research Center (PARC) near the Stanford University campus in Palo Alto, California. Government

Angels Took a Pounding Too

Angels took as much of a pounding in the dotcom meltdown as did the small individual investor. In February 2000 Paul Allen, a co-founder with Bill Gates of Microsoft who left that company in the mid-1990s to spend full time in technology start-ups, invested $1.65 billion in a telecommunications company called RCN.

Allen made the investment through his investment firm, Vulcan Ventures. He took preferred stock convertible to 26.6 million common stock shares of RCN. At the end of 2001, Allen's stake in RCN was worth less than $100 million, a loss of over 90 percent.

Of course, Allen doesn't need to hold a rent party to pay his living expenses. He still owns 138 million shares of Microsoft, valued at the end of 2001 at over $9 billion.

research grants for technological innovation, which began around World War II, were given to major universities such as Massachusetts Institute of Technology, Carnegie Mellon University and California Institute of Technology.

Beginning in the 1950s, some of these labs started to spin out civilian uses of their technologies into dozens of entrepreneurial companies, most of which were located within a few hours' drive of the university or major corporations. Today's Silicon Valley is the culmination of the Stanford and PARC effect, and the Massachusetts high-tech belt east of I-495 around Boston is the outgrowth of four or five generations of MIT spin-offs and spin-offs of those spin-offs.

> Angels became a fixture in the popular culture of business in the late 1970s and early 1980s when they began funding the generation of garage start-ups in the personal computer hardware industry.

With each successive generation of talented entrepreneurs that left larger companies to start their own and try to bring their genius to market came an ever larger need for private investment to fund the start-up and early years. Although angel investors continued to exist and operate throughout the century, they did so quietly. They began to come to the surface with the advent of the "garage" entrepreneurs of the 1950s and 1960s. Such entrepreneurs as David Packard and William Hewlett, who started Hewlett-Packard, and Ken Olson, who founded Digital Computer, had help from deep-pocketed investors.

Angels became a fixture in the popular culture of business in the late 1970s and early 1980s when they began funding a generation of garage start-ups in the personal computer hardware industry, such as Apple and Compaq; and in the software world, such as Lotus, Microsoft, and Software Arts. Angels also were involved in many start-ups in the biotech industry.

During the dotcom gold rush of the late 1990s, angels were somewhat pushed out of the picture as venture capitalists threw ever-larger pots of money at start-up companies that promised new, Internet-based business models. These companies burned through billions of VC dollars as they tried to prove that business was about "eyeball share" (how many visitors a Web site attracts) rather than actual profits.

It is almost ironic that one of the Web-based markets that has held up in the dotcom meltdown is the one for Internet matching services that put angels looking for deals together with entrepreneurs seeking funding to bring their innovations to market. Once again, as venture capitalists have pulled back, angels are finding their role where it used to be, in providing seed- and early-stage financing. This business model, as well as others, will be explored in detail in chapter 7, "Finding Angels."

As venture capitalists have pulled back, angels are finding their role where it used to be, in providing seed- and early-stage financing.

Key Characteristics of Angels

Although each angel is unique, it is possible to draw six broad general characteristics of these investors. Angel investors:

1. Have discretionary wealth. Whether angels are considered "wealthy" or not depends on your definition of wealthy. However, they must meet the SEC guidelines for "sophisticated investors."

   These individuals are considered qualified (sophisticated) by virtue of their net worth and/or income. They must have a net worth of over $1 million and/or an annual income of over $300,000 for a couple or $200,000 for an individual. In the United States, the area around New York City, including the suburbs in northern New Jersey and Fairfield County, Connecticut, has the highest concentration of households that meet these criteria.

   Because of their status, angels can be approached about investment opportunities not fit for ordinary investors concerned with risk of failure and loss of capital. People raising capital (you) and their brokers or agents are free to market unlisted securities to angels.

Angels usually have much more wealth than the entrepreneurs they fund; this wealth mismatch can have implications for the relationship.

> Angels usually have much more wealth than the entrepreneurs they fund.

2. Travel increasingly in flocks. Over the past 20 years, angel clubs, networks, and other organizations have flourished. They serve as centralized clearinghouses for angels to meet entrepreneurs, obtain business plans, and explore investment possibilities. Some are more formally run than others.

   Many of these groups have been organized by university business schools or satellite organizations, such as the MIT Enterprise Forum.

   In Silicon Valley, in northern California, it is possible for an entrepreneur to approach 50 to 100 angels with a single presentation to such a group.
3. Are solo investors. Despite breaking bread together to survey the entrepreneurial field, when it comes time to make investments, angels tend to go it alone. If they wanted to be members of investment pools, they wouldn't put the time and effort into sizing up investment opportunities. Instead, they would just plunk their money into a VC fund and be done with it.
4. Tend to invest close to home. The vast majority of angel organizations are geographically based. Many started out as breakfast clubs where entrepreneurs, angels, and managers and professionals looking for job opportunities with entrepreneurial companies got together to network. Some still work that way, although many have become more formal by hiring professional association management or by becoming part of a university-based center for entrepreneurship. Since many angels

like to stay intimately involved with their investments, they tend to invest in companies within driving distance.

5. Are Internet savvy. The Internet has opened up vast, new worlds for both angels and entrepreneurs to move beyond their local area and find opportunities across the country and even overseas. A number of Internet sites cater to angels and the entrepreneurs looking for their money.
6. Differ regionally. In the Silicon Valley and around Boston, angels are disproportionately technology-oriented, and often willing to put money into new concepts. In the New York area, angels primarily come from a finance background and are more risk averse, and therefore less likely to invest in a business with unproved technology.

Chapter Key Points

- Angels invest in entrepreneurial business where they have no prior personal relationship with the entrepreneur.
- Individual angels are usually willing to risk more capital in a business than are friends or family members.
- Angels are often used as "bridge capital" from the small amounts needed to start up a company to the large amounts needed to take a fully developed product to market.
- Angels often travel in flocks but usually invest on a solo basis.
- Angels are often themselves entrepreneurs and willing to invest in a business for reasons that go beyond bottom-line criteria.

CHAPTER

7

FINDING ANGELS

INTERNET WORKING IS EFFECTIVE FOR FINDING ANGELS

Finding angels, especially in the Internet age, is relatively easy. Finding the right angel, and making the deal work, is far more difficult.

You should structure your search for an angel by referring back to your entrepreneur profile and especially to the question that asks what is special about you, as an entrepreneur, or about your company. Remember, many angels are entrepreneurs themselves and wish to invest in businesses, technologies, and innovations that dovetail with their own background and/or current businesses. Some women angels may wish to limit their investments to female entrepreneurs, and minority angels to only minority entrepreneurs.

Aside from looking for angels who mesh tightly with your unique characteristics or those of your business, you should also look for angels by conducting a targeted search. Remember, you want to minimize the "distance" you need to cast your net by leveraging your relationships with friends, family, business associates, and professional advisors in order to reach other potential angels they may know. You hope to reach people—in this case angels—through personal contacts. First try those who you are closest to, then people with whom you have a more tangential connection.

These various degrees of connection are like the concentric circles on a shooting target (see figure 7-1). Each circle outside the center is a universe of more distant relationships.

FIGURE 7-1 Targeted Search for Angel Investor

Web-Based Angel Networks
offroadcapital.com
ACE-Net
garage.com
angeltips.com
UniversityAngels.com

Regional Angel Networks
Business Incubator
Regional ACE-Net Node
Regional Angel Club

Community Resources
Chamber of Commerce
Breakfast Club
Business Publication
Local University Business School
Trade Association, Magazines, Shows

Professional Advisors
Attorney, Accountant, Banker, Friends and Family

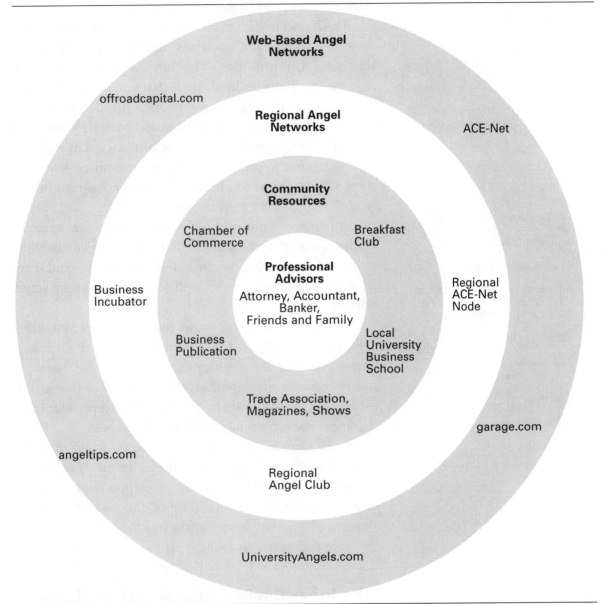

In the bull's-eye of the target are your company's professional advisers, especially your accountant, attorney, and banker, as well as your friends and family. Accountants and attorneys have clients, some of whom have the wealth and desire to be venture angels and are looking for private-equity investments.

In the second circle are what we call community resources. These are resources from both your local and business communities. The key to your acceptance among members of this circle is that you are a part of the local community. Circle members who may introduce you to individuals looking to invest include your local chamber of commerce, the editor of the local or regional business newspaper, and faculty at local university business schools. You can also check out any business breakfast clubs that exist in your area.

Remember the "millionaires next door." They live like you. Do not cross anyone off your list of potential angels because he or she "does not act like s/he has money."

Business community resources you can turn to include any trade association that your company belongs to or that deals with the same kinds of products and services as your company, as well as trade magazines and shows.

The third circle represents regional angel networks. There are literally dozens, if not hundreds, of such networks around the country. They tend to be clustered around major metropolitan areas and/or universities, especially those known for producing entrepreneurs and business ideas from its faculty and students.

In the fourth circle are the Internet-based investor networks. These are placed on the outer rim of the target because through them you can reach potential investors far and wide. However, some of the most successful Internet-based angel networks are those that focus on specific regions or alumni of particular universities.

The Inner Circle: Professional Advisors

Your professional advisors can provide you with some sound leads. They can also help you cut through the angel/entrepreneur meet-and-greet phase of courting by making personal introductions. In fact, without their involvement, a referral may not deal with you.

The Millionaire at the Keyboard

A man in blue jeans and a cotton shirt walked into a piano store. The senior salesman, seeing how the man was dressed, asked a new, young salesman to handle the "customer." The young salesman asked the man what he wanted. The man said he wanted a Boesendorefer grand piano. So the salesman took him to the $85,000 floor-model Boesendorefer.

The man played it for a few minutes and said, "I want to buy it." The salesman said there were none in stock, and it would take a month to get another delivered. The customer said, "I'll take this one." The salesman asked what credit card the man would like to use to charge the piano, and the man pulled out a roll of bills and said, "I don't like credit cards."

Informal investors reached through your professional advisors are more likely to infer that the venture has a "Good Housekeeping seal of approval," even if the person making the referral tells both you and the prospect that they are in no way validating the investment quality of the venture. While professional investors will do their own due diligence on your business plan, others will assume that the professional advisor would not have referred the opportunity without thinking it appropriate.

Many people who have risk capital available ask their accountant and/or lawyer to be on the lookout for investment opportunities. Professional advisors know your personality and business-operating style, as well as the particulars of your business, and can often help match you with an angel of the appropriate temperament and personal style.

Many people who have risk capital available ask their accountant and/or lawyer to be on the lookout for investment opportunities.

Bankers are another good source of referrals for angel investors. They are often eager to help new and young companies secure equity capital from an angel they know and trust; this kind of a relationship can help raise the bank's comfort level and make it that much easier for you to get a bank loan in the future. Banks do this because they want you to prosper and remain a customer.

Banks also hope that an angel investor might be willing to guarantee a loan for you, in addition to providing you with capital in exchange for an equity stake.

In a private loan guarantee, the guarantor provides a letter of credit from his or her bank (whether or not it is your bank as well) or another financial company. The bank holds the letter of credit as collateral against your company's loan. The guarantor's bank usually holds collateral in the form of a certificate of deposit or financial securities against the letter of credit.

Banks also hope that an angel investor might be willing to guarantee a loan for you, in addition to providing you with capital in exchange for an equity stake.

If you work with a large commercial bank, speak to a lending officer who specializes in small-business lending (in most banks, this means loans of less than $1 million). If you have your banking relationship with a smaller bank, speak with the president, who is often wired into both the community of wealthy individuals who use your bank, as well as banking leaders throughout the community.

Small-business lending specialists and small-bank presidents may also know of local or regional investment groups you can get into and might even bring you along as a personal guest if they attend meetings of such a group. They tend to have good contacts with the local chamber of commerce, real estate owners (this helps when you look for space), and businesses that service other businesses, such as office-equipment dealers.

The Second Circle: Community Resources

If you live in a metropolitan area, check out the chamber(s) of commerce. Many sponsor venture investment groups, and if they don't, they should know who does.

Don't always assume that the largest city in the area has the largest or best chamber for this kind of relationship.

For instance, the Boston chamber of commerce is actually smaller than a number of suburban chambers located along the Route 128 and I-495 high-tech belts to the west of the center city. Venture capitalists and angels tend to hang out with the tech crowd, because that's where much of the innovation is. If your business is in health care, retail, or services, and the people you call tell you their venture group doesn't focus on those areas, ask if they know which group does.

Small business development center (SBDC) executive directors are also often tied into the angel and venture capital network. A call to the local SBDC is well worth the effort. The Small Business Administration (SBA) Web site, www.sba.gov, has a listing of SBDCs around the country.

Leads to angel networks may be obtained from a local university's business school, a VC firm, the state economic development office, or a local government. Since you are not asking any of these sources for money, most should be willing to help.

Your state or regional economic development agency can also be a help, as can the Secretary of State's office. The dean of the local business school, as well as the faculty who teach entrepreneurship and finance should be wired into any venture investing networks in the area.

Contact the editor of the local business newspaper; newspapers love to compile lists and business newspapers are heavily oriented toward service articles. There may have been a "best of the angels" article published in the previous year that the editor will gladly send you, or maybe she'll refer you to on the paper's Web site. Who knows, the editor may want to do a story about your company.

If any local companies have floated initial public offerings (IPOs) of their stock, you should get a copy of the prospectus and read it. It will include a list of principal shareholders. These are the angels and venture capital funds that invested early and cashed out by selling their stock at the time of the IPO. If they've cashed out recently, they may have money available to go into a new venture with you.

Your business community is an important resource. Your industry's trade association, trade magazines that cover your industry and the markets you hope to sell into, and trade shows that you attend or display at are all vehicles for meeting potential angel investors.

Finally, there are resources for the angel community you should know about. *Angel Advisor* is a bimonthly magazine, and Angel Forum is a conference and tradeshow series. Both are operated by Angel Society, which can be reached at www.angelsociety.com.

When you create a chart of either friends and family or angels, put all of them on one chart and color code those who are in one category and those who are in more than one.

The Third Circle: Regional Angel Networks

Regional angel networks are often more formal than a chamber of commerce subcommittee or an angel-investor breakfast club. Many are sponsored by centers on entrepreneurship that are affiliated with a university's business school (see sidebar).

Regional networks are also forming through an Internet network called the ACE-net, which can be reached at www.ace-net.sr.unh.edu. ACE-net is the Internet domain name for the Access to Capital Electronic Network, a program started in the late 1990s by the SBA's office of advocacy.

Although ACE-net is a tool for entrepreneurs to list their proposals and for individuals to search for possible investments, it has also spawned over 60 regional "nodes." These regional nodes, or subgroups, allow angels and entrepreneurs located in the same geographic area to find one another more easily. The national ACE-net site has a listing of all the regional ACE-net nodes. Each node operates independently and somewhat differently. Some regional nodes also sponsor off-line events for entrepreneurs and angels to interact. Entrepreneurs pay $450 to post their business plan on the Ace-net Web site.

For instance, the Connecticut ACE-net node held a competition in early 2001 in which over 60 entrepreneurs submitted proposals for a round of funding. Six were chosen for a face-to-face meeting with a group of potential angels, at which they presented more detailed business plans. Each entrepreneur paid not only to get their proposal on the site but in front of the dozens of angels who utilize the Connecticut node.

Angels also often flock to business incubators. An incubator is either a nonprofit or for-profit company that offers spaces and services to small new companies. Many have office and laboratory facilities of different sizes in their building, so if a company grows it can move from one place to another and stay in the incubator. Incubator services often include a central copy center for large printing jobs; an auditorium with state-of-the-art presentation media for gatherings of investors, business partners, and others; conference rooms; and even with a caterer. Some incubators have a law, accounting, and/or marketing firm on-site, although tenants are not obliged to use these services.

Angels also often flock to business incubators.

The National Business Incubation Association (NBIA) has over 550 members. Its Web site, www.nbia.org, can tell you where to find the closest one to you. Over half the member incubators provide formal or informal access to early-stage financing, according to the association.

Some national organizations ride the circuit as well. The MIT Enterprise Forum, run by the university, visits more than a dozen cities in the United States each year. At these meetings, entrepreneurs who have been prescreened present their business plans to a panel of venture capitalists who critique both the plan and the presentation to help each entrepreneur hone his pitch. These events include before and after program networking time. Many

Angels on the Web

Here is a list of some of the best places to find potential angel investors. Many of these sites provide web links and other ways to contact local and regional angel networks as well.

- acenet.sr.unh.edu
- angelmoney.com
- angelsociety.com
- capcon.com/worldfinance/who01
- financehub.com
- garage.com
- investorangels.com
- internetangels.com
- mit.edu/entforum
- nbia.org (business incubators)
- offroadcapital.com
- universityangels.com

angels are there to check out the pitches and work the crowd. The forum's Web site, web.mit.edu/entforum/, lists where the Forum will pitch its tent in the coming year.

The Fourth Circle: Web-Based Angel Networks

In addition to ACE-net, there are a number of Internet-based angel networks, as well as Internet-based matching sites.

Perhaps the best-known Internet-based sites for entrepreneurs looking to match up with angels are OffRoad Capital, at offroadcapital.com, and Garage.com, at garage.com.

In its first year, from mid-1999 to mid-2000, OffRoad signed up 5,000 investors and raised $42 million for seven companies. OffRoad is a hybrid angel/professional venture capital site, where wealthy angels often piggyback their investments with those made by professionally managed VC funds. OffRoad offers some deals in conjunction with an investment banking firm Robertson Stephens.

OffRoad and Garage.com go beyond mere networking to facilitate relationships. But they differ in the model they use.

OffRoad operates on an underwriting model. It accepts a deal from an entrepreneur, then opens the deal up to its network of investors to bid on (based on how much they will invest for how little equity). Before the offer closes, potential investors can view the company's financial results and engage in Web-cast question-and-answer sessions with company executives. The entrepreneur pays for the underwriting service, and membership fees to investors are minimal.

Garage.com uses a blind matching service model. Investors pay an annual fee to enter a password-protected area of the web site called "Heaven," where entrepreneurs have posted business plans. If an investor is interested in the proposal, Garage.com forwards the investor's information to the entrepreneur. If the entrepreneur is interested, Garage.com gets the parties together for a handshake. In 1999, its first full year—Garage.com helped 40 companies raise about $101 million.

Garage.com uses a blind matching service model.

A unique organization, which is Internet-based but community-oriented, is universityangels.com. Founded in 1999 by four Harvard Business School graduates, the company is an umbrella for university-specific Web sites. On each site, alumni entrepreneurs from that university's business school meet up with alumni angels. By April of 2001, over 75 universities had instituted sites under the universityangels.com umbrella, and over 2,000 alumni angels had signed up to help fund ventures started by their peers. The UniversityAngels company has also created a pool of $20 million that it will invest in follow-up rounds for companies that originally get funded through one of its Web sites.

Brokers and Finders

Brokers and finders are middlemen who help entrepreneurs raise capital. They promote themselves as individuals who have a broad range of contacts in the financial community and industry, which they use to find you funding.

This is a broad category. We distinguish brokers and finders from friends, family, professional advisors, and other acquaintances by the fact that a broker or finder wants compensation—either cash or a stake in the company—in exchange for helping you find capital.

If someone is offering to do something for you, ask how he or she would like to be compensated. If someone is in a position to help but you are uncomfortable asking, start off by saying you would like to ask for help, but you want to compensate the person appropriately. Often people will do things without being compensated; your offer shows them that you are serious.

How Do Brokers and Finders Differ?

Brokers usually advertise their services and have a set business model on which they operate (i.e., they expect predetermined compensation for performing particular services). For instance, they may charge a small cash fee for each referral they bring you, and then a larger fee (all cash, cash and equity, or all equity) for every referral who actually makes an investment.

Brokers usually conduct a number of different tasks having to do with small businesses. They often find buyers for small companies, and business owners looking to sell for potential buyers. They also assist in mergers of like businesses. In the course of these activities, they create a network of individuals with capital to invest—people who have perhaps sold a business and want to become more passive investors or possibly consultants to another business.

In some states, brokers need to be licensed with the secretary of state, and all who operate under a corporate or "Doing Business As (DBA)" name can and should be checked out with the Better Business Bureau.

Finders are a more elusive group. They may be business consultants, stock brokers or other investment advisors, or angel investors themselves who have access to a network of other risk investors.

Accelerators, discussed in detail in chapter 17, may also perform the "finder" tasks as part of their more complete role.

The Maryland PIN

Since the advent of venture networking groups in the late 1970s and early 1980s, many organizations have developed a more formal approach to matching entrepreneurs who seek funding with angel investors. A number of these groups are managed by entrepreneurship programs at university business schools. One such program is the Private Investor Network (PIN) sponsored by the Dingman Center for Entrepreneurship at the University of Maryland in College Park.

The Dingman Center's PIN is a network of over 100 SEC- accredited private investors looking to invest in companies in all industries. PIN investors invest in companies in the mid-Atlantic region; companies looking for funding through the PIN must be based in Maryland, Virginia, Delaware, or the District of Columbia. The company should be trying to raise between $250,000 and $3 million.

Each month, the PIN holds a breakfast meeting where a number of entrepreneurs make their pitch for funds. Two-page submissions about the company, which must adhere to a strict format, are reviewed on a rolling basis. Any submission that arrives by the 25th of the month is reviewed for a subsequent month's breakfast.

If the two-page proposal is accepted, the Dingman Center staff work with the entrepreneur to hone his or her formal pitch to the group, which lasts ten minutes. The two-page briefs for all of the presenting companies are given to investor participants in a three-ring binder. Presenters can provide additional handouts if they wish.

After the presentation, individual investors contact the entrepreneur on their own. Most PIN investors put $50,000 to $250,000 into a venture. They sometimes syndicate a deal with other PIN members.

Entrepreneurs pay a $200 reading fee along with their two-page submission, and an additional $200 fee if they are chosen to make the full 10-minute pitch.

The PIN is an incorporated entity of the Mid-Atlantic Venture Association (MAVA). It is operated through the Baltimore-Washington Venture Group (BWVG).

Accelerators are one-stop shops for a number of business services for entrepreneurs; they may help find capital, personnel, and office, lab, and/or product-development space, and provide consulting services of various kinds. Some accelerator organizations even have a physical location in which to incubate their entrepreneurial clients.

Finders are not licensed and often negotiate different terms and conditions for each arrangement they make with an entrepreneur.

Sometimes it may be necessary to convert a member of your inner circle into a paid finder. You will have to judge whether a referral is being provided for you on a "friendly" basis or whether you sense that the person making the referral is seeking some kind of compensation if the referral works out.

It's important to determine this early and to be very up-front about it. Then, if the person does want compensation, engage in serious, businesslike negotiations about how he or she will be compensated. Down the road, when your company is successful, you don't want your old college buddy or your uncle to tell people "others got taken care of, but not me."

> Family and friends are not immune to becoming angry and even suing if they feel they were supposed to be compensated for providing successful referrals, even if nothing was ever put in writing.

Family and friends are not immune to becoming angry and even suing if they feel they were supposed to be compensated for providing successful referrals, even if nothing was ever put in writing. Oral agreements are often upheld in court, and the state of mind of the parties who allegedly made an agreement is a key element in determining if a defensible agreement was put in place. So, if you are going to create a "finder" relationship with someone from your informal network, be sure to pay a lawyer to have a proper, formal contract drawn up. The agreement can and probably should be short and simple, but it must be done correctly.

"Professional" finders always want a written agreement that outlines their compensation. Many want to be compensated for "expenses." This is often the trickiest part of the contract, since defining project expenses you pay as compared to normal operating expenses the finder covers as part of running his or her business can be difficult. Others ask for unspecified "charges," which you must have defined clearly. Your contract should always state explicitly what expenses you are paying for.

Compensating a Broker or Finder

Broker or finder compensation generally has three elements to it.

1. Fees for searching for capital. Most brokers or finders want an up-front fee for undertaking such an assignment; they will not work purely on a contingency basis.
2. Payment of expenses the broker or finder pays out in the quest for capital. These should be defined clearly to make sure you are not paying normal operating expenses or expenses that will also be billed to another client (e.g., if the broker has four clients he is trying to find capital for, and travels to another city to meet with potential funders, each client should be charged for one-fourth of the trip's expenses).
3. Payment of a "success fee" if the search is successful in obtaining capital. This fee can be either a fixed amount or, more commonly, a percentage of the amount raised.

In some states, only brokers who are registered with the secretary of state are allowed to take the fee in either cash or an equity stake in the company (in the form of stock, warrants that allow for the purchase of stock at a later date, or a combination), while finders must be paid success fees in equity.

One common success fee formula is 5 percent for the first $1 million raised; 4 percent for the next million; 3 percent for the next; 2 percent for the next; and 1 percent for anything over the first $4 million. Other brokers and finders work on a straight 3 percent commission for all money raised.

When the deal involves allocation of funds for several purposes or by different parties, the fee issue is more complex. For instance, an investor may agree to provide funding for particular activities but not others, or may release portions of the funding over time as particular milestones are reached.

In such a case, you should pay the broker or finder at the time you actually take control of the funds, not when the funding agreement is made. However, you might put the full fee in escrow. If you are paying cash, this puts it out of reach for other purposes. And if you are paying in equity, this assures that it is issued at its value when the deal is signed, not at a variable value.

Chapter Key Points

- Finding angels is relatively easy. Finding the right angel, and making the right kind of deal with an angel, can be difficult.
- Your professional advisers, such as your lawyer, accountant, marketing consultant, or business consultant, are the best place to begin your search for angels.
- Because many angels like to invest locally or regionally, it is important to make contacts with organizations such as chambers of commerce, local investor clubs, and local business schools.
- Alumni associations, especially those from business schools, are increasingly becoming a hub where angels and entrepreneurs meet.
- Be careful working with those who charge to find investors for you. Make sure anyone earning a fee as a broker or finder is explicit about fees and expenses, and set performance criteria and definitions of success in the contract.

CHAPTER

8

WHAT DO ANGELS WANT FROM YOU?

MONEY ON WINGS COMES WITH STRINGS

What angels want out of any investment depends on their motivation for becoming a risk-capital investor. Professional managers of VC funds have a fiduciary responsibility to their passive investors, and their primary—if not sole—motivation is the highest possible financial reward they can obtain for their fund.

Angels, on the other hand, are investing only for themselves and may have a broad range for their acceptable rate of return. However, other motivations may have a major influence on investment decisions. While they still seek a high return, they are often willing to take less return or assume more risk in order to fulfill one of these other motivations.

What makes angels so difficult to capture is that each one is different. Therefore, your presentation and offer must be customized in such a way that the angel sees your company and its opportunity through his or her particular point of view.

Understanding what angels want is no different than understanding what your market wants. Within the marketplace are different customer segments, and each segment places different relative values on the various attributes of your company's product or service. It is not enough to show a customer what the product or service is and what its features are. Rather, the customer must understand the benefits of the product or service.

You must look at each angel you contact about an investment opportunity in your venture as a market of one. In raising capital, you are selling your company, and when raising capital from angels you are selling highly particular attributes of your company that mesh with the attributes each angel finds most important when making the investment decision.

The Angel and the Early-Stage Company

There are four principal types of relationships a potential angel may seek with the company he or she invests in.

> *If you agree that an angel will take a position in your company, work out a job description and compensation plan at the outset.*

1. A job. Some angel investors are actually looking for a job and willing to buy their way into one through an early-stage investment in an entrepreneurial company.
2. An opportunity to "run" an entrepreneurial business from outside. Some angels do not wish to be involved in day-to-day management but want to exert some level of control over the company's activities by serving on the board of directors or an advisory committee, or as a consultant.
3. An opportunity to diversify an investment portfolio through high-risk passive investment.
4. An opportunity to provide some kind of social good.

No matter which of these relationships a potential investor is seeking, part of the motivation is always a desire for "action." Just as some people bet on the horses, go to casinos, or day-trade the stock markets, some individuals like to try to pick the winners from the hundreds of thousands of Americans who start new businesses each year.

A Job

There have been several rounds of corporate downsizing since the mid-1980s, and with each one, huge numbers of corporate executives and middle managers have been put out of work. In addition, large corporations have moved toward pushing their executives to retire between the ages of 55 and 62, in order to make room for younger executives to climb the corporate ladder.

These retirees often have money to invest and a desire to continue working. Some of them join angel clubs and become passive investors, taking on much of the due diligence work those clubs perform before investing. But others wish to find one company to invest in where they can also get a job.

They will often work for little or no pay at first. Then, when the company begins to find solid ground, they expect to be put on the payroll at a salary near what the founder earns, and in a top executive position.

For the entrepreneur, finding such an individual can be a prayer answered. If your company goes through the early stages of growth and attracts significant VC funding on the way to an IPO of common stock, the venture capitalists may move to replace you and other founders with seasoned professional managers. Having an angel on board with management skills and who is willing to continue working with you can help you keep some level of management control over your company as it enters adolescence, instead of being pushed out the door.

Having an angel on board with management skills and who is willing to continue working with you can help you keep some level of management control over your company

"Run" an Entrepreneurial Business

Many angels are entrepreneurs themselves. They have started one or more businesses, taken them through the early stages of growth, and may even have cashed out in an IPO or a sale to a larger company.

As you know from running your own business, entrepreneurs want to be in control. And entrepreneur angels tend to demand a high level of control in the company they invest in. They usually do this from their position on the board of directors, a seat they demand in exchange for their investment. At the first sign of financial trouble, they may push for the board to install new management, possibly even themselves.

Such micromanagers can be a pain in the backside. However, they are sometimes willing to pay for the privilege by making investments larger than other angels might. While some micromanagement-style angels are serial entrepreneurs, others are born wealthy and simply believe that everyone will cater to their wishes, as the maid and butler did when they were growing up.

Diversify a Portfolio

High net-worth individuals have learned since the 1980s that private equity investments usually have a higher rate of return than those in publicly traded stocks and bonds. The very wealthy may have a portion of their investment portfolio in private equity opportunities such as real estate, leveraged buyout funds, hedge funds, and venture capital.

There can only be one boss but any number of advisers.

Most of these will be passive investments, but some might be active. If investors don't want to manage their own real estate portfolio, the other option for active involvement is usually venture funding. And so rather than become passive investors in a professionally managed VC fund, they turn to angel investing.

Many people who are angels solely to diversify their portfolio are not interested in active involvement in the company. However, there are two exceptions.

One is former entrepreneurs who believe they can add value to your effort by sitting on the board of directors but have no interest in managing your company for you. These people can be true angels. They have a wealth of knowledge and experience from which they allow you to draw and can keep you from making the same kind of mistakes they made in similar situations. They also have substantial contacts that can help move your company forward with a minimum of effort.

One angel describes his contribution in the May 2000 issue of *AlleyCat News*, a magazine about venture capital and the dotcom world in New York's Silicon Alley: "If I do anything, I cross-fertilize. If I need to make a call to a CEO, chances are I know the executive on the other side of the line. I have contacts that are relevant and relationships with real companies. That's valuable."

The other exception is angels who invest in new businesses with products or services they are intimately familiar with. This happens a lot in the medical technology and biotechnology businesses, where doctors and scientists often put their investment capital.

These angels usually don't want a seat on the board but may want some kind of position on the scientific advisory committee. If you keep them focused on the technology, they can be a great help. But if they begin to delve into the business's management, they can be difficult, simply because they often don't realize that the company has to go through lean times before it makes money.

Research on risk-capital investments has shown that the majority of venture funding flows from white men to other white men.

Provide a Social Good

Research on risk-capital investments has shown that the majority of venture funding flows from white men to other white men. Since the mid-1990s, minority and women entrepreneurs have more means of bringing investments into their ventures.

Some are simply offering their own money, experience, and management talent to other entrepreneurs like themselves. Others have created focused angel clubs and even VC firms that direct investments solely toward minority or women entrepreneurs.

For instance, in 2000 Kay Koplovitz, the former CEO of USA Networks, created Springboard. The idea behind Springboard is to train women entrepreneurs to better present their business plans to angels and venture capitalists. Springboard programs are sponsored by the National Women's Business Council, of which Koplovitz is president, as well as local sponsors where each event is held.

Enhancing the role of minority and women entrepreneurs is not the only social good angels are willing to invest in. William Wetzel, a professor at the University of New Hampshire business school, began studying what he called "informal risk-capital investors" in the early 1980s and published a number of studies of New England angels.

One study showed that 45 percent of survey respondents were willing to accept less return or more risk in order to support entrepreneurs in their region; 39 percent to contribute to the development of socially useful technology; 37 percent to help add employment to their geographic area; 19 percent to aid urban-based entrepreneurs; 17 percent to support women entrepreneurs; and 14 percent to help minority entrepreneurs.

Enhancing the role of minority and women entrepreneurs is not the only social good angels are willing to invest in.

And just as there are "green" mutual funds that only hold stocks in companies that are environmentally friendly, there are venture funds and angels who invest in ventures that enhance the earth's environment. Funds such as Calvert Partners in Washington D.C. have made this type of investing not only acceptable but desirable.

Qualifying the Prospective Angel

Given that it is difficult to generalize about angel investor motivation, it is important for you as an entrepreneur to "qualify" any potential angel investor to make sure his or her motivations and desires mesh with your objectives and the role the angel may play. Understanding an angel's motivation is key to a successful relationship and possibly even to the success or failure of your business.

For example, one seed investor whose financial contribution entitled him to 20 percent of the company's equity demanded and received 50 percent of the voting authority on all major decisions (essentially a veto power). This investor saw himself as a capable manager and wanted to preserve the value of his investment.

Regardless of the investor's management abilities, he did not know the industry in which the company was engaged. The investor often overrode company executives's decisions and effectively stymied the company's growth.

To qualify potential angel investors, ask the following nine questions, then do some background checking as well to see if their answers jibe with how others see them.

1. What is your background (i.e., business, professional) and how much of that experience is in my company's field?
2. Do you meet the SEC guidelines as a "sophisticated investor" ($200,000 annual income for an individual or $300,000 for a couple, or $1 million in household net worth)?
3. What is your experience investing in entrepreneurial businesses? (Ideally, you will not be getting too much money, if any, from first-time angels.)
4. What type of business do you want to invest in? What products and services, and what stage of a company's life cycle interest you?
5. What type of involvement do you want to have in the company's operations? Is it active or passive, consultative, board, or management?
6. What investment range are you considering?
7. Do you want to be the single investor at this stage, or a "co-investor" with people you know?
8. What are your financial criteria for making an investment (equity, debt, or debt-to-equity position, time frame for returns, minimum acceptable rate of return, and preferred exit strategy)?
9. Do you have any other important criteria for investing?

Valuation must be reasonable because it is subjective and, just like expectations, personal. It must be agreed on, and it must take into account terms of the investment, whether or not the investor will be available for subsequent investments, and other circumstances.

Some individuals, especially those new to private equity investing, may object to providing some of this information. You need to explain that you don't want to waste their time if the two of you are not a good match, especially since this will be a long-term relationship. Stress that if you two are a potential match, you want to be able to make a formal presentation that speaks to the specific benefits the investor might obtain by investing in your company. Also, tell the investor that you must be sure you are in compliance with securities laws. Just as with the discussions with friends and family prospects, blame the need to ask on your lawyer and federal securities regulations.

Unless management control is carefully determined, you may end up having a 50-50 partner. Know how much power you wnat any angel to have.

What Angels Need

Because angels are usually investing at the early stages of a company's lifecycle, their relationship with the entrepreneur must differ from a professionally managed VC firm's. Most angels enter negotiations with an entrepreneur around five topics. To some angels, all are important; to others only some are and, as we have already said, the relative importance of each is different for each angel.

1. More than just common stock
2. A reasonable and realistic valuation of your company
3. A seat on the board of directors
4. Some degree of management control
5. A clearly defined exit strategy

More than Common Stock

Most angels want a position in the investor hierarchy that gives them preferred rights above those held by common stockholders. They usually do this in one of two ways. They either give the entrepreneur a loan that converts to stock if particular benchmarks are met, or they take convertible preferred stock.

In the first option, if the company folds early on, you are on the hook to repay the loan. However, some angels invest on an interest-only basis and defer interest payments for one or two years. During those first years, as each performance milestone is met, some of the loan, and the deferred interest, converts to stock. If the company hits all of its milestones over the defined period, the entire amount of the loan converts to an equity position for the angel. This conversion is usually to common stock, although some loans may be converted to preferred stock. Some angels retain their creditor status until there is a public offering.

In the second option, the angel usually waives payments of dividends due on the preferred stock for a period of time, possibly even until the company is profitable. As performance milestones are met, some or all of the preferred stock and the waived dividends can be converted to a common-stock position. Or, the investor can wait to convert until there is a public common-stock offering or the company is sold to a publicly held company and the angel becomes a stockholder in that company.

The reason for taking preferred stock in the first place is to protect against the company going belly-up; if it does, holders of preferred stock (the angels) get their money out before holders of common stock (usually the founders and early employees who have been given some common stock in exchange for less cash compensation).

The reason for taking preferred stock in the first place is to protect against the company going belly-up.

If an angel does accept common stock, he or she may want warrants that allow for the purchase of more common stock at the same price for a set period of time into the future. The angel may also ask for a clause that says the entrepreneur cannot initiate a buyback of shares from the angel with income from future rounds of private financing.

You need to create a plan with milestones and an exit strategy. The peak time for entrepreneurs to terminate their business is the fourth or fifth year. Better to plan for an unsuccessful end than to be caught by events.

Reasonable and Rational Valuation

Valuation is one of the trickiest parts of negotiations between an angel investor and an entrepreneur. An angel or syndicate of angels usually wants between 20 and 30 percent of the company's equity.

Because many angels or syndicates generally wish to invest between $500,000 and $1.5 million, they seek out companies with valuations of $1 and $6 million. Of course, this is not a hard and fast rule, but it's a good set of parameters to work within.

If a company's valuation is less than $1 million, friends and family and other "bootstrap" funding is usually needed to boost that valuation above the $1 million level. If the company is valued at over $6 million, angels are rarely able to provide enough capital to reach the next stage growth , and owners ought to be looking more to professional venture capitalists.

Matching the amount of funding needed to take the venture to the next level with the size of the equity stake the angel(s) wish to have and the valuation is an exercise in triangulation.

Early-stage companies usually lack hard data on sales, cost of goods sold, and margins on which to determine company valuation. Many not only have no revenues but also no prototype product or customer base.

Some companies also have competitors who are further along on the same path they are, which limits their chances of success unless they can prove their technology of process superior.

There are a number of models angels can use to determine a rough valuation for your company. Some angels rely on a formal discounted cash-flow model, although this is difficult because of the short history entrepreneurial companies have and the challenge of making good predictions about income and expenses. Others use less-formal models. Some prefer to hold off on the valuation until after some performance milestones have been met.

One long-time angel, John Ason, explains in an article posted on angelsociety.com how he values entrepreneurial companies that he is considering making an investment in. He assigns the following valuations:

- A good idea: $1 million
- A working prototype: $1 million
- High-quality management: $1 million
- Meaningful revenues: $1 million
- Strong relationships in the company's industry and with potential clients: $1 million

With this down-and-dirty methodology, he comes up with a "positive valuation" for a company of between $1 and $5 million. Then he begins taking value away for what he calls "valuation demerits," such as a lack of market focus, inability to forge alliances, bad deal negotiating, and poor attitude toward angel investors. Too many demerits can kill a potential deal, not just reduce its value.

About half of individual angel investors want to sit on your board of directors.

Board Representation

About half of individual angel investors want to sit on your board of directors. An investor syndicate usually appoints one or two members to sit on the board.

From this perch, they can oversee how the company is progressing and determine if and when it will hit the performance milestones that trigger either conversion of debt into equity, preferred stock into common, or other events such as a need for more capital or a decision to seek a buyer.

A seat on the board also gives the angel the ability to influence major management decisions and effect changes, if needed. Because of the power an investor has as a board member, you should grant this position only for large investors or a representative of a group of smaller investors. Also, make sure there is a personal "fit" between you and the investor or investors' representative who will have a seat on the board.

One CEO of a small company tested each prospective member of his company's board with a single question: "If I wanted to do something, how would you vote?"

Unsophisticated angels may ask for a board seat because they have been told that investors are always appointed as directors. Sophisticated investors know that getting a board seat depends on the size of the investment.

Seasoned angels also know that serving on the board exposes them to liability. Investors, vendors, and others who believe they have been mislead by a company may take their grievances to the courts and try to hold officers and directors, as well as managers, responsible. Most companies provide director and officer insurance. But this is expensive and does not cover instances of willful misconduct or misrepresentation.

Seasoned angels also know that serving on the board exposes them to liability.

The board should be composed of individuals who make a substantial contribution to the company's success—in their knowledge and experience as well as in terms of their ability to provide large amounts of funding. Entrepreneurs should view board seats as a premium not to be given lightly.

Management Control

Some angels demand a degree of management control (usually termed veto rights over particular issues) as a condition of their investment, even if they are on the board and don't take an active role in operational management. They might seek to control:

- Changes in compensation, especially stock options, for the company's top executives
- Executive hiring, including the CEO and chief financial officer
- Sale of the company or crucial or substantial assets
- Changes in the company's bylaws or articles of incorporation

- The annual business plan
- Contracts for over a particular amount (e.g., 25 percent of the amount the angel has invested)
- Borrowing over the amount of the angel's investment

The angel may also request other rights, such as:

- The right to countersign any checks over a particular amount (e.g., 10 percent of the amount the angel has invested).
- An antidilution clause, such that within a certain period, if stock in the company is sold for less than the price the angel paid, the company will issue additional shares to the angel to maintain his or her percentage of the equity ownership.
- "Tag-along" rights. In the event that a member of the management team receives an offer to sell or exchange any of his shares, that offer may be accepted only if the angel has the right to participate in the sale or exchange, on a prorata (equal percentage) basis.
- To invest in further rounds of financing in order to maintain the investor's percentage equity interest in the company, or even the right of first refusal to provide funds for any subsequent rounds of private financing.
- "Put" options on the stock he or she holds. A put is the option to force the company to buy back the stock at book value or at a set price at a specified time.
- An "unlocking" provision, whereby if there is a bona fide offer to purchase the company and the angel wishes to accept the offer while the entrepreneur does not, the company must purchase the angel's interest on the same terms as the offer to buy the entire company was made.

An angel usually will seek to protect his or her investment by piggybacking rights onto those of the founders. For instance, if the entrepreneur wishes to sell more than 10 percent of his or her stake in the company, the angel would be able to piggyback an equal percentage of his or her stake in the sale, at the same price. A similar situation exists if the company registers its common stock for sale to the public; the angel would want piggyback registration rights in order to sell some or all of his or her stake in order to cash out at the time of the IPO.

The most important issue angels and entrepreneurs face at the time of investment is defining the exit strategy.

An Exit Strategy

Perhaps the most important issue angels and entrepreneurs face at the time of investment is defining the exit strategy. It is generally agreed that out of ten investments made by the most savvy angel, three or four will go bust and the angel will be lucky to recover any of the initial investment. Another three or four will become ongoing concerns that earn mediocre results, and the angel will probably recoup all of the investment out but without much return. Only two or three will provide a profitable exit.

A thorough understanding of the various exit options, and the likelihood of each, is important at the beginning of the capital raising process. Different exit mechanisms have an influence over what an angel investor can expect as a time frame, and as the annual rate-of-return for the investment.

Contrary to popular mythology, an IPO is not usually the final outcome for a successful venture. Most companies are purchased by larger publicly traded companies before they can go public. Buying a privately held company is a whole lot easier than buying a publicly traded one.

During the 1990s, global publicly traded companies scoured the world looking for private companies to buy. This was especially true in the telecommunications and

Socially Conscious Angels

Just as there are mutual funds that only invest in companies with particular environmental or worker-rights policies, or product attributes, there are also angels who seek to invest in such companies.

One national angel investor network—Investors' Circle (IC)—based in San Francisco, tries to match its members with entrepreneurs seeking funds for companies that have a combination of good financial outlook, environmentally friendly policies, and social consciousness.

Since its inception in 1992, IC members have invested about $75 million through the group, with investments currently running in the $500,000 to $1.5 million range. Each company that passes muster through the IC due diligence process is presented to members for their consideration. Groups of four members (a member can be an individual, an institution, or a pool of up to three individuals) invest in each deal as a syndicate.

One angel commented on his socially conscious funding: "This is a unique opportunity to create a legacy, an existence that will transcend my own."

pharmaceutical/biotechnology industries. Most of these purchases were driven by the technology developed by the entrepreneurial company, as larger companies sought to add bits of technology to their portfolios for less money and more quickly than they could by developing the technology in-house.

In the telecommunications industry, Cisco, Lucent, and Nortel together spent *literally tens of billions of dollars* between 1995 to 2000, purchasing dozens of companies with innovative technology in the telephone and Internet switching industry. Young software companies were also gobbled up by the dozens.

Many of these sales were driven by investors in the entrepreneurial companies who had structured their investments in ways that gave them leverage to force the entrepreneurs to accept buyouts if the investors wished to.

Preferred stock, debt-to-equity conversions, nondilution clauses, and right-of-refusal clauses all provide angels with stronger assurance that they will exit with a profit—or at least won't lose everything—than a purchase of straight common stock. That's the rule of capitalism—he who has the gold gets to make the rules.

These protective terms need not be given as a condition of investment. They are there to be negotiated only when requested by the investor. Ideally, you as the entrepreneur will have a standard term sheet with a fair set of terms (discussed in later chapters). The standard term sheet is, in itself, a barrier to anyone wishing special consideration. Once an exception is made, the venture may be stuck with making the same condition available to all investors, at least all future investors.

Chapter Key Points

- Angels often have nonbottom-line motivations for making a particular investment. These can include: a job, an opportunity to run an entrepreneurial business, an opportunity to diversify their investment portfolio, or an opportunity to provide a social good.
- To "qualify" an angel, you need to ask about his or her motivation for the investment in your company and determine if your goals and desires for the relationship with an angel match the angel's goals and desires for the relationship with an entrepreneur.
- Angel investors structure their investments to give them a preferred position in case the company is forced to liquidate, and an exit strategy that provides them options and leverage.
- Angels use different methods to determine an entrepreneurial company's proper valuation.
- An angel's degree of management control and whether or not the angel gets a seat on the company's board are important negotiating points.

CHAPTER

9

WHO ARE VENTURE CAPITALISTS?

WITH VC FIRMS, YOU'RE PLAYING IN THE MAJOR LEAGUES

Venture capitalists (sometimes called institutional venture capitalists) are the professional managers who invest in risky, entrepreneurial businesses that have some track record and a prospect of becoming a publicly traded company. Since their advent as a distinct class of investors in the mid-1970s, venture capitalists have shown the world a new way to grow companies.

Over the past quarter century, they have developed a model for spurring the development of new ideas and providing the resources to develop those ideas into successful commercial ventures. Through the exchange of large blocks of capital for significant equity in young growing companies, venture capitalists have provided entrepreneurs a way to see their ideas blossom and grow while maintaining significant control over those efforts.

Since the late 1970s, the flow of VC funds to small entrepreneurial companies has been like a spigot turning higher and lower but never turned completely off. Successful investments bring in more venture capitalists and more investors in their funds. This money then spreads out to a larger pool of entrepreneurs. Many of these investments are made hastily, with little due diligence, on ventures that should not be funded. Success rates drop, and VC money slows to a trickle.

After the excesses of the dotcom era and the resulting shakeout from 2000 to 2002, VC firms are in a "back-to-basics" mode. The investment pace has slowed. They are rarely putting money into start-ups. Early-stage is much more broadly defined. VC firms are looking for strong management, especially previously successful entrepreneurs, industry expertise, and the ablility to execute. In many cases they are only speaking with entrepreneurs who come through referrals from sources they respect.

> *After 25 years the VC business as we know it has some characteristics of a mature industry combined with the traits of independent entrepreneurs. The established quality firms are conservative and follow evolved guidelines and processes, while those born in successful times go with trends.*

Venture capital as we know it today is a phenomenon of tax-law changes in 1976, which established great advantage for capital gains derived from investments over ordinary income. In 1978, about $3.5 billion was managed by firms in the embryonic VC industry (firms such as Venrock Associates, established by the Rockefeller family, and the Bessemer Trust). By 1983, this amount had more than tripled to $12.1 billion.

The VC community had also grown, and a number of new firms had started. Rather than tapping into smaller amounts of old money, these firms began actively soliciting wealthy investors who were willing to put money into professionally managed pools for investment in risky private-equity ventures rather than the public stock markets. VC firms sprouted in what has become the east coast version of northern California's Silicon Valley near Stanford University, around Boston near Harvard and MIT, and in New York City.

In the early 1980s, many VC investments turned out to be failures. Many went south because investors did not do enough due diligence and threw money at technological innovation that proved not to have a profit-making business model (not unlike the dotcom mania). Euphoria over this new scheme for making money diminished. VC firms started shifting their investments to entrepreneurs who could show progress in developing their products.

By the mid-1980s, venture capital for seed and early-stage financing had been significantly reduced to only about 3 percent of total VC funding.

Another shake out in the industry came in the early 1990s because VC investments made in the late 1980s were failing.

Large and well-publicized returns from successful VC investments made in the 1980s brought many more people into the VC field. Younger employees of VC firms struck out on their own, utilizing their association with their old firms' track record to raise large amounts of capital for their funds. Some of these newer venture capitalists were good; others were not.

A "tiering" effect occurred, both in the VC world and in the world of entrepreneurs. Senior managers from successful entrepreneurial companies were able to go off, start their own companies, and raise money from top-tier VC firms. Less well-known entrepreneurs sought money from firms with less prestige. As part of their contract with investors in their funds, venture capitalists are obliged to put their money to work within a certain amount of time, and less prestigious firms were often caught between the need to invest funds quickly and an insufficient number of high-quality opportunities.

With each round of adversity, the VC industry has instituted new measures to improve its success rate and manage risk more effectively. The result is that companies funded by venture capitalists today have a higher probability of success than those funded 20 years ago.

Again, as low-quality VC firms failed to perform enough due diligence on prospective investments and subsequently did not obtain high enough returns, they closed up or merged. By the early 1990s, due diligence in the VC industry had become more rigorous. More firms moved away from making seed-capital investments and toward investing in later-stage companies that had already proven their business model concept using their own money and the money provided by friends, family, and individual angels.

There was yet one more cycle. By the late 1990s, business plans touting new e-business revenue models were flooding VC firms. A few early dotcom "successes" opened the floodgates, as investment bankers and stock analysts touted early dotcom IPOs, and stock values for companies like Amazon.com, eBay, and Yahoo skyrocketed. By 1999, venture capitalists were throwing money at dotcom proposals, funding rank start-ups with $50 or even $100 million.

The term "burn rate"—the rate at which a dotcom was burning through its venture capital cash—came into use. The Dilbert cartoon of January 15, 1999, shows an entrepreneur in a venture capitalist's office. The venture capitalist says:

> Despite your cool ponytail, you seem to have squandered our investment. You'll get no more funding unless you mutter empty Internet words that make us swoon.

The entrepreneur says "e-commerce," and the venture capitalist swoons.

By 2001, even empty Internet words could not make venture capitalists swoon. When publicly traded internet stocks dove to the bottom and the IPO market dried up almost overnight, the venture capitalists cut off the flow of funds to many early-stage companies.

The venture capital model has moved from one of informality to formality over the past quarter century.

Venture Capitalists Today

The venture capital model has moved from one of informality to formality over the past quarter century. From a willingness to make deals based on an entrepreneur's enthusiasm, track record, and "guesstimates" of a market, venture capitalists have come to a point where they conduct rigorous evaluation of a business's prospects before making an investment.

You are in a better position to receive financing if you obtain the VC firm's screening criteria before submitting a proposal.

Veteran venture capitalists have always done this. But now their options have increased since successful entrepreneurs come back to the venture capitalists who funded their previous efforts. (The exception to this new model occurred with dotcom companies, where we learned that even cold-eyed venture capitalists can get taken in by investment manias.) There are three key attributes of today's venture capitalists that are worth exploring.

1. They have created ways to quickly develop a short list of prospective ventures to invest in.
2. They are increasingly specialized.
3. They establish investment consortiums with other venture capitalists and even with angels.
4. They have become more disciplined, looking for solid business fundamentals.

Quick Short Lists

Beginning in the early 1980s, venture capitalists began requiring a written business plan from any entrepreneur looking for money. No longer would they engage in a discussion without seeing the particulars written down.

With a batch of business plans in hand, the VC professional can begin the difficult task of sorting, screening, and evaluating. This three-stage assessment puts business plans through an ever-finer analysis, and at each step looks for any "fatal flaw" that will make the venture fail.

It is important to remember that this kind of analysis is more art than science. There is no one scheme that always works for picking winning ventures. There are venture capitalists who turned down the opportunity to invest in such companies as FedEx and Dell computers.

The three-stage analysis can be viewed as a funnel, as shown in figure 9-1. A large number of potential venture investments enter the funnel's wide mouth, but only a few exit the narrow mouth as part of the VC firm's portfolio. One of the secrets to VC success is to maintain a steadily increasing number of submissions since only one of dozens or hundreds will emerge as a funded company. This is commonly known as the "deal flow."

You are in a better position to receive financing if you obtain the VC firm's screening criteria before submitting a proposal.

FIGURE 9-1

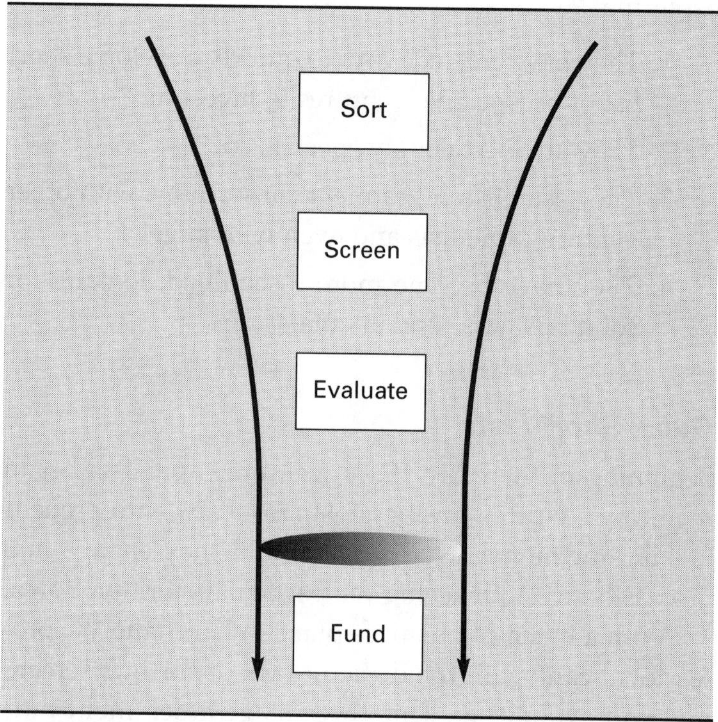

Sorting provides the filter through which ideas are given a simple yes or no based on a few straightforward criteria.

Sorting. This provides the filter through which ideas are given a simple yes or no based on a few straightforward criteria. Analysts consider whether the idea fits the venture firm's chosen business areas for investment, the level of funding requested and stage of the venture, the technology and technical feasibility, and the potential market.

Screening. Screening examines the prospective ventures that have passed the initial sort. It applies more subjective standards, such as the quality of the management, the size and ease of reaching the market, the product and its competition, the state of the technology necessary to make or properly use the product, and some rough financial projections for both capital needs and revenue.

Evaluating. In the fine evaluation, each of these areas is developed more closely to see if it will stand up to the scrutiny of an in-depth analysis necessary to make the decision to invest. At this level, the management team is evaluated for its business and entrepreneurial experience, and compatibility with one another. The market is analyzed for market channels, current competition, and potential customer base.

The product is analyzed to see whether it has advantages over competition, and whether any intellectual property rights can and should be established. Technology is analyzed to see if it is available, feasible, and cost-effective.

The financial projections are analyzed to see what the profit margin would be at various price points, what the cost is to produce the product in various quantities, what the return on investment might be, and what the payback period for the investment might be. Finally, the venture is analyzed for potential regulatory problems, legal issues, union or other worker relation issues, environmental concerns, or other intangible but potentially fatal land mines.

Guidebooks and listings of VC firms usually contain the firms specialization, as well as other worthwhile information.

Most of the prospects that today's senior venture capitalists take on previously successful entrepreneurs who are seeking money for a new venture. They also get prospects from qualified sources making referrals. Today, more and more venture capitalists are asking for a two-page synopsis of an entrepreneur's business plan. Many are even screening through a five- or ten-minute verbal pitch and Power-Point presentation.

Others have a two-stage auditioning system, where prospects make a two-minute presentation without slides. Those who make the cut are then given four or five minutes and a limited number of PowerPoint slides to tell their story. Only entrepreneurs who make it through these first two phases are asked to submit fully developed business plans for evaluation, as depicted in figure 9-2.

FIGURE 9-2

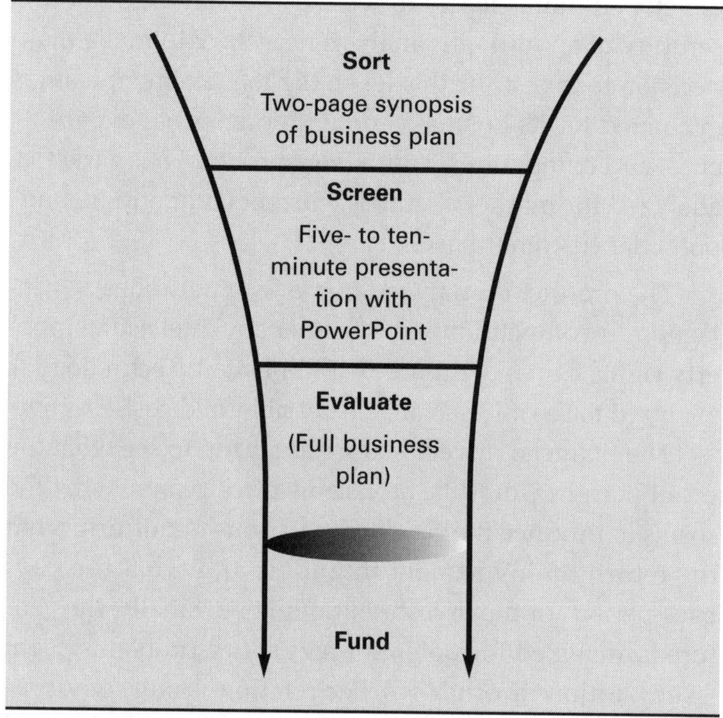

> The ever increasing complexity and subspecialization of technology has forced venture capitalists to specialize in their investments.

This methodology speeds up the analysis process and increases the number of deals considered; in essence it accelerates the deal flow. (This new methodology will be discussed in greater detail in chapter 10. What venture capitalists want for presentation material at each stage of the process will be covered in chapter 11.)

Specialization

The ever increasing complexity and subspecialization of technology has forced venture capitalists to specialize in their investments. As technology has expanded and the commercial possibilities of narrower technology have become apparent, venture capital firms have had to develop or have access to more scientific expertise to analyze potential investments.

Because the size of a VC firm's management team must be small in order to effectively run the investment portfolio, it is impossible to obtain expertise in every potential technology. Of course, it is possible to hire outside expertise to analyze technologically complex ventures, and some firms do this. Many have specialists on retainer to perform these analyses.

But it is not financially practical to have outside analysts performing a large portion of the total venture analysis. This analysis is subjective, and overuse of outside experts makes it more difficult to analyze ventures against the same criteria, and against each other, for a limited investment pool.

VC firms that invest heavily in companies with sophisticated technologies usually focus on only a handful of technologies at most.

> *Entrepreneurs should expect that a consortium will be created if the required investment exceeds a VC firm's limit or the level of technical know-how required goes beyond a firm's capabilities.*

Consortiums for Investment

Specialization, as well as the increased amount of money it takes to bring many technology innovations to fruition, has forced VC firms to work and invest together more than they did in the past.

It used to be that when an investment was larger than the amount a fund was willing to risk, a venture firm might ask other firms to participate in the investment with them. In most cases, the fund initiating the investment partnership would take the lead role, as well as the seat or seats on the company's board of directors to manage the investment for the group of investors. It would also maintain the records of the investment for the group.

Today, if a firm thinks a venture might be promising but does not have the experience or knowledge in the particular technology, it usually co-invests with a firm that does have the expertise and makes more investments in that area. If the analysis is positive, the firm that brought the proposal will be the subordinate investor, with the firm that has the expertise becoming the lead investor taking on oversight, investment management, and board participation. Sometimes, the experienced firm that decides the investment is worthwhile will invest on the condition that the initial firm takes the lead, while the experienced one provides counsel to the other. Effectively, the VC firm uses its co-investor to do the due diligence and make the critical investment decisions.

One VC firm states in its plan that it seeks to make 35 investments a year (which is a lot) but that all require a co-investor. This firm uses its sorting process to not only make an initial cut but to move potential investments to the proper partner.

Chapter Key Points

- Venture capitalists are the professional managers who invest money for others in high-risk entrepreneurial companies.
- Venture capital has been around since the end of the Second World War, with large increases in popularity in the late 1970s and mid-1980s, and then again from the mid-1990s until today.
- Venture capitalists use a three-step analysis process—a sorting, a finer screening, then a detailed evaluation—to decide on which companies to invest in.
- Venture capitalists require a constant and large "deal flow" to find enough promising companies in which to invest their funds.
- Today, more and more venture capitalists will not look at a business plan or speak with an entrepreneur unless he or she has been referred from a reliable source of referrals.

CHAPTER

10

FINDING VENTURE CAPITALISTS

MORE AND MORE, YOU NEED A REFERRAL

The best way to look for institutional venture capital is by conducting a targeted search, just like one you'd conduct for an angel investor. Remember, there many different kinds of VC funds, including:

- Private VC firms made up of a small group of individuals, who invest money pooled from wealthy individuals pension funds, university endowment funds, and/or foundations. Each "fund" managed by the VC firm has a limited number of investors and a set amount of money, and is closed when the desired amount of capital has been raised.
- Public VC funds, which operate like closed-end mutual funds, and have a large number of investors who put in smaller amounts than investors in private firms.
- Small Business Investment Companies (SBICs) and Specialized Small Business Investment Companies (SSBICs), which are private VC funds that are registered with and regulated by the SBA, and can borrow at below-market rates to supplement the private capital they raise for investment.
- VC funds operated by investment banks. These banks are responsible for underwriting initial public offerings of stock and often use their VC funds as ways to create a relationship with entrepreneurial companies. Their goal is to get the IPO business, as well as ownership of a block of the pre-IPO stock.

- Corporate VC funds owned and managed by publicly held corporations, which often take equity positions in companies that are experimenting with innovative technology. This provides an inside track to that technology through a technology license, a technology purchase, or an outright purchase of the company at a later time.
- State governments and occasionally local governments that have developed VC funds to keep or bring business into the state or city. These funds are usually managed by a professional VC firm. Cities and states use equity investments as one of their portfolio of enticements—along with loans, grants, and tax breaks—to get companies to locate in their state and provide jobs.

Your target should take into consideration four variables: geography, specialization, your company's current stage of maturity and growth, and the amount of funding you are seeking.

Figure 10-1 resembles figure 7-1, the angel investor target. Again, you begin your search close to home, with those you have the most intimate contact with, and widen it using available tools and resources.

Inside the first circle are your company's professional advisers, especially your accountant, attorney, and banker. You can often leverage these people's contacts to reach professional venture capitalists who might be their clients, or who have previously funded their clients. Remember, venture capital is a world of relationships, and venture capitalists love to invest in networks that have proven profitable in the past.

The second circle includes the same community resources you used to find angel investors. These could be chambers of commerce, local and regional business publications, local university business schools, breakfast clubs, and informal networks where angels and venture

FIGURE 10-1 Targeted Search for Venture Capital Investors

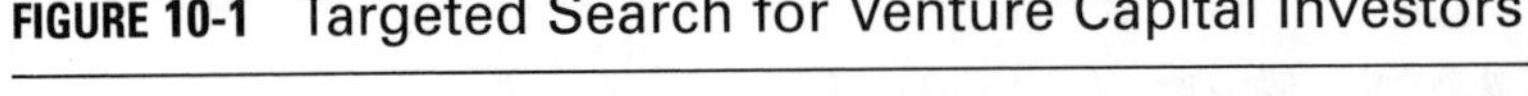

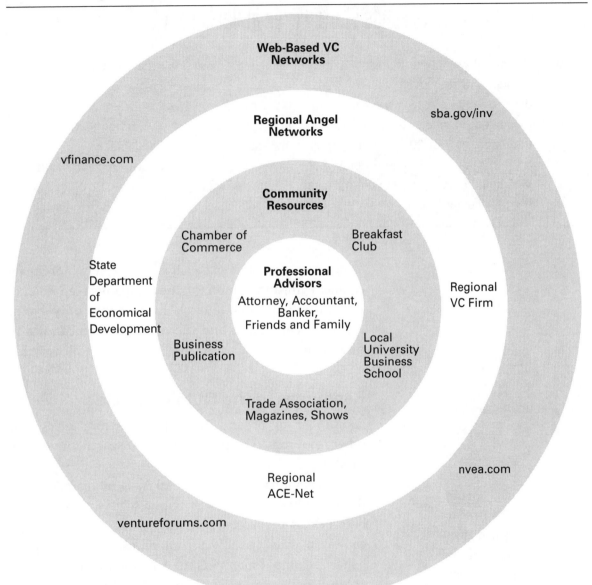

capitalists congregate. They also include your industry community—the trade magazines you read, associations you belong to, and conferences and shows you attend.

The third circle has local and regional VC funds. Many venture capitalists like to invest as close to home

VC Funds Started Even in Recession

Over $55 billion was committed to 200 new VC funds in the recession year of 2001, according to VentureWire, a research firm that tracks venture capital. This was down from the record year of 2000, when $70 billion was committed to 250 new funds. But 2001 was still the third-largest year for raising money for new VC funds.

Another key finding in the VentureWire report was that investors were moving away from funds that invest in telecommunications and the Internet, putting their money instead into funds established to invest in biotechnology, medical devices, and health care technology.

as possible, since this makes it easiest to stay in intimate contact with, and to monitor, the company being funded.

In the final outside circle is the entire universe of other VC companies and the resources you can use to find them.

A number of organizations provide directories and other resources to help you with your search for venture capital.

Resources in the Outside Circle

A number of organizations provide directories and other resources to help you with your search for venture capital.

The National Venture Capital Association (NVCA) is the VC industry's trade association, with over 400 members. NVCA members represent the majority of venture capital invested in all U.S. companies. The NVCA publishes an annual membership directory, which is available on paper for $150 or on CD-ROM for $300. The directory can also be searched online for $99. The NVCA also publishes an annual yearbook that details the venture industry's disbursements to companies, future commitments made, and IPOs and acquisitions of companies funded by members. Paper and CD-ROM directories may be ordered online, at www.nvca.com.

The NAVF runs conferences at which entrepreneurs make presentations to potential funders. It posts a calendar of upcoming venture forums, as well as proposals by ventures looking for funding, on its Web site, venturefo rums.org. The Small Business Administration has a complete list of SBICs available at sba.gov/inv.

A privately operated Web site, Vfinance.com, also provides a listing of VC providers through its VC resource library, which includes listings of hundreds of firms, with contact name, number, and a one-paragraph description of the firm and its investing model.

Many of these blurbs also link to the Web page of the firm described. Vfinance.com also has a search tool, vSearch, that can use a number of criteria to zero in on what you're looking for and produce a short list of VC firms for $1 per name.

Venture Economics company, (ventureeconomics.com) publishes the monthly *Venture Capital Journal* and the annual *Pratt's Guide to Venture Capital Sources*, which lists over 1,400 firms. Both are available on the Web.

Identifying venture capitalists is easy. But in the post dotcom era, their caution requires a stamp of credibility before they review a business plan. This means you need a reference.

The New Venture Capital Road Show

It used to be that a "road show" described when an entrepreneur took his or her presentation on the road and pitched it to individual VC firms over a two- or three-week period in order to line up investors.

Today it is more common for venture capitalists to come to entrepreneurs. These meetings follow one of two distinct models:

1. The venture forum
2. The venture capital firm cattle call

Venture Forum

A venture forum is a meeting attended by both a large number of venture capitalists and a large number of

VC Spooks

The Small Business Administration isn't the only place in the federal government to look for venture funding.

In late 1999, the Central Intelligence Agency created a private, not-for-profit VC company called In-Q-Tel to make investments in companies developing technology that can be utilized in security, intelligence gathering, and counterintelligence work.

The terrorist attacks on September 11, 2001 made In-Q-Tel a hot VC (400 entrepreneurs inquired about funding in the final three months of 2001, four times the normal number of inquiries). At the beginning of 2002, In-Q-Tel was looking seriously at 60 companies, mainly start-ups, for possible investments. The firm closed nine deals in 2001 (five were disclosed, the others remain classified), investing over $15 million total.

At the start of 2002, the Army and the Office of Homeland Security were considering establishing their own VC efforts.

entrepreneurs looking for funding. Investors or their intermediaries (i.e., attorneys and accountants) are often in attendance. These forums often include networking sessions and display halls, as well as an opportunity for a limited number of entrepreneurs to make their pitch to the assembled venture captialists.

In a cattle call, a single VC firm advertises throughout the entrepreneurial community that it is looking for business plans.

VC Firm Cattle Call

In a cattle call, a single VC firm advertises throughout the entrepreneurial community that it is looking for business plans. The model is similar to the one used by some angel clubs, and some are supported by or accredited by a local organization.

Entrepreneurs pay a fee to make the presentation. Presentations can be done in one round or two. If done in one round, all entrepreneurs are given about five minutes (and five presentation slides) to make their case. With two rounds, entrepreneurs have only two minutes (and no slides) to make their case. Then, after the cut is made, the presenters who have made it to the second round get a longer time and are allowed to show a half dozen slides. Only a handful of entrepreneurs whose presentations are deemed best are asked to submit documentation.

Fees collected from entrepreneurs making presentations help the VC firm cover expenses for travel and rental fees of the facility in which the presentations are made. Some firms that run this kind of program provide counseling and assistance in shaping the presentations before they are made.

A viable alternative to venture capitalists is to talk to a corporate venture capital department or to the R&D department of a corporation that has parallel or complementary technology/products. If your technology advances the company's efforts and products, it may fund you.

Chapter Key Points

- You need to undertake a targeted search for venture capital funding, just as you do for angel funding.
- As when looking for angel funding, use your professional advisors (accountant, lawyer, marketing consultant, business consultant) to introduce you to venture capitalists.
- There are a number of different kinds of VC firms (private, public, SBICs, investment bank, corporate, and government-sponsored). Each offers advantages and disadvantages.
- A number of Web sites are available to help with the search for venture capital.
- You can take part in the new venture capital road shows, where venture capitalists come looking for entrepreneurs.

CHAPTER

11

WHAT DO VENTURE CAPITALISTS WANT FROM YOU?

BE PREPARED TO SING FOR YOUR SUPPER

Professional venture capitalists want a lot. But that's all right. They provide a lot, too.

Over the past quarter century (save for the bursting of the dot-com bubble in 2000–2001), professional venture capitalists have consistently provided their clients (wealthy individual investors and institutions) with the highest rates of return of all investment vehicles.

These professional financiers have also developed finely honed skills and techniques that allow them to properly assess whether or not an individual entrepreneurial company will succeed over a five-year period. They have created a model for investing in those companies to the greatest advantage of their limited-partner investors.

They also have learned how to evaluate and quantify risk, and thus place a value on a closely held entrepreneurial business. This allows them to provide an appropriate level of funding in exchange for equity interest and to provide a "risk premium" (a higher rate of return for a more risky investment) for their investors.

These financiers have made their investors—and many entrepreneurs as well—very wealthy indeed.

In order to "do a deal," a professional venture capitalist has to be convinced that there is a far better than even chance the investment in the new venture will create a compound annual return of 30 percent or better for a five-year period (in other words, a 250 to 400 percent cumulative return on the invested capital over five years). In order to achieve this return for their investors, venture capitalists must closely assess risk and invest in a portfolio of companies that offers opportunities for blockbuster economic growth and various ways for the economic gain to be realized. (This will be discussed under "exit strategies" later in the chapter.)

So what do these professional, institutional venture capitalists want from you?

In general, they want ten things, which are listed below. There are exceptions, which we'll take up as we go along. Some of these exceptions have to do with the particular structure of some VC firms; others with firms that are targeted to special types of entrepreneurs (i.e., women or minorities). But these differences are usually related to form, not substance.

The first five items a professional venture capitalist wants are necessary to get you into serious discussions over the size and terms of an investment. The second five are the major terms the professional venture capitalist negotiates around. We call the first set the stage setters and the second set, the deal makers.

Venture capitalists demand integrity above all else.

The Stage Setters

Professional venture capitalists receive inquiries and business plans from hundreds of thousands of entrepreneurs each year, yet they make only about 5,000 new investments each year. Many of these are follow-on investments in companies they have already invested in, and many are in new companies run by entrepreneurs they have dealt with before in other companies. So the odds of a new entrepreneur receiving an investment are smaller still.

Each VC firm, no matter how it receives inquiries (venture fairs, business plans arriving "over-the-transom," or referrals), sees, speaks with, or reads proposals from hundreds of entrepreneurs, all seeking to be one of the handful of investments that firm makes during the year.

Once you get a VC firm to consider a proposal, there are five key stage setters a professional venture capitalist needs in order to be interested in beginning serious negotiations about an investment in your company. They are:

1. A viable business, not just a dream
2. An experienced, professional management team
3. A set of polished presentations for each of the different phases of the venture capitalist's analysis
4. Realistic projections
5. Good karma

Most institutional venture capitalists do not invest in pre-seed or seed rounds of financing.

Viable Business

Most institutional venture capitalists do not invest in pre-seed or seed rounds of financing. Of course, there are exceptions to this rule, especially among the smaller regional firms and SBICs, which are discussed in more detail in chapter 20.

For the most part, however, institutional venture capital wants to come on board after you have proven your business model and product concept; developed any innovative product (at least in prototype); and done some significant amount of market testing regarding size and receptivity of market, and sensitivity to pricing in the market. (An exception is in the area of biotechnology, where some venture capitalists are willing to come in during the early phases of new-drug research, after it has gone from the laboratory bench or computer models into animal testing.)

If your business is at the gleam-in-the-eye stage, you need to work on your own bootstrap capital (see chapters 23 to 28); investments from friends, family, and/or business partners; and possibly an angel investor.

Management Team

Institutional VC investors invest primarily on the strength of the management team and the numbers. The difference is in the relative weight different venture capitalists give to the two variables (with about two thirds of the weighting going to the dominant variable, and one third to the nondominant variable).

All institutional venture capitalists, whether they focus primarily on the management team or the numbers, want the team to be composed of professionals with a demonstrated track record in business management (especially as successful entrepreneurs) as opposed to technology. If the whole management team is technical, the venture capitalists may insist that any negotiations and ultimate investment will be predicated on finding a suitable chief executive to run the company.

Management and business viability is the foundation of venture capital interest.

The great exception to this is start-ups founded by whiz kids right out of school, recent graduates from either a top-notch MBA program or a first-rate technical program. But even in these cases, the professional venture capitalist will want to make sure it has significant influence both in the decisions made by the management team as well as the decision to change management at any time.

Polished Presentations

More venture capitalists are asking for three different, and distinct forms of presentation. These presentations correspond to the three-stage analysis (sort, screen, evaluate) performed by venture capitalists, as described in the previous chapter.

Most no longer accept unsolicited full-blown business plans. If you send in a plan, they will send it back or put it in a "slush pile," to be read by a lower-level associate as time allows.

Rather, the first presentation they want is a succinct summary—usually limited to two or three pages—of your business plan. This should be one or two pages that list the company's product, industry and market, competitive advantage (especially if it involves proprietary technology or process), senior management team, major accomplishments since founding, and major goals and objectives for the immediate future for which financing is being sought. The final page is a profit and loss (P&L) spreadsheet that goes back two years in annual increments and projects forward for two years by fiscal quarters and another three years on an annual basis.

The second presentation, if the first has piqued the venture capitalist's interest, will probably be a brief oral presentation. This might be at the firm's offices, at a regional meeting the firm holds to bring a number of presenters together, or at a third-party-sponsored venture fair the firm will be participating in.

> Some VC firms are running two- or three-day presentation festivals where they bring together dozens of entrepreneurs who have made the first cut (or sort cut) to compete against one another.

Some VC firms are running two- or three-day presentation festivals where they bring together dozens of entrepreneurs who have made the first cut (or sort cut) to compete against one another. Some of these firms are providing coaching and mentoring ahead of these presentation festivals. Many are charging entrepreneurs a fee if their proposal brief is accepted and they are asked to present; this fee offsets the firm's costs to host the event and to provide any up-front assistance to the presenters.

Such a presentation will usually be limited to five to ten minutes (some firms limit them to two minutes in a first round, then cut the field again before the longer presentations). Most ask you to give a PowerPoint presentation with your talk and to provide hard copy of the PowerPoint slides to listeners (you will be told how many to make). The size of these PowerPoint decks are also limited by the firm. PowerPoint is a simple graphics and text software program that creates presentation slides that can be projected onto a screen directly from a computer.

The third presentation is a full-blown business plan, which is the basis for an in-depth evaluation. If your company passes this evaluation, the firm can use the business plan as the basis for a detailed due-diligence investigation of your company, should it decide to pursue the investment.

Due diligence involves not just picking apart the business plan but also doing a detailed investigation of the entrepreneurial team, including personal, financial, and even criminal background checks.

Remember, professional venture capitalists are in the business of picking business plans apart.

Realistic Projections

Remember, professional venture capitalists are in the business of picking business plans apart. They have finely tuned antennae and substantial experience with which they can detect the slightest hint of exaggerated claims regarding attainable market share and pricing.

Venture capitalists also know there are no truly new ideas. If you claim there is no competition for your product, that probably means there is no viable marketplace for your product.

What venture capitalists want to see in a business plan is a product or service that exploits a market niche that large companies are ignoring, or a problem in an industry that has until now been too expensive to solve or is technologically unfeasible.

But even if you are developing the first real solution to a problem, that doesn't mean your solution will be the only one tried, or even the only one that works adequately. You will never achieve 100 percent market penetration, and you must achieve a balance between pricing and market penetration.

Venture capitalists demand realistic projections on the expense side, as well as on the revenue side. How much time and money will it take to get your product or service concept to the market, and how much will it cost to make the market aware of your product or service?

Remember, venture capitalists like to make follow-on investments. But they also weigh each new investment

How Well Do You Struggle?

A start-up software and device company was referred to a VC firm. A member of the firm said he was interested in meeting with the management team and discussing the opportunity. After the meeting and discussions with his partner, the venture capitalist told the entrepreneur the firm was extremely interested in the opportunity.

But the VC firm did not want to invest the full amount the company was seeking. The venture capitalist informed the entrepreneur that he should seek other investors, and tell potential investors that one firm was willing to invest $500,000 of the $2 million needed.

In the meantime, the start-up was in danger of running out of money before it could arrange all of this funding. Company management called the VC firm to find out if it could receive some of the funding to carry the company until it found other investors.

But the VC would not put up any money at this point.

When asked why this was, the venture capitalist replied that he and his partners were testing the entrepreneur's creativity by seeing how well he operated in a crisis and how quickly he could marshal his resources to find the necessary additional funding.

on its own risk-reward scale. If you set a record of making bad projections—by being too aggressive on income projections or not fully accounting for the time and money required to reach each milestones—your investors will make sharp adjustments to your projections and possibly your capital stream.

The world of professional venture capitalism is small, and all of the guys in it talk to one another. A reputation for insisting on unrealistic projections will make it that much harder to find funding in other places.

Good Karma

After the numbers have been crunched and the management team inspected up and down, there is still an intangible element to the relationship between a investor and an entrepreneurial business. You have to be able to work together.

Some people call it personal chemistry. We call it good karma.

The venture capitalist needs to feel that you are not just engaging in a fee-for-service relationship but that there is a basis for a deep level of trust and bonding.

Good karma is not as important for a professional venture capitalist as it is for an angel investor, who often allows these intangible relationship issues to have a greater influence on his or her willingness to invest. But it does play a role.

Think of it this way. With angels, the intangible is often a positive: they are more willing to invest because of a "good feeling" about the entrepreneur. For professional venture capitalists, the intangible can only be a negative: Despite good projections, professional management, and terrific presentations, "bad feelings" about the entrepreneur or the team can lead to a decision to pass on the investment opportunity.

Distressed ventures have an avenue for obtaining new funding because some VC firms search for companies with depressed valuations in which to make cheap investments of fresh money.

The Deal Makers

Once you've made it through the preliminaries, and the institutional venture capitalist has proven through due diligence to himself and the firm's partners that you and your company are worthy of investment, you are halfway home.

This may seem disappointing; after all that work you should be at least 80 percent of the way to getting a check. But there is a lot of negotiation (which can be difficult, although it should never be testy) to go through before the paperwork can be signed.

Section V provides a detailed discussion of the parts of the investment agreement and the specific issues surrounding negotiations. Here, we just want to touch on the five keys that venture capitalists look for to make the deal work for them (and, they hope, for you). They are:

1. A reasonable valuation of your company
2. A deal structure that protects the venture capitalist
3. A major influence on the board of directors
4. A significant equity position to make the investment fruitful
5. A set of viable exit options (known as an exit strategy)

Reasonable Valuation

The benchmark for many financiers is to determine some expected multiple on their investment over a specific period of time.

Valuation of an entrepreneurial company is very difficult. A publicly traded company is valued every day, in the marketplace. The number of shares outstanding multiplied by the price of the stock provides the company's valuation.

At the other end of the scale, a small business of long standing is also relatively easy to value. It has hard assets, regular predictable revenues and cash flow, and goodwill built up among its customer base.

But a rapidly growing entrepreneurial business, based on an innovative product or service (possibly even a technological breakthrough) is, by its very nature, a subjective valuation question.

While angels typically use informal valuation techniques (e.g., $1 million in valuation for each of five variables, up to a possible $5 million total value; good idea, working prototype, good management, meaningful revenues, and industry relationship), professional venture capitalists still depend more on valuation techniques used by investment bankers and taught in business schools. These include calculating the payback period and working through a series of discounted cash flows. The more innovative your technology, process, or product, the more difficult it is to make reasonable sales forecasts.

The benchmark for many financiers is to determine some expected multiple on their investment over a specific period of time (e.g., three times the investment in five years). This rate of return works out to be more than 30 percent per year, compounded. It is about what venture capitalists who invested at the end of the 1970s (after tax-law changes) received. During the 1980s, the rate of failures increased and average compound rate of return declined. The rate of return increased steadily during the 1990s and went through the roof in the years 1997 to 1999, but then declined rapidly as the dotcom bubble burst and many investments failed.

Some venture capitalists are beginning to use a tool known as "option pricing," an economic model that helps value the price of a financial market option, based on an assessment of the probabilities of future uncertainties.

Whatever valuation technique(s) are used, these negotiations are the starting point in any discussion over a professional venture capitalist making an investment. Entrepreneurs usually begin with their valuation, which is usually a number plucked out of the air (or one related to a prior valuation created during an angel investment).

The entrepreneur also considers the equity he has already sold and other factors that determine the viability of the venture. Only after the valuation is determined, and the venture capitalist sees how much equity is owned by other parties (you and other founders; friends and family; and angels), can he or she determine if there is a reasonable opportunity to make a meaningful investment and receive an equity position in exchange.

In the early venture capital days, some VC firms had an orderly method for arriving at the valuation, while others arrived at the result haphazardly.

Assumptions Necessary to Value Start-Ups

In the early venture capital days, some VC firms had an orderly method for arriving at the valuation, while others arrived at the result haphazardly. It is fairly straightforward to value a company that is a viable entity and has revenues and even profits. Standard discounted cash-flow calculations and other methodologies help to create a valuation, then the venture capitalist can simply say, "I will invest 25 percent of the current valuation in exchange for X percent of the total equity." This amount is always less than a straight percentage of the pre-investment amount, since the company will have a larger valuation with the new money invested.

For instance, if the venture capitalist values the company at $4 million and is willing to invest another $1 million, that's 25 percent of the current valuation, but only 20 percent of the post-investment (or "post-closing") valuation, which would be the percent of the company the venture capitalist is buying.

Another factor for the venture capitalist deciding whether to make an investment is the number of existing equity holders.

More recently, when venture capitalists were funding companies that were little more than an idea or even a dream, it became more difficult to reconcile venture capitalists' valuations with those of entrepreneurs. Without sales, analytical methods are based mainly on market definition and expenses until product launch, and wrapped up in projections.

If a company is not operating, or has been set up but is engaging in product development, creating a context for valuation requires answers to a host of questions, such as:

- Is the company entering an established industry, or one that is relatively new?
- Is the product or technology new to the industry?
- How will people or companies in the customer universe accept the product or technology?

Yet another factor for the venture capitalist deciding whether to make an investment is the number of existing equity holders. If a venture capitalist is extremely interested in the venture, yet uncomfortable because there are many other investors, he or she may work with the entrepreneur to develop a plan for buying some other investors out of the venture.

Finding Common Ground in Forecasts

Venture capitalists today want to invest in companies that not only have good management, but that can generate $100 million in annual revenue within five years.

While entrepreneurs often project such earnings, venture capitalists usually discount them by at least 50 percent on the assumption that entrepreneurs always overestimate both their product's market penetration and the price and gross margin the product can sustain.

The financial statements should show an ability to eventually generate revenues sufficient to return the venture capital investor his investment compounded at 30 percent or more for his percentage of the equity. Cash flow is used rather than net profit from the profit-and-loss statement, because net profit can include depreciation, tax-loss carry forwards, and other reductions. Cash flow is a concrete measure for determining whether the investor's share has the desired return.

Even though the venture capitalist will not usually take out his or her earnings (we'll discuss this in more detail in the section on exit strategies) the cash flow shows whether the investment is earning the desired rate of return. Again, this measurement is only taken after the fifth or sixth year the investment is in place (unless the company has been sold or gone public before then). Through the early years, the company may actually be losing money even if it has revenues, due to the costs of developing products and bringing them to market.

Today's venture capitalists are not inclined to make a simple purchase of common shares in exchange for their investments.

Deal Structure

Today's venture capitalists are not inclined to make a simple purchase of common shares in exchange for their investments. They hope to take a convertible preferred stock position and conduct the conversion from preferred stock to common stock over time or just before an IPO is undertaken.

Venture capitalists, like many angels and even some friends and family, will want this preferred stock investment because it both provides better downside protection than common stock and better potential for upside return than straight debt.

Founders, as well as friends and family and other early investors, retain their common stock. The venture capitalists thus receive returns ahead of founders and earlier investors, both if the business fails and if the company does well but not well enough to pay off everyone.

The venture capitalist also wants to determine the terms of the conversion to common stock (i.e., the events that will trigger the conversion), as well as any conditions that, should they occur, would allow him or her to get out of the deal.

Usually the amount of money a venture capitalist brings to the deal is sufficient to accomplish several milestones in the company's business plan.

Some of the other terms of the venture capitalist deal concern SEC registration rights once the company goes public (the ability to sell out of all or some of the equity position as part of the initial public offering at the same time the company sells its new shares to the public). In addition, there will be other conditions set by the venture capitalist.

Even though the venture capitalist will have one or more seats on the board (but usually not a majority), he or she will have a number of veto rights provisions (i.e., the company can't incur debt without the investor's express permission; changes in the company's charter and by-laws must be approved by the investor; and changes in the nature of the business must be approved).

As we have said before, venture capitalists prepare the term sheet. As an entrepreneur, you will be put in the position of negotiating the terms. However, the venture capitalist is at an advantage. You may be unwilling to pass on the deal—even if you don't like the terms—because you are desperate for the cash.

Usually the amount of money a venture capitalist brings to the deal is sufficient to accomplish several milestones in the company's business plan. This allows the company to achieve a higher valuation and have an easier time raising the next round of capital. It usually makes it more palatable for an entrepreneur to accept somewhat onerous conditions placed on the deal by the venture capitalist.

Board Influence

Venture capitalists also often seek to structure deals so they get substantial influence on the board of directors in order to protect their investment. For instance, if your company has a nine-person board, a venture capitalist may wish to have three seats, even though it has only purchased 20 or 25 percent of the company.

A properly defined exit strategy is perhaps the most important thing to a venture capitalist.

Significant Equity Position

In order to receive this disproportionately generous treatment, venture capitalists need to be able to acquire a large enough equity stake in the company. Even if 25 to 40 percent of the company has been sold off to friends and family and angels in prior financing rounds, it is not unusual for venture capitalists to purchase another significant portion of the company, leaving the founders with well less than a majority position.

The venture capitalist wants not only to make it possible to force out the founders, if necessary, but wants all prior investors to be less influential going forward.

Exit Strategy

A properly defined exit strategy is perhaps the most important thing to a venture capitalist. The exit strategy allows the venture capitalist to get out of the investment position "whole" (including a premium rate of return) before the entrepreneur recognizes any profit.

While you may have the vision flashing through your mind of becoming an instant billionaire through IPO, venture capitalists know that the IPO route is the least likely of all outcomes. Less than 10 percent of successful

A VC Firm for Slow-Growth Companies

The dotcom fizzle forced many VC firms to change their *modus operandi*, but few were willing to admit it. One has.

Ignition Corporation, a VC firm started in 2000 by former executives from McCaw Cellular and Microsoft, raised $285 million for investments in start-ups in wireless communications, business software, and Internet infrastructure.

But in its public announcement of the fund, Ignition said it would try to bring public the companies it funded as quickly as it had in the past. Rather, it would take a patient tack, mentoring the entrepreneurs and nurturing the companies in an effort to make them profitable before looking for an exit.

All eight Ignition founders have operating experience in communications or software. They will work closely with the entrepreneurs of businesses in which Ignition makes investments.

A strategic buyer will want to purchase the company in order to acquire something it doesn't have—most often technology but sometimes market presence or market share.

entrepreneurial companies issue an IPO within their first five years. And five years is the magic time horizon for a professional venture capitalist. (Since at least half of all new businesses fail within the first five years, according to SBA research, less than 5 percent—only one in 20 entrepreneurial businesses—will ever issue an IPO.)

So what are the other ways for a venture capitalist to exit its investment in your company?

1. Sale to a strategic buyer
2. Sale to a financial buyer
3. Earn-out (sale back to the company)

Sale to a Strategic Buyer

A strategic buyer will want to purchase the company in order to acquire something it doesn't have—most often technology but sometimes market presence or market share.

In fast-moving industries, such as telecommunications and pharmaceuticals, larger players are always taking equity positions in, or buying outright, small, nimble companies working on promising technologies. From 1998 to 2000, the three giants of North American telecommunications equipment makers—Lucent, Cisco, and Nortel— spent over $20 billion to acquire privately held companies rich in innovative technology.

Occasionally, a strategic merger will occur between two smaller companies looking to join forces in order to better battle larger industry participants. The valuations provided in these "merger of equal" transactions are hardly ever as rich as when a smaller company is bought by one of the big players. They do, however, allow passive investors such as VC firms and angels to recognize a significant return on their investments.

Occasionally, a strategic merger will occur between two smaller companies looking to join forces in order to better battle larger industry participants.

Sale to a Financial Buyer

There are a number of private-equity partnership firms that purchase operating companies after they have established a track record. These include Hicks, Muse; Kolberg, Kravitz; and Forstmann Little.

Financial buyers sometimes purchase a number of smaller companies and combine them to achieve economies of scale in operations.

Sale to a financial buyer is a more likely outcome for a company that is not involved in cutting-edge technology but has capitalized on an opportunity to fill a profitable market niche that larger players in the industry do not want to try to exploit.

Earn-Out

An earn-out is when the entrepreneurs within a business gradually buy back the equity position taken by passive investors, including payment of a premium return on the investment.

Earn-outs do not occur frequently. They are most common in companies that are exploiting an industry niche rather than dealing in innovative technology.

They are most likely to occur after a period of time when it is determined that the business will produce steady, predictable, and generous revenues, but is not the kind of blockbuster company that can produce a public offering. A candidate for earn-out is also a candidate for purchase by a financial buyer, if there is one that deals with companies in its industry.

Chapter Key Points

- When venture capitalists evaluate a potential investment, they look at ten criteria. The first five can be thought of as "stage setters" and the second five as "deal makers."
- The stage setters are: a viable business; professional management; polished presentations; realistic projections; and good karma.
- The deal makers are: reasonable valuation; advantageous deal structure; board influence; significant equity position; and viable exit options.
- Valuation is usually the starting point for investment negotiations.
- Perhaps the most important criteria for venture capitalists is a multitude of exit options.

CHAPTER

12

EQUITY-INVESTOR ARRANGEMENTS

NITTY-GRITTY LEGAL LANGUAGE IS IMPORTANT

Any time you sell a portion of your corporation to an investor, you are engaging in the sale of "securities." Sales of securities (stock shares, which are warrants that allow the holder to exchange them for shares, or bonds) are highly regulated, both at the federal level through the Securities and Exchange Commission (SEC) and at the state level.

This high degree of regulation requires that the documentation laying out the terms and conditions of the arrangement between you and an investor incorporate specific legal language. There are four different kinds of transactions for selling stock in exchange for an investment of capital:

1. Private Placement
2. Direct Public Offering (DPO)
3. Initial Public Offering (IPO)
4. Reverse Merger

Private Placement

There are two different forms of private placement, a term sheet or a private placment memorandum (PPM).

A term sheet is used when the investor is a professional venture capitalist or an angel who has been involved with private equity investing for a long time. A PPM is used for investments by friends and family and by less sophisticated angels. A PPM provides investors with more detailed disclosure about the nature and risks of the business than does a term sheet.

Term Sheet

A term sheet is a document created by a venture capitalist that lays out the terms of a capital investment by a single investor or a consortium made up of a small number of individual investors. (The parts of a term sheet will be discussed in greater detail in chapters 30 and 31.) The term sheet can be drawn up for a single investment, or for multiple investments that will take place over a timeline or when predetermined milestones are reached. These pretimed or predetermined investments by the same investor(s) are called "tranches."

Most of the required documentation in an investment offering can be found in the business plan.

The two most important things to remember about the term sheet are:

1. It is prepared as a one-time document.
2. It is subject to negotiation between the entrepreneur and the investor(s). But because term sheets are usually drawn up by the venture capitalist or angel, in reality the entrepreneur has little leverage to change the terms.

If the investor is an angel, the level of negotiation depends on how experienced the angel investor is (the more experienced, the more he or she will want, and the more tightly he or she will want it spelled out in the term sheet) and how much has been negotiated prior to writing it down in the investor agreement. The relationship between the angel and the entrepreneur is closer to parity than the relationship between entrepreneur and professional venture capitalist, because the entrepreneur needs the money but the angel may have more than strictly financial motivation for making the investment.

When the investor is a professional venture capitalist, the VC firm prepares the term sheet, and the entrepreneur must review it and comment on it. The entrepreneur enters any negotiations as the weaker party. The venture capitalist-entrepreneur relationship is clearly one where the venture capitalist holds the power. Most venture capitalists are not at all shy about declaring that "he who has the gold makes the rules" and term sheets between venture capitalists and entrepreneurs are rigid documents.

Private Placment Memorandum (PPM)

A PPM is a document drawn up to solicit investors for a sale of stock that is "exempt" from registration with the SEC. This exemption cuts down drastically on the amount of paperwork that must be generated, as well as on the cost of preparation. The Small Business Investment Incentive Act of 1980 expanded the exemptions in the original Securities Act of 1933.

While private placements are exempt from the SEC's registration requirements, they are not exempt from registration under some states' so-called blue-sky laws. Nor are they exempt from the antifraud provisions of the Securities Act of 1933.

Sale of secu- ritities are governed by both the federal securities laws and the securities laws of individual states.

Securities Laws

Sale of securitities are governed by both the federal securities laws and the securities laws of individual states. State securities laws are often referred to as "blue sky laws." They describe the guidelines and methods under which people can market within each individual state financial securities that are not registered with the SEC. The two sets of regulations are tightly intertwined, and states regulations do not supercede those of the SEC.

Federal Securities Laws

Registering an offering of stock with the SEC is necessary if you are offering your stock to the general public through either an initial public offering (IPO) or a direct public offering (DPO). But it is not necessary for a PPM. PPM's are issued under one of numerous "exemptions" to the Securities Act and Securities Exchange Act. PPMs are written explicitly so they qualify for one or more of these exemptions.

The regulations for sales of stock to small groups of qualified investors are commonly referred to as Regulation D offerings; Regulation D is an SEC regulation that was the outcome of interactions between the SEC and various state securities regulators. The three most often cited portions of Regulation D are Rules 504, 505, and 506.

> The regulations for sales of stock to small groups of qualified investors are commonly referred to as Regulation D offerings

Under Rule 504, known as the Small Business Exemption, nonpublic companies (those not subject to the reporting obligations of the Securities Exchange Act of 1934) can issue a private placement of up to $1 million in securities over a 12-month period and can sell the stock to an unlimited number of investors. Investors do not need to be "accredited."

Accredited investors include individuals who meet the SEC's criteria for being a "sophisticated investor" as well as institutional investors, private business development companies, tax-exempt organizations, a trust with more than $5 million in assets, or an entity in which all of the equity owners are accredited investors. (Since the mid-1990s, many institutional investors, including universities and pension funds, have set aside a portion of their assets for investment in private placement offerings.)

The company issuing the stock cannot be an investment company (one that simply invests in other companies rather than operating on its own for profit) or a "blank check" or "blind pool" company. (It must inform potential investors in the private placement memorandum what its operations are and what the proceeds of the stock offering will be used for.)

Under Rule 505, a company that is not an investment company (but which may be a public company under the Securities Exchange Act of 1934) may issue up to $5 million of securities over a 12-month period to an unlimited number of accredited investors and up to 35 nonaccredited investors.

Rule 506 is the most common rule under Regulation D that small companies use to prepare a PPM and issue a private placement of stock. Under Rule 506, a public or nonpublic company can sell an unlimited amount of securities to no more than 35 nonaccredited investors and an unlimited number of accredited investors.

State Securities Laws

Every state has blue sky laws designed to keep frauds that sell "the blue sky" to unwary investors from gaining a foothold in their state. Under state blue sky laws, a company that wants to sell equity investments under a uniform set of terms to more than a few individuals must register with the state's securities regulators (this may be the state securities commission, attorney general, or secretary of state), unless the investment falls within one of the exemptions of that state's particular law.

> Every state has blue sky laws designed to keep frauds that sell "the blue sky" to unwary investors from gaining a foothold in their state.

If you are going to market your company to potential investors, you must check with the securities regulator in each state in which you will conduct the marketing effort to determine what regulations your offering falls under.

You generally don't need to register an offer made to a venture capitalist, an individual angel or small group of angels, or to a small group of friends and family. However, private-equity investments such as limited partnerships that are being marketed to a larger number of potential investors whom you do not know must be registered in every state where the offering is being made. (This falls under the SEC Regulation D.)

Most states only allow unregistered stock to be sold to investors who meet the SEC's definition of an "accredited" or "sophisticated" investor. These are individuals who either have an annual income of $200,000 ($300,000 for a couple) or a household net worth of $1 million. These people are accredited to make risky financial investments because they have a financial cushion should a high-risk investment turn to dust. Because they are qualified, and presumably knowledgeable in investing, companies don't have to provide in their prospectus the same detailed description of risk that is necessary for the general public in an IPO or DPO.

Qualified investors receive a PPM, which provides limited information about the venture and its risks (essentially a business plan framed in proper regulatory language). A PPM is much less detailed than a full-blown prospectus, which must be produced for an IPO.

Create an equity distribution plan with a securities attorney in advance of raising capital.

Dialing for Dollars

Some entrepreneurs use telemarketers to raise money from investors as part of a private placement. Such an effort needs to be undertaken with great care. Solicitations should be made only to a targeted list of prospective investors and not to the general public, which would nullify the exemption from the securities registrations. It is also important not to violate the provisions of any state's blue sky laws.

Telemarketers generate more than $200 billion in sales annually, including financial products and securities. They buy lists or information from brokers, and have access to various databases, which they use to construct lists of potential buyers of private placement investments. Some companies use telephone book white pages, combined with listings of automobile registrations and local and state government real estate records to find homeowners who might fall into the right price range to buy a securities investment.

Brokerage houses are sometimes enlisted to sell these private placements to their clients. They usually sell in minimum investment blocks of $1,000, $5,000, $10,000, or even $25,000. Brokers are supposed to explain to their clients that these are unregistered, illiquid investments in high-risk ventures.

Some companies that only sell private placements use telemarketers armed with a variety of lists from market research firms, nonprofit organizations, and list generation services. List services are notorious for selling old lists, or phone book-type lists that have been "salted" with a few good names.

Some ventures have successfully used telemarketing to raise money in small amounts from strangers. But it still makes many people queasy. If you are going to look for stranger-angels, it's probably better to use one of the Internet-based matching services, where at least the potential investors have self-selected and not been called out of the blue by a silver-tongued telemarketer.

Some ventures have successfully used telemarketing to raise money in small amounts from strangers.

Restrictions on Transferability

Whether issued through a term sheet or a private placement memorandum, privately issued stock has restrictions on its resale or transfer. Because the securities have been sold to a limited number of investors, there is no public market for them. Any resale or secondary transfer must comply with both the SEC regulations under the Securities Act of 1933 and any applicable state securities laws.

Direct Public Offering

A direct public offering (DPO) is the direct sale of shares in a company to individuals; it does not rely on an investment bank to underwrite the offering or market the shares. Shares issued through a DPO are subject to the same SEC registration requirements as shares issued through an IPO that has an investment bank as an underwriter.

Once the shares are in the hands of individual investors, they can be traded through brokerage houses. Depending on the number of shares issued and the volume of shares that trade on a daily basis, they may trade on an exchange, through the NASDAQ, or in the thinly traded "over the counter" marketplace between brokers.

A DPO is a costly way to raise capital but not as costly as an IPO since there is no underwriter taking a fee. The

Internet has created a vehicle for many companies to undertake DPOs that were not previously possible. Much of the cost of a DPO comes from the regulatory burden placed on these offerings.

A DPO is sometimes used to raise capital prior to a larger public offering undertaken with the assistance of an underwriter and as an alternative to a private placment.

Understanding securities law restrictions is necessary to prepare a good strategy for raising capital.

Initial Public Offering

An initial public offering (IPO) is the more traditional way of opening a company up to investment by the general public. It is usually the culmination of the process of "growing" a new company. Venture capitalists invest in young and growing companies with the express desire of liquidating their investment in four to seven years, either through an IPO or sale of the company to a larger, publicly traded company. In either case, with their assets becoming liquid, they can exit the investment and return the cash to the investors in the fund, or reinvest it in other growing companies. Angels also often use an IPO as a time to exit the company, although they retain some investment position more frequently than do venture capitalists.

The IPO process is time-consuming and expensive, since fees must be paid to both the underwriter(s) and the attorneys who prepare the voluminous documentation, including a detailed prospectus.

Reverse Merger

In addition to issuing stock either through an IPO or a DPO, a company can also become publicly traded through a process known as reverse merger. This is when a privately held company merges into a publicly traded but dormant company (sometimes referred to as a shell company).

A reverse merger is much less expensive than issuing new stock through an IPO or even a DPO. It also takes a lot less time to accomplish and relieves you of the anxiety of having your IPO dragging along through the registration process while the market is moving down or your industry is being hit by bad news.

Your attorney or accountant, or a contact they have, might have access to a "clean shell" that you can buy. A clean shell is a company without a lot of legal liabilities hanging over it (e.g., you don't want to buy a company that ceased to exist because of asbestos-related lawsuits). In addition, you may be able to find a shell that has a significant tax-loss carry forward.

A clean shell is a company without a lot of legal liabilities hanging over it.

If the public company's previous operations were continually money-losing, the company may have ceased to operate but still have tax losses that can be used in future years to offset taxable income. That income doesn't have to come from the same line of operations but can come from your operations after you have bought the shell.

Once you have gone public through a reverse merger, you still need to raise additional capital; remember, you have simply bought the corporate shell. You can now issue shares through a secondary public offering (a stock offering after the initial one that made the shell public). You can issue warrants to current shareholders, allowing them to purchase more shares at a set price for a set period of time.

Also, once you have acquired a public shell, many more investors might be willing to engage in a private exempt stock offering.

Of course, there are some pitfalls to reverse mergers. Once you resuscitate a dormant public company, shareholders from the past might come out of the woodwork. These shareholders often maintain a constant downward pressure on your stock, seeing any increase in the share price not as evidence that you are going to make good but as an opportunity to get out of a dud investment for at least a few pennies on their original investment.

Creditors from the previous operations can also make claims against you and drain capital that would be better spent building the business.

Finally, there is always the possibility that irregularities occurred in trading of the stock in the past. This is most likely to have occurred toward the end of the previous entity's operating life, especially if the stock was at one time "delisted" from an exchange and forced to trade on so-called "Pink Sheets" or the "OTC Bulletin Board," two mechanisms for brokers to buy and sell low-value stocks. These are the least regulated tiers of the stock market, and manipulation, either by brokers or the company's previous owners and managers, may have occurred. This also will not help your relations with stockholders.

Before engaging in a reverse merger, it's important that you and your attorney, accountant, and/or other business advisor research the entity carefully.

Before engaging in a reverse merger, it's important that you and your attorney, accountant, and/or other business advisor research the entity carefully.

Accredited Investor Questionnaire

The following questionnaire, or a similar one, is used by companies along with private placement memorandums to make sure potential investors meet SEC requirements. All of these legal tests are, of course, subject to change by the SEC at any time.

1. Are you a natural person (as opposed to a corporation) whose individual net worth, or joint net worth with your spouse, exceeds $1,000,000?
2. Are you a natural person who had an individual income in excess of $200,000 in each of the two most recent years, or who had joint income with your spouse in excess of $300,000 in each of the two most recent years, and who has a reasonable expectation of reaching the same income level in the current year?
3. Are you any organization described in Section 505c(3) of the Internal Revenue Code of 1986, as

amended, or similar business trust, not formed for the specific purpose of acquiring (your company name) stock, with total assets in excess of $5,000,000?

4. Are you a trust with total assets in excess of $5,000,000, not formed for the specific purpose of acquiring (your company name) stock, whose purchase of securities is directed by a "sophisticated person" as such terms are defined in Rule 506 promulgated pursuant to the Securities Act of 1933?
5. Are you a private business development company as defined in Section 202(2)(22) of the Investment Advisers Act of 1940?
6. Are you a bank as defined in Section 3(a)(2) of the Securities Act of 1933, or any savings and loan or other institution as defined in Section 3(a)(5)(A) of the Securities Act of 1933 in its individual or fiduciary capacity; any broker or dealer registered pursuant to Section 15 of the Securities Exchange Act of 1934; any insurance company as defined in Section 2(13) of the Securities Act of 1933; any investment company registered under the Investment Company Act of 1940; or a business development company as defined in Section 2(a)(48) of the Securities Act of 1933; any Small Business Investment Company licensed by the U.S. Small Business Investment Act of 1958; any plan established and maintained by a state or its political subdivisions, or any agency or instrumentality of a state or its political subdivisions, for the benefit of its employees, if such plan has total assets in excess of $5,000,000; any employee benefit plan within the meaning of the Employee Retirement Income Security Act of 1974, if the investment decision is made by the plan fiduciary, as defined in Section 3(21) of such Act, which is either a bank, savings and

loan association, insurance company, or registered investment advisor, or the employee benefit plan has total assets in excess of $5,000,000, or, if a self-directed plan, with investment decisions made solely by persons that are "accredited investors" as such term is defined in Rule 501 of the Securities Act of 1933?

7. Are you an entity in which all of the equity owners are accredited investors?

Chapter Key Points

- You can sell stock in your company to investors in one of four ways: a private placement, a direct public offering, an initial public offering, or a reverse merger and secondary public offering.
- Private placements of stock to venture capitalists and some angels are handled through term sheets, while private placement of stock to friends and family and less sophisticated angels is carried out through a private placment memorandum.
- Sales of stock are regulated through both federal and state laws.
- Private placment transactions (both term sheets and PPMs) are covered under Regulation D of federal securities laws and are exempt from most filing requirements.
- PPMs are more heavily regulated than term sheets and must have within them a clear description of the company's goals and objectives, as well as a discussion of the risks involved in making the investment.

SECTION II

▲ ▲ ▲

BUSINESS PARTNERS

CHAPTER 13

SUPPLIERS

GOOD CASH-FLOW MANAGEMENT IS MONEY IN THE BANK

Suppliers don't normally provide capital for your business in the form of a cash investment in exchange for equity. However, they do offer credit to their customers, and working closely with your suppliers can help you capitalize your business by better managing your cash flow.

Suppliers (also known as vendors) are the people and companies that provide you with the materials, components, and other production-oriented goods that go into your product, as well as the goods and services you need to run your business.

If you have a product-driven business—i.e., you produce, distribut, or retail products—there are three ways suppliers can help you manage cash flow and reduce the need for working capital in the form of cash.

1. Buying on credit
2. Buying on consignment
3. Supplier-managed inventory

Buying on Credit

Most suppliers of goods (and some suppliers of services) are willing to provide favorable credit terms to capture new business. Of course, the best credit terms are usually extended to companies with the best credit history. And, as a new or young business, your company will have a short—or nonexistent—credit history. Still, there are suppliers who will work with you to provide manageable credit terms.

First, most suppliers do not charge interest on payments made within 30 days (and sometimes 60 days) of the date you purchase the material. This means that if you have a quick production process, or a distribution or retail business that moves purchased materials quickly to your customers, you will have a short lag between the time you get paid for your sales (assuming you offer similar terms) and the time you must pay for the goods you have purchased from your suppliers.

Relationships can be established with your supplier that range from very favorable transaction terms to outright investment in your company.

You may even find suppliers willing to extend interest-free payment for a period of time longer than it takes you to move goods. In this case, you can collect interest on the money you have earned before you must pay it to your suppliers, a situation known as "playing the float."

Playing the float is how supermarket and fast-food outlets keep their prices and profit margins low and still make money for their owners. The profit margin on a fast-food meal, for example, is essentially 0 percent. That means it costs the franchise owner of a Burger King or Wimpy's or Dunkin' Donuts as much to buy the food and paper goods, lease the space, hire the help, and take a salary every month as the store takes in from customers.

Yet the franchisee still earns a profit if suppliers give 30 or 60 days to pay with no interest charge, the rent only comes due monthly, and paychecks are cut every week. Every night the day's cash goes into a cash-management account at the bank where it earns interest until the bills fall due.

Even if your throughput time (the time your inventory is in your facility, be it production, distribution, or retail) is such that you must pay your suppliers before your customers have paid you, most suppliers will extend you credit at a rate lower than you would pay for an unsecured bank loan, and certainly lower than for your credit card.

CBS and iWon

Occassionally, a "supplier" will actually invest in a company by providing goods or services in exchange for equity.

In 1999, CBS invested $85 million in the Web portal company iWon. CBS put up $15 million in cash and provided iWon with $70 million in services in the form of advertising time.

iWon's unique offering in the crowded Web portal space was to give away a chance at $25 million worth of cash sweepstakes prizes every time a user clicked onto the portal. The company's ads, which ran on CBS from 1999 to 2001, were catchy and garnered iWon a following.

The company kept its operations lean, remained privately held, and survived the Internet bubble implosion. In November 2001, tiny iWon purchased the excite portal from Excite@home, which was liquidating through a bankruptcy proceeding, for only $10 million.

Buying on Consignment

Some suppliers are willing to sell you production materials on consignment, meaning that you only pay for what you use, and can return unused materials over a set period of time. Consignment raw material inventory is usually offered by companies that deal in products with an infinite life, such as steel or plastic resin. If you return the unused inventory six months after you take possession of it, the supplier can usually find another customer.

Consignment buying is based on the honor system; you write a check to the supplier every month for the amount of material you actually used.

Sometimes a supplier will sell you a standard amount of material every month based on your best estimate of production and provide you with more material (safety stock) on consignment in case you have higher demand than predicted.

Many suppliers also sell to retail outlets on consignment. This is typical in the clothing industry, where the financial risk has always been on the brand-label companies rather

The objective of conserving capital forces you to explore every avenue for delaying cash outflows. You have to pay your bills, but later is better.

than the retailer. If an item falls out of fashion between the time it is designed and the time it appears on retail store racks, the brand-label company is stuck with a lot of unsellable goods.

Inventory management and other transactions with suppliers demand careful record keeping to avoid errors in either party's accounts.

Supplier-Managed Inventory

Supplier-managed inventory is a technique used in manufacturing, where a supplier accepts a large order for a certain amount of raw materials, components, or subassemblies that will be used over a long period of time. Then, the supplier delivers to the purchaser only the amount of goods needed to meet a week or a day of production, holding any inventory in its own facilities. A supplier who manages your inventory may also store parts or components from other suppliers, and "kit" materials from many suppliers for delivery to you.

Suppliers charge a premium to manage your inventory for you, but it is often cheaper to pay the supplier to do it than it is to finance and build a facility for holding your own production-oriented inventory. Whether you hold the inventory or the supplier does, the payment for the goods themselves will be the same.

Maintaining good supplier relations and managing inventories with your suppliers is only one aspect of sound cash management. Another is timely receipt of accounts receivable and daily posting of income into your cash-management account.

Good cash management can win you the respect of banks and other lenders, which in turn can allow you to borrow early in your company's growth cycle and at favorable terms. In addition, banks will often consider references from suppliers, who are sometimes called trade creditors, when considering a loan in the future.

Chapter Key Points

- Suppliers infrequently take an equity stake in an entrepreneurial company.
- Good cash managment is key for small and growing companies.
- If you operate a product-oriented company, a supplier may allow you to buy on credit or consignment, and may give you favorable credit terms.
- Supplier-managed inventory can save you the cost of financing and building space to store your raw material and component inventory.
- Good credit references from suppliers can be helpful in the future, when you seek bank financing.

Other ways of minimizing cash outflow is to be Spartan in facilities, stretching inventory, using barter, and hiring consultants for necessary but not full-time services.

CHAPTER 14

CUSTOMERS

IF POSSIBLE, PIGGYBACK ON A BIG CUSTOMER'S TECHNOLOGY

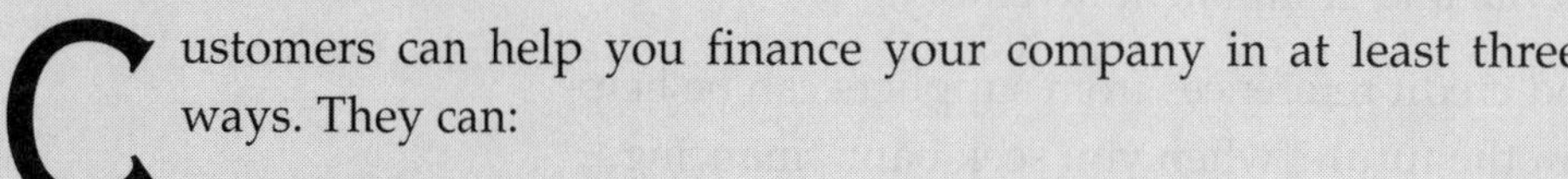

Customers can help you finance your company in at least three ways. They can:

1. Adhere to your credit terms.
2. Provide you with services through a Web-based enterprise portal.
3. Take an equity position in your company.

Customers are much more likely to invest in your company than are suppliers, especially if you provide them with critical components, software, or knowledge.

Large technology and pharmaceutical companies have for many years invested in start-up companies that can potentially provide the larger company's customer base with complementary products. Sometimes this is done through some sort of a strategic alliance (see chapter 18), and sometimes it's done through providing capital and taking an equity position.

Adhering to Your Credit Terms

For a new or young company, the flip side of working with suppliers to stretch your payments and obtain the best possible credit terms is getting your customers to pay you promptly.

It is often more difficult to work with customers than with suppliers. Suppliers are often willing to work closely with a new customer that is a young and growing company since there is a good chance the kindness will be returned when the customer becomes large and well established. Filling small orders, extending no-interest payment from 30 to 60 days for the first year, and providing favorable credit terms are all potential "loss leaders" for suppliers.

But in the world of business, what goes around comes around. Whatever you try to work out with your suppliers, your customers will try to work out with you. Many, if not most, of them have more leverage with you than you have with your suppliers. While you are hunting for suppliers who offer the best terms and conditions, so too are your potential customers.

> In the world of business, what goes around comes around. Whatever you try to work out with your suppliers, your customers will try to work out with you.

Before you open your doors for business, you need to define a payment policy that brings in cash in a timely fashion yet doesn't turn off potential customers. One of the most frequently cited reasons for small businesses closing is excessive accounts receivable and the need to pay their own suppliers, which in combination drains operating cash.

If you are operating a retail store, managing incoming cash is little or no problem. Customers will pay by cash, credit card, or check. But once you operate in the business-to-business realm and have to sell on credit, whether to other companies in a product's production chain or retailers as a distributor, you need to manage incoming cash flow closely. Always take the following four steps before you sell on credit:

- Determine the "grace period" for no-interest payment (30, 60, or 90 days).
- Determine the interest rate for payments made after the grace period.
- Create a set of standard collection documents (first letter, second letter, demand letter, etc.).
- Set a policy for when you will send an account to a collection agency or attorney.

Enterprise Portal Access

One of the hottest items in the world of business-to-business e-business is the implementation of enterprise portal software by large companies. Many companies installing enterprise portal software are increasing its usefulness by extending portal access beyond the company's own employees to other companies throughout the value chain.

An enterprise portal is front-end software (the software a computer user interacts with). It uses Web-browser technology and allows the user to have access to a host of software applications, information sources, and services that the hosting company packages. Like a consumer portal, it allows the user to move back and forth from one application, information source, or service component quickly without having to log onto each use separately.

> Large companies are beginning to use their enterprise portals to cement relationships with suppliers and B2B customers.

By extending the use of its enterprise portal to its business partners, a company that hosts a portal can streamline the information flow up and down the product value chain, and reduce its own costs along with those of its business partners.

As a small company, you don't have the resources to implement an enterprise portal. But being new, you probably are implementing computer systems throughout your company's operations. Much new software for small and medium-sized businesses can be "plugged into" other companies's enterprise portals.

Large companies are beginning to use their enterprise portals to cement relationships with suppliers and B2B customers. They are offering more and more software applications, business information, and Web-based services to their business partners. While plugging in to this may seem to make you a captive partner (and in some ways it does), it can provide you with computer horsepower that you simply can't afford on your own.

There are two ways to utilize a customer or supplier's enterprise portal to your advantage.

As a Supplier

Suppose you have created an electrical component that utilizes new technology you developed. Your product has uses in all kinds of "controls," from avionics for planes and helicopters to devices for automobile dashboards, boats, elevators, and lawn tractors. Your company will not manufacture these components but does the design engineering for them so they can be integrated into larger systems and used in various products.

DaimlerChrysler issues a request for proposals (RFP) for a new dashboard system for a car that will become available to consumers in two years. You receive a call from a major developer and manufacturer of systems for cars (called a Tier-1 supplier), such as Johnson Controls or Honeywell. The company wants to incorporate your technology into its proposal.

Piggybacking on corporate customer programs gives your company visibility and credibility, in addition to enabling you to stretch available dollars.

Such a company is big enough to implement an enterprise portal. This portal provides employees (and select business partners) with access to a variety of corporate information, software applications, and Web-based services.

You receive a code that allows you to get into the portion of the company's enterprise portal on which collaborative design takes place. Using this platform, the proposal's project manager downloads to you a copy of the RFP, with the parameters for your component highlighted.

You tinker with the basic design of your component to get it to meet the design specifications, then upload your design to all the other designers and engineers working on this project, both at the Tier-1 company and the other subcontractors.

Unfortunately, engineers at another company have designed their piece of the major system so it is incompatible with your component. The sophisticated design-management software on the Tier-1 company's in-house computer system (to which all participants have access for this project) points out the incompatibility. Before this kind of software, such an incompatibility might not have been discovered until the final system went into testing.

This problem is taken up at the regular Tuesday conference call with all of the engineers from all the partner companies. Instead of having to paw through a desk piled with design documents, each person uses a computer screen to display the items being discussed. The problem is ironed out and you go away to work on the redesign.

Toward the end of the three-month design project, the project manager calls for a face-to-face meeting (in the past, you may have been at meetings every two weeks). All project partners are given access to the company's travel service through the enterprise portal to make arrangements for planes, hotels, and rental cars.

By consolidating travel arrangements, the Tier-1 company, which is responsible for travel costs, can reduce its processing expenses by simply paying its travel service rather than reimbursing individual project partners. In addition, by logging into the travel service, each project partner creates a permanent record of preferences for future travel they may do with the company.

The system you helped design is chosen. You are asked to fill an order for 400,000 units over the next two years, with the first delivery due in nine months. As a design engineering firm, you have no manufacturing capabilities.

However, that's not a problem. The Tier-1 company puts you in touch with a contract manufacturer that has worked on sophisticated components in the past. You will work with the manufacturer to build a production line for the component, source the raw materials and parts, design and implement a quality control process, and fulfill the order.

All of this, as well as coordination with the production management team for the entire system at the Tier-1 supplier, will be done through the enterprise portal. The contract manufacturer's internal computer systems have already been integrated into the portal, so you can have access through your computer at your facility to production and inventory information. Third-party logistics providers are already on board, and their computer systems have been tied in, so you can track delivery of components to the Tier-1 supplier.

You will provide electronic invoicing to the Tier-1 supplier at the time of delivery. You will receive electronic payment and be responsible for electronic payment to the contract manufacturer, who is technically your subcontractor.

All this will be done through the enterprise portal.

Oh, and by the way, since you are now a fully integrated business partner, you can continue to have access to travel services and the same volume discounts that apply to the Tier-1 company, because you are a "subaccount." You will receive bills and make payments for your travel electronically.

Customer

Let's say your business is automotive repair and maintenance. You have a dealership agreement with a particular brand of tire (e.g., Firestone), meaning you only sell that company's tires and third-party tires that company wholesales.

Again, that company is large enough to have an enterprise portal available to its employees and business partners. These partners include suppliers of materials for tire manufacturer (steel belts, rubber, white-wall material, plastic air stems, etc.) as well as its authorized dealerships, of which you are one.

Through the enterprise portal, you can place your orders for tires and tire equipment such as balancing hardware, replacement stems, repair kits, and patches. Ordering, billing, and payment can all be done electronically. You can

A Good Reference

One company with a new technology and a well-defined market, but little money to market its idea, created an effective technique to reach its audience. It demonstrated the value of its technology to a nonprofit association that represented many of its potential customers.

The association endorsed the company's technology to its members. One member company gave the start-up an order large enough to begin production.

track the status of your order and find out when to expect delivery.

The company providing you with server access is responsible for maintaining your records' confidentiality; this is often done by having a third party manage the enterprise-portal servers.

Of course, none of this is very special; you could do it simply through a company's Web site. But an enterprise portal enables the company to increase its communication with you by "pushing" information instead of you always having to "pull" it (search for it) on a passive Web site.

Enterprise portal software allows a company to send out alerts and other important information to its portal users that is specifically tailored to them. For you, this can include new wholesale prices, special incentives to dealers and consumers, and shipping offers from the logistics carrier for orders placed at a certain time.

The enterprise portal can also save you money. Say the tire company makes a deal with a company that provides Web-based accounting software to set up a computer server dedicated to the company's distributors. Now you don't have to pay for accounting software or a computer with enough storage capacity to hold your accounting data. You simply log on to the enterprise portal, find the software, perform your accounting chores, and upload your data to the server. The company providing you with server access is responsible for maintaining your records' confidentiality; this is often done by having a third party manage the enterprise-portal servers.

The company may also allow you to gain access through its enterprise portal to a third-party e-business marketplace where distributors of auto parts, mechanics tools, or computerized diagnostic equipment sell directly to businesses like yours.

Taking a Position

Large companies, especially those in technology-based industries, sometimes take an equity position in smaller, more nimble, innovative suppliers. This was a common practice in the telecommunications industry throughout the 1990s. Cisco, Nortel, Lucent, and other large corporations bought stakes in dozens of small companies as a way to acquire access to technology that complemented their own or allowed them to challenge each other.

> Large companies, especially those in technology-based industries, sometimes take an equity position in smaller, more nimble, innovative suppliers.

In lieu of taking a position, a customer may ask you to customize a product or provide an opportunity for you to prototype a product for its customer.

Sometimes these equity stakes include an option to purchase all of the smaller company's stock within a predetermined window of time. When such purchases are carried out, it allows company founders and venture capitalists to cash out their investments without risking an initial public offering of stock.

Although some large companies do take equity positions in small companies, it is more common for them to invest in smaller innovative ones through some kind of strategic alliance (see chapter 18) or technology licensing arrangement (see chapter 19).

Chapter Key Points

Every kind of arrangement you may try to make with your suppliers, your customers may try to make with you.

- While large companies can afford to extend favorable credit terms to small companies as a "loss leader," small companies must be aggressive in collecting all of their bills.
- Defining your payment policies before you begin shipping product, and adhering to them, assures adequate cash flow.
- If you provide goods or services to a large company, tagging along on that company's enterprise portal can save you time and money in contract management, invoicing, and receiving payments.
- Large companies sometimes make investments in smaller, more nimble, innovative companies.

CHAPTER 15

EMPLOYEES

IN THE POST-DOTCOM WORLD, USE STOCK OPTIONS WITH CARE

Employees can help finance your company by accepting an equity stake in exchange for less cash compensation.

This usually means providing employees with a grant of stock options. But it can also be accomplished by creating an employee stock ownership plan (ESOP), a vehicle that transfers all or part of the company's ownership to employees over time.

Stock options are only valuable if the company's stock will become publicly traded. ESOPs make sense if the company will remain privately held and allow an owner to "cash out" or diversify her investment portfolio. ESOPs are especially useful for family-owned businesses if there are no members of the next generation who wish to own and operate the business, or if there are family tensions that might cause the business to be sold upon the owner's death.

Stock Options

A stock option provides an individual with the right to buy a share of stock at a set price for a predetermined period of time. The use of stock options as an incentive for employees of young entrepreneurial companies became widely used in the 1990s.

Huge grants of stock options were used to hire, retain, or lure away from other companies talented individuals. Many management-level employees were hired for relatively low cash compensation in exchange for the chance to become wealthy through stock options.

Since most entrepreneurial companies either fail or are sold to larger companies, rather than to the public through a stock IPO, few people granted stock options actually are able to exercise them. And since many of those companies that went public had a lock on their employee's stock—a time after the IPO when employees could not sell their stock—many of those who became paper millionaires ended up going bust.

After the dotcom bust of 2000–2001, many prospective employees of entrepreneurial companies are now saying "Forget the options, show me the money."

> There are some tricky accounting and tax implications for stock options.

Stock options in a start-up or young privately held company may give employees the right to purchase a share of stock for $2 or $3 any time within the next five years. The assumption is that the company will become publicly traded before then, and the price at which the stock is sold to the public will be set above $2 or $3.

If, for instance, a person were granted 40,000 options to buy stock at $2 in his first year of employment, the company's founder could argue that the employee is, in effect, receiving a deferred payment of $80,000. The employee's hope is that the stock will become public, be issued at $10, $15, or even $20 a share, and continue to climb. At any point until the option expires, the employee can exercise all or a portion of them (i.e., purchase the share of stock on which the option is held) and recognize an immediate gain above the deferred payment.

There are some tricky accounting and tax implications for stock options. They are not taxed at the time they are issued, but rather at the time they are exercised. The difference between the price at which an individual is able to buy the stock, known as the strike price (i.e., $2 or $3 a share) as provided for in the option and the market price at which it was purchased is taxable as ordinary income for that year. This often drives an employee into a higher tax bracket than normal.

For instance, an employee is granted 100,000 options at $3 per share in exchange for taking a low salary with a start-up, and the stock goes public two years later in an IPO at $10 per share. The owner of the options has not declared them as income in the year they were issued—after all, they had no real value then since these was no market for the stock. The employee decides to exercise those options and purchase the 100,000 shares of stock for $300,000. The stock is worth $1 million. The $700,000 difference between the market value and the price actually paid ($1,000,000 – $300,000 = $700,000) is taxable in the year the options are excercised as ordinary earned income.

For most employees to exercise stock options after a company goes public, they usually have to borrow the money from their stock broker's firm. The prudent thing to do at this point is to immediately sell enough of the stock to pay back the loan and to set aside the cash necessary to pay the taxes the next year. However, in the heady years of the late 1990s, a lot of brokers urged their clients who exercised stock options to keep the stock in a brokerage account and use it as leverage to maintain the loan they took out to buy the stock, and borrow more from the brokerage house to pay taxes (known as maintaining a margin account).

More companies have lost valuable employees through inequitable treatment than any other way.

Margin accounts must have stock equal to at least two times the amount of the outstanding loan. During the market tumble of 2000, many of people were wiped out when their stock holdings lost value and portions were continually sold to pay off some of their margin loan and maintain the margin account's ratio of value to loan amount.

Of course, if the company goes belly-up or never achieves the necessary traction to be anything but a modest-size privately held company, the employee has received a deferred payment worth $0. He or she never has a chance to become a paper millionaire or to lose everything to margin calls.

In the case of entrepreneurial companies that get sold to larger publicly traded companies, it is possible for employees who have been given stock options to make serious money. Usually they may exercise their options at any time up until the sale closes. They buy their own company's stock, then convert their shares into shares of the publicly traded company at whatever the conversion rate is (the same conversion that founders, angels, and VC investors get).

> In the case of entrepreneurial companies that get sold to larger publicly traded companies, it is possible for employees who have been given stock options to make serious money.

Regardless of how well the employee makes out, the company has not had to pay $80,000 in cash for each year of employment.

Employee Stock Ownership Plan (ESOP)

ESOPs are not that common in entrepreneurial companies today. They are much more frequently set up by established family-owned businesses. But they were somewhat popular even with start-ups from the 1980s until the middle of 1990s, when they fell out of favor.

ESOPs provide a privately held company's owners a number of tax advantages over other kinds of employee retirement plans such as profit sharing prior to the advent of 401(k) plans and SIMPLE plans for small businesses.

Profit-sharing plans, 401(k)s, SIMPLE plans, and ESOPs are all referred to as defined contribution plans. This means the amount put into the retirement plan is set, but the amount the employee will receive is not. Traditional pensions are defined benefit plans, meaning that the benefit is predetermined and based on a formula that combines years of service with pay. The employer must put in as much money as necessary to meet the defined benefit each year.

Small companies were never able to establish pension plans. Profit-sharing plans became popular in the

1970s. Under such a plan, the company would put a certain amount of money in each year, which would be divided up into individual employee accounts proportional to each employee's salary or wages. If an employee stayed long enough to become "vested" in the plan, upon leaving the employee would receive the amount in his or her profit-sharing account.

Let's say a company makes a $400,000 contribution to a profit-sharing plan for employees. The $400,000 is deductible as compensation. But the company loses the productive use of that $400,000, since it is in a trust account for the benefit of employees. If the company instead establishes an ESOP, it can make the profit-sharing payment to the ESOP, and the ESOP then turn around and buys shares in the company at an agreed-upon price. The shares are held in trust, the company gets the same tax deduction and has access to the $400,000, which means it has to borrow $400,000 less for operations and saves $40,000 or more in annual finance charges.

ESOPs can also be "leveraged," meaning the company can borrow money to fund them, and the ESOP increases its percentage of ownership in the company as the loan is paid down. Such leveraged ESOPs can be used by owners of privately held companies to cash out in a tax-advantaged way.

ESOPs can also be "leveraged," meaning the company can borrow money to fund them, and the ESOP increases its percentage of ownership in the company as the loan is paid down.

On the face of it, ESOPs look terrific. But what if the company fails? Employees are left with worthless stock as their retirement proceeds.

In fact, today employees who contribute to their company's 401(k) retirement savings program are urged not to buy company stock in their 401(k). The premise is that they are already heavily "invested" in their company by depending on their company for weekly earnings. They should use their 401(k) to diversify.

Many companies, however, "match" the employee's contribution in the form of company stock. Some even have provisions that don't allow employees to sell holdings in company stock until they have reached a certain age. Such rules existed in the case of Enron, the giant gas pipeline and energy trading company that filed for bankruptcy in December 2001. Thousands of employees who had become paper millionaires in their 401(k) plans when Enron stock traded at $90 a share in 2000 were wiped out as the stock price dipped to 40 cents a share just before the bankruptcy.

Chapter Key Points

- Employees can help finance your company by accepting an equity stake in exchange for less cash.
- Stock options are granted to employees by companies that think they will eventually sell their stock in an IPO.
- Employee Stock Option Plans (ESOPs) are a more common tool to provide employee ownership in companies that believe they will always be privately held.
- Exercising stock options creates tricky accounting and tax implications for an employee.
- Since most entrepreneurial companies don't go public, most employees who accept stock options never get a chance to exercise them.

CHAPTER

16

EMPLOYERS

DON'T TAKE A BUYOUT, CREATE A SPIN-OUT

Let's say you are not running your own business. Instead, you are working for a large company.

You have a terrific idea for a product or an innovation that appears to work. Or, you manage a business process and find yourself saying "I can do this better than the company is doing it. If I were freed from this corporate bureaucracy I could make a profit ."

What do you do?

You might try getting the corporate management to nurture your idea as a new internal corporate venture. Or, you might work a deal where your endeavor is "spun out" of the company and established as a new business, with the larger company participating in some way. The company could take an equity stake in your business (supply venture capital), work with you in a strategic alliance (see chapter 18), or license your product (see chapter 19).

Corporate Venture

Most larger companies have had internal development programs for many years. Some of these programs generate revenue by providing technologies, products, or processes.

While most companies simply add these efforts to already operating divisions, departments, or strategic business units, some establish major new revenue generators as independent ventures. Such ventures are generally

The Network Manager

A large telecommunications corporation tried to develop a network management system for itself and its clients. After spending $2 million, it abandoned the project.

The project manager thought the software had potential and was disappointed with the company's decision. Figuring he couldn't lose, he asked the company if he could take the project outside the company and pursue it independently.

He didn't have the cash to pay for the intellectual property, so the company agreed to take an equity stake in his new venture and to receive a modest percentage on all products sold using the technology for the first seven years.

Corporate venturing, a popular strategic tool in the 1980s, was created as a way for large corporations to stem the tide of entrepreneurial employees leaving the company and chasing after venture capital dollars.

different enough from the company's mainstream or even ancillary businesses that they don't fit neatly into its current product portfolio.

These intrapreneurial efforts can be held within a portfolio and managed as a professional venture capital firm might manage a portfolio of companies it has a stake in. Some companies even establish a program to which employees can bring forward their proposals outside the formal hierarchy. The process is designed to sort, screen, and evaluate these projects as potential new ventures to be funded.

Corporate venturing, a popular strategic tool in the 1980s, was created as a way for large corporations to stem the tide of entrepreneurial employees leaving the company and chasing after venture capital dollars. A number of companies had strong corporate venturing programs, including IBM (where one author of this book worked), which created 37 new ventures under its Independent Business Unit program in the 1980s.

By 1990, more than 100 major American corporations had corporate venturing programs; some of the most successful ones were those at 3M, Merck, and Corning. But the majority faded away within a few years, due to a lack of enthusiasm on the part of major corporations and an inability to blend an entrepreneurial business model for corporate venturing with a more traditional model for running ongoing business units. (We laid out a business model for corporate venturing can be found in our book, *New Corporate Ventures: How To Make Them Work*, published by John Wiley & Sons, 1988.)

Corporate internal ventures have been difficult to start, and few have been successful. However, for the entrepreneur the advantage of available resources is a prize not to be quickly dismissed. A good idea is worth the sweat it takes to get your employer interested. It could be just as tough on the outside, with greater risks.

Three Operational Options

There are three ways a corporation can structure its relationship to employee-developed entrepreneurial ideas:

1. Create a small stand-alone unit that reports to a key executive and serves as the "holding company," which grows and nurtures entrepreneurial efforts. Establish a "board of directors" for this unit.

   Initially, the entrepreneurial effort is housed within this unit. Because it is "off-line" from traditional development efforts, it can cut through the need for projects to fight for resources with others in departments, divisions, or business units.

   If the entrepreneurial effort grows and acquires critical mass, it can be pushed out and reconstituted as a separate business unit within the corporation.

2. Establish the entrepreneurial effort as a 100-percent owned subsidiary of the corporation.
3. Establish an independent entity, called a spin out, that transforms the intrapreneur into an entrepreneur. The corporation receives an equity position in the new company in exchange for its prior investment and for transferring ownership of the technology, product, or process. It can also purchase more equity to give the entrepreneur financing with which to take the company forward. (Spin outs are discussed in greater detail in the next section.)

What's Behind Spin Outs?

Corporations recognize their need intrapreneurs. However, most have not learned how to manage such employees or innovation programs within the corporate structure. The truth is that venture capitalists make their investment decisions and manage their portfolios in a way that is totally foreign to corporate management.

The dot-bomb highlights the need for sound business fundamentals. With large corporations more concerned about their resources, an intrapreneur must present a sound and compelling story.

Corporate executives are uncomfortable creating different rules for people whose endeavors are selected for internal venturing. Some of the issues that keep them from trying to operate entrepreneurial efforts within their company include:

- Milestone funding
- Sharing rewards
- Cutting losses

Milestone Funding

Corporations are used to budgeting annually. They ask all employees with budget-making authority, "What do you need to operate next year?"

However, the appropriate question for an entrepreneurial business is, "What do you need to get to the next milestone (i.e., idea to prototype, prototype to finished product, product to market, etc.)?" And milestones don't fit neatly within years.

It is possible for companies to "escrow" enough funding to get the venture through its growing stages by drawing from the escrow account as milestones are reached. This is, to some degree, what venture capitalists and angels do when they make a deal for staged funding.

But the way corporate accounting is done, the entire amount committed is booked as an expense for the year in which it was committed, and many corporations are unwilling to show that much of an up-front "loss" on their books for a venture.

Sharing Rewards

Corporations have difficulty believing that anyone who works for them deserves an equity stake in an individual venture. Sure, they want their employees to own company stock and "align their goals with that of the company." But corporate accounting makes it difficult for people to have a big piece of the action in one particular project or entrepreneurial effort.

Again, this is completely opposite to the thinking of venture capitalists. Venture capitalists want entrepreneurs to feel "ownership" of the effort. They insist that the entrepreneur put up some of her own money to fund the company, a concept known as having "skin in the game." They want entrepreneurs to get rich, because only then do venture capitalists becomes rich.

Some corporations have established programs in which employees bring their ideas to an independent review panel to see whether they qualify for resources.

Cutting Losses

Once a corporation has put a lot of money into a project, it is often loath to stop funding the effort. The corporate default position is always to take the product to market and count on marketing efforts to create success, even if the technology has been overtaken or the perceived market for the product has dried up.

Not so with venture capitalists. They constantly analyze the entrepreneurial company to see if it is achieving milestones and creating a revenue-generating and profit-making enterprise that brings them their 30 percent compounded annual rate of return (even if they don't pull their funding). If the company isn't progressing, the venture capitalist begins to look for ways to turn the situation around or to get out of the investment.

Culture of Money

These issues all have to do with the culture of money. Corporate money culture is annual-budget driven, linked to cost-accounting methods, and inherently risk averse.

Venture capital money culture is result-driven, linked to return on investment, and inherently risk taking.

In most corporations, the inevitable force of the traditional corporate culture of money eventually squashes any small efforts to run what is in effect a venture capital fund for internal innovation.

Spin Out

Just because most major corporations are unable to operate an internal venture capital function doesn't mean they don't understand the value of risk-taking entrepreneurial efforts. They simply have determined that such efforts need to be taken outside the context of the corporation's day-to-day operations.

Some companies have large portfolios of spin outs, sometimes referred to as corporate incubators.

Rather than try to corral intrapreneurship and house it inside the corporation, more and more companies are helping employees take their innovative ideas outside and set them up as stand-alone entrepreneurial businesses. This way, the company becomes a passive stake-holder through an equity investment or some other means of staying close.

Some companies have large portfolios of such spin outs, sometimes referred to as corporate incubators. In a corporate incubator, the company sets up a deliberate program of nurturing and growing ideas or concepts to the point where they can stand alone, then spins them out as stand-alone companies and takes an equity stake in each one.

To foster spin outs, a corporation creates a venture capital pool from which it makes investments in companies started by employees. These companies are based on ideas, product concepts, new processes, or technological innovations developed by the employees that the company does not want to pursue to completion but believes are viable.

Management must consider two things before spinning out an internally developed technology or product. There must be:

1. Substantive and sustainable reason for pursuing the effort.
2. Potential for large incremental value to the corporation.

Any venture spun out of a company is set up as a separate legal entity rather than a corporate subsidiary. The individual who develops the idea—and therefore "founds" the new company—may be asked to make a token cash investment in exchange for an equity stake (some make substantial investments). But the largest way he or she puts skin in the game is through the "law of no return" that most companies have set up (i.e., if the new company fails, the employee is not automatically rehired into the company). For someone who may have spent years or decades in corporate life, this is a huge risk.

Most large corporations have research and development operations and facilities for bringing an idea to fruition and demonstrable prototype.

Making the Business Case

An intrapreneur who has the potential to take her project outside the corporate walls begins developing the business case by listing the reasons the company should pursue the idea. He or she also uses each of these reasons to test and validate the idea. This is sometimes referred to as providing "proof of concept."

Of course, for each reason the intrapreneur makes for pursuing an idea, the company can make a counterclaim for not pursuing it. Major reasons might include:

- The corporation has already made a substantial investment, and this is the best way to obtain a return.

  The counter to this, of course, is that the corporation should cut its losses rather than sinking more capital into the idea as a stand-alone entity.

  In order to neutralize the counter argument, the intrapreneur needs to show that the reason the idea is not further along is not because it is bad, but because it was stifled in the corporate bureaucracy or funding was insufficient to reach the necessary milestones.

Also, in the corporate arena, many times development efforts are taken very far before being examined against the size of the potential market. If the intrapreneur has done some market testing and can show the corporate VC fund's leadership that the market potential is larger than expected, this can free up funding.

- The new company's management, having been a part of the corporation, can relate well to corporate management. Their understanding of the corporation's goals and operating guidelines reduces the "getting to know you" time that an entrepreneur would take with professional VC funders or that a corporate VC team would need if it funded a company run by entrepreneurs they had not worked with before.
- As a passive investor, corporate management will have to spend less time than in the past on managing the venture. However, the corporation can remain close to the venture and offer direction. In addition, by taking an equity position, the corporation can effectively freeze competitors from taking advantage of the new company's efforts by placing restrictive language in the investment agreement.
- Given the nature of the enterprise and its management's previous relations to the corporation, it would be easier to fold the new company back into the corporation at a later date (if appropriate) than it would be if the venture were being operated by individuals who had never been related to the corporation.

Unfortunately, real-life experience shows that most former employees who become entrepreneurs do not relish the idea of working for the corporation again. When such ventures are brought back in-house, they often leave. And, as with any entrepreneurial company, if the founder leaves, this may reduce the value of the venture.

- If the effort has already reached some of its milestones, an argument can be made that the corporation has a lot less risk investing here than in a start-up company from outside.
- Finally, by investing in the effort, the corporation is investing directly in a technology it believes is promising (or else it would not have approved the development effort being born inside).

Taking the Spin Out to the Next Level

Once a spin out has been effected, the entrepreneur may need to raise more capital to get the company to the next level. (If the corporation were providing all of the new company's capital needs, it would probably have set it up as a subsidiary.)

There are a few different ways to raise capital in this situation. Friends and family funding is not appropriate, and even if it were, it could not provide adequate funding.

The primary means of raising the next infusion of capital is through angels or, better yet, professionally managed venture capital. This is complicated by the fact that the new company already has a significant corporate equity investor, which may scare off some venture capitalists. Corporations in general have different objectives than venture capitalists, and VC firms are reluctant to work with corporations on corporate-sponsored ventures. Many do not understand the VC mindset. The conflicts between return on equity and micro-managing technology development may be too much to reconcile.

The primary means of raising the next infusion of capital is through angels or, better yet, professionally managed venture capital.

An internal venture may become the basis for a later strategic alliance between your company and your old employer.

Financial institutions may be inclined to consider the opportunity. Because a major corporation is involved, the new company has some implicit validity. An equity investment by an insurance company or a major loan from a bank or other financial services company such as GE Capital, is not out of the question. Also, the relationship with a major corporation could make it easier for the new company to borrow in the public credit market or issue stock to the public. The former parent company could even guarantee a loan.

The new company may solicit other corporations that could benefit from the technology, product, or process, or want to make VC investments. Of course, those who could benefit include competitors of the corporate benefactor, which would have to approve any approaches made to other corporations.

Another corporation with complementary technology and outside the corporate benefactor's market and industry may be willing to establish a partnering relationship (see chapter 18).

Finally, the technology, product, or process could be licensed to other companies, with the advances against future license royalties being used to complete work on the effort.

Spin Outs and Other Investors

Having corporate involvement may make finding other funding easier. While some venture capitalists believe large corporations will try to interfere with a spin out's operations and therefore dislike co-investing with them, other venture capitalists and many angels like such co-investment opportunities.

They often consider that the corporation's internal investment and spinning off of the entity is analogous to the seed- and first-round financing that entrepreneurs have to obtain. Therefore, a venture spun out

Take this Product Line

A medium-size company had been supplying components to a large corporation for one of its assemblies. The large corporation was the only customer for this particular product, and the company was moving into other product areas.

The owner of the supplying company approached the line supervisor for the product, whom he knew wished to go into business for himself. He offered to help the man start a company that would produce and sell these components. He would sell the equipment to manufacture the product and take an equity position in the new company but would have no day-to-day operational control.

from a corporation has already demonstrated the level of viability they look for when analyzing potential investments.

The corporation may represent a waiting market for the company's technology, product, or process. There is a strong possibility the corporation will further strengthen its ties to the spun-out company either by licensing any final product or process or by entering into a strategic alliance. This may include providing technical support. All in all, an angel or venture capitalist has to believe that the corporation has not spun the company out to simply fend for itself.

If the corporation actively solicits investments from a variety of sources, the entrepreneur's job is made easier.

The corporation might be willing to reaquire the company in the future, which helps the venture capitalists create a viable exit strategy. The venture capitalist may engage in discussions with the corporation to obtain a guarantee that it will reaquire the company if certain milestones are met.

If the corporation actively solicits investments from a variety of sources, the entrepreneur's job is made easier. He or she does not have to spend so much time rounding up money, and the corporation's goodwill in taking this effort makes the job of "selling" the venture to independent investors easier.

Spinning Out Dotcoms

By 2001, the e-business spin out craze had ended due to a couple of reasons.

In 1999 and 2000, a number of large corporations created e-business strategies that called for them to create an e-business venture to parallel the corporation's business, and spin it off as a self-contained company.

Corporations that chose to structure their e-business strategy this way did so because during that time, stock markets were valuing pure e-businesses at much higher multiples than they were valuing bricks and mortar companies, even those with e-business sales channels or e-business connections to suppliers.

By 2001, the e-business spin out craze had ended, due to a couple of reasons.

One was the crash in stock prices of pure e-business companies, and the reacceptance among stock market participants that even e-businesses had to make a profit. Bricks and mortar companies that had shown a steady history of making profits—especially those that

Both a Buyer and a Seller Be

A department within a large corporation had been working on a contract for another major corporation for four years. The customer questioned whether the scope of the work being performed was drifting beyond the original intent of the contract and might be inconsistent with the contract's mission. The customer didn't object to the work being performed, only that it had not been contracted for.

In light of the prospect that the contract might be cancelled, the program manager proposed to both her organization (the selling company) and the buying company that a separate business be started to perform the work being done both under and beyond the scope of the contract.

She suggested that both companies take equity positions in the company, which they did.

showed they could bring in revenue and reduce costs using e-business technology—came back into favor.

The second was that so many e-businesses that had spun out of bricks-and-mortar companies had done worse than either pure-play e-business start-ups or bricks-and-mortar companies with an e-business component.

The dotcom frenzy created a number of unique business models. One was a company called Intend Change. The start-up company, backed by $11 million in venture capital from Softbank Technology Ventures, Crosspoint Venture Partners, and USWeb/CKS, sought to help start e-business pure-play start-ups or link with e-business start-ups being spun out of bricks-and-mortar corporations.

The dot-com frenzy created a number of unique business models.

Intend Change debuted in 1999, aiming to find opportunities among Fortune 1000 companies. The process, which they called "venture construction," was theorized to work in the following way:

Intend Change would find a large bricks-and-mortar corporation looking to create a parallel e-business venture. IC would help arrange venture funding (if the venture was an e-business pure-play start-up) or work with corporate executives to devise a strategy for an e-business start-up/spin out. IC could also bring venture backing into a bricks-and-mortar e-business, so long as it was guaranteed to be spun out over time.

Over six months to one year, the e-business venture would be developed and readied for launch. At launch, Intend Change and its backers would take a 10 to 20 percent equity stake in the new business, as well as a seat on the board of directors. The company also would help the newly launched company recruit a new management team. Finally, the newly hatched e-business would operate on a lean model by outsourcing digital-business services such as IT logistics, marketing, and branding to USWeb/CKS.

Like so much of the dotcom world, this model had more sizzle than steak. Although Intend Change did help a few companies get going, none of them are household names.

Chapter Key Points

- There are many opportunities for employees to become entrepreneurs with the employers' assistance.
- Some corporations have internal venturing programs that foster "intrapreneurship."
- Companies recognize the need for entrepreneurs, but they have a difficult time managing such employees.
- Recognition that they are unable to manage internal ventures has led many corporations to "spin out" entrepreneurial companies.
- Spin outs may have difficulty moving from the stage of being funded by the entrepreneur and his or her former corporate employer to the stage of acquiring angel or VC funding.

CHAPTER

17

PROFESSIONAL SERVICE PROVIDERS

USE EQUITY TO GET ALIGNED WITH YOUR SERVICE PROVIDERS

In the heady dotcom days of 1998–2000, everyone wanted to be either an entrepreneur or a venture capitalist. Even without an idea of their own or $1 million to invest, many became successful through a kind of venture bartering arrangement.

Instead of being paid in cash for services provided to entrepreneurs, some professionals took some of their fees in the form of equity. Lawyers, accountants, marketing and public relations professionals, and management consultants are the most likely to agree to an equity stake. But even landlords have been known to take equity.

Today, with the entrepreneurial economy in the doldrums, it may be tougher to talk helpers into rolling the dice along with you and your business, but it can be done.

Some professional service providers are willing to take equity because they feel an equity stake will some day be worth more than the cash they could have taken today. They work on the notion that $1 in income today is only $1 of sales and far less than $1 in profit. But $1 taken as an equity stake in a company can some day be worth $5, $10, or more, with everything above the first $1 being pure profit.

Others take an equity stake because they have excess capacity in their businesses and prefer to gamble on some return on the other end of the deal rather than sit around waiting for cash-paying business to come through the door.

Most of those willing to take equity don't take their entire fee that way. They usually take enough in cash to cover their costs, and then take the portion of their fee that makes up their profit in the form of equity, gambling that their stake will increase in value over time. And they don't take an equity stake in any business, only in those they feel have a real potential for serious payback.

Service-providing professionals are usually in a position to do due diligence about a business while doing their work. Accountants and lawyers are privy to a company's intimate financial details. Management and operations consultants understand how the company actually does its business. Marketing and public relations consultants are able to see how the company is viewed by customers, suppliers, competitors, and other important outside groups. They all can develop some "gut feeling" about whether the business will flourish or flounder in the long run.

Service-providing professionals are usually in a position to do due diligence about a business while doing their work.

In the red-hot dotcom years, a deal for a professional service provider to take an equity stake was usually made up front, ahead of any work being done. Today's cooler economy is different. If a service provider wants to discuss taking a portion of fees in equity, that is a vote of confidence you should cherish.

Finders and Brokers

Finders and brokers are the people who help entrepreneurs find financing. In many states, brokers must be registered, while finders don't have to be. Usually, they are well-connected to a network of angel investors; professional venture capitalists are less likely to be brought into a deal by a broker or finder. Business consultants, stock brokers, and investment advisors often act as finders.

Finders and brokers, in states where they are allowed to do so, often like to take a portion of their compensation in equity. Most insist that the retainer portion of their fee and their expenses be paid in cash, but some are willing to take a portion or all of their "success fee" in the form of equity.

One often-used success-fee formula is 5 percent of the first $1 million raised, 4 percent for the next $1 million, 3 percent for the next $1 million, 2 percent for the next $1 million, and 1 percent for anything over $4 million. Thus, a broker or finder who raises $5 million would be due $150,000. If he or she were willing to take this in the form of equity, you would have enough cash to hire more employees.

Many entrepreneurs spend valuable dollars or equity satisfying part-time needs with full-time resources. You need to figure out how much work a professional service provider will do, and the amount of time you need the services, before developing an offer.

Incubators and Accelerators

Incubators and accelerators are also often willing—or even request—some of their fee in equity. Incubators have been around longer than accelerators. Incubators nurture new companies over time, while accelerators act to supercharge new companies.

Incubators

In the late 1980s and early 1990s, incubators were in vogue. Many were started by universities to support faculty-driven start-ups and to provide other entrepreneurs with access to faculty. Others were created by large corporations as a way to get and stay close to small innovative companies.

Incubators are essentially real estate that's loaded with extra services. They have always worked well for life science companies, which would have to invest heavily to build or retrofit space into laboratories.

Instead of a small company simply renting space, fitting it out as a lab and hiring its own service providers and staff, it can take space in an incubator that includes lab and office space, and shared services such as marketing and accounting, and common spaces such as conference rooms, auditoriums, and a cafeteria or on-site restaurant.

During the dotcom frenzy, companies such as Idealab and CMGI sprouted, and referred to themselves as incubators. They were essentially holding companies funded by VC money that in turn invested in equity stakes in small dotcom businesses. Having to fulfill their own funders' goals, they were driven to try to get companies from concept to initial public offering (IPO) in less than one year. However, most of the small companies and the incubators failed with the dotcom meltdown in 2000 and 2001.

All incubators are not equal. Incubators run by profit-making companies have different terms and conditions than university- or not-for-profit operations.

Corporate incubators have been more successful than dotcom incubators. Paul Weaver, chairman of the global technology program at PricewaterhouseCoopers, argues that there is more money being spent on incubating new ideas at large companies than at independent incubators.

Corporate incubators work with outside entrepreneurs who have technology or products that dovetail with their own. Such companies as AT&T, Dow Chemical, and Sony all have active incubator programs.

Existing corporations' incubators have an advantage over independent incubators, Weaver believes, because corporations are inherently strategic in their thinking, incubating efforts that relate to their core businesses. The independents' business model is purely financial, essentially venture capital with added services.

In a January 2001 survey of over 150 technology companies, PricewaterhouseCoopers found that 39 percent have formal investment programs with guidelines as to what kinds of efforts to pursue, both inside and outside the company, while 15 percent have wholly developed business incubator programs. Companies with incubator programs, the study found, have generated five-year revenue growth rates three times the average for their various industries. "They are looking for a hands-on stake in start-ups likely to pay off big dividends down the road," Weaver told the Web site UpsideToday.

Accelerators

Some 898,000 new businesses were formed in 1998, a record according to the U.S. Small Business Administration (SBA). To get their companies off the ground, some entrepreneurs turned to a growing group of accelerators to provide everything from financing to marketing.

Accelerators were spawned by the same need for speed that the for-profit incubators touted. With so many ideas—especially Internet-related ones—chasing venture capital and angel money, only those who got there early got funded.

Some accelerators are individuals, while others are groups of independent professional service providers who team up to offer "one-stop shopping" for entrepreneurs in need of services. Some larger management consulting companies have also formed accelerator-type organizations to work with smaller, entrepreneurial companies.

An accelerator can add value in many ways. In addition to rounding up financing, accelerators can find real estate, provide legal and accounting assistance, and even mentor young entrepreneurs in the rudiments of running a business.

Some angels act as accelerators. These "value-added" angels often take an active role in a company's day-to-day management and put their network of contacts to work for the entrepreneurial company.

Some for-profit incubators take equity (e.g., 3 to 5 percent) because they select companies that have the promise to grow big and look for venture capital.

Equity for Service Providers

You should probably think of service providers as participants in either a friends and family or an angel-driven round of financing. This is important when determining how much equity to sacrifice. Remember, you always need

Watch out for Double Dippers

Accelera Concepts contracted with Software Systems Co. (SoSysCo) (not the companies' real names) to secure any or all of the following:

- a strategic alliance
- additional financing
- a combination marketing-finance agreement

Accelera received a retainer to cover expenses, as well as a success fee if it brought any arrangement to fruition.

Four months later, Accelera asked SoSysCo to sign a revised contract agreeing that it would move forward to create a strategic alliance with another of its clients, and obtain financing from yet another client. Accelera also asked for a monthly fee of $5,000, larger than its current fee, as well as a substantial upward revision of the success fee.

The upshot was that Accelera was already collecting fees from the other two parties as well. When Sosysco discovered this clear conflict of interest in negotiations, the agreement was terminated.

> If you find an angel who is also acting as an accelerator, you need to factor that in when determining how much equity the angel will receive for his or her investment.

to leave enough in the pot for future rounds of financing, so you have some significant equity left at the end of the day.

If you find discrete service providers who will take some equity in the early stages of your business, don't let go of more than a total of 10 or 12 percent to them and the friends and family combined.

You probably don't have to throw around large amounts of equity to satisfy professional services providers. At this point, they know they are "taking a flyer."

If you find an angel who is also acting as an accelerator, you need to factor that in when determining how much equity the angel will receive for his or her investment. Remember, the angel's investment of time may not be equally valuable to his investment in capital.

For instance, suppose an angel wants to take 25 percent of the equity for a $500,000 investment and will provide personal services worth another $100,000 over the next year. A 25 percent stake for $500,000 assumes that the company's value is $2 million. Therefore, another $100,000 in professional services should be worth another 5 percent.

But you are taking a salary of $60,000 a year for a position that would pay $150,000 at an established company. This is based on the assumption that your low pay will be compensated on the back end through additional value in your equity position when your company is bought or goes public.

In this case, you could ask the angel to consider taking 40 cents on the dollar in extra equity for his or her efforts, or another 2 percent for $100,000 worth of professional services.

Chapter Key Points

- Some professionals (accountants, attorneys, consultants, and others) are willing to provide services to entrepreneurs in exchange for some cash and some equity in the new business.
- Brokers and finders, who try to find investors for a new business, are sometimes allowed to structure their fees as a combination of cash and equity.
- Incubators provide lab or office space, as well as ancillary services, for start-up companies. Many accept part of their fee in equity.
- Large corporations are running incubators to help both their own company's intrapreneurs launch businesses, as well as entrepreneurs who have concepts for products or services that fit well with the corporation's.
- Accelerators go beyond incubators by mentoring entrepreneurs and helping them become more attractive candidates for VC investment. Accelerators seek to provide entrepreneurs with "one-stop shopping" for many business services.

CHAPTER

18

JOINT VENTURES AND STRATEGIC ALLIANCES

MAKE YOUR COMPANY VALUABLE AS AN ALLIANCE PARTNER

People often think joint ventures and strategic alliances are the same thing. In both cases, two or more companies join together to pursue a common objective. The difference is in the degree to which the joining together results in creation of a new entity to carry out the pursuit.

In a strategic alliance, the parties join together to pursue a common and specific purpose such as marketing a product or developing a new technology. Generally, within such a collaboration, each company invests resources to support its own scope of work, carried out in its own facilities. If additional funds are necessary, they are financed by the company that needs them, and ownership of any outcome (i.e., a patent or a product) is usually shared.

A strategic alliance can be transparent to outsiders, such as customers, suppliers, and other business partners. They do not have to know about your relationship with your partner, since their relationship is with you, although any product can be designated as jointly developed.

In a joint venture, however, the partner companies contribute tangible assets (i.e., people, hard goods, finances) to a separate legal entity (a company with its own facilities and administration).

Creating a Strategic Alliance or Joint Venture

Start-up and young companies are generally better candidates for strategic alliances than joint ventures. Joint ventures are usually created by two or more large companies that want to create a platform on which all of them can gain.

Good examples of joint ventures are the industry-consortium model e-business marketplaces. These are buying and selling platforms in a particular industry created by a small group of large players who consolidate purchasing, and sometimes collaborative design throughout the industry's value chain.

Such e-business marketplaces as *Covisint* in the automotive world and *Transora* in packaged goods, are joint ventures made up of three to five large industry players and two or three technology companies. Each of these joint ventures is an independent business and does not provide any of the partners a trading advantage (although they do provide the partners a trading advantage over the suppliers, who are often being forced to use these marketplaces to work with the partners).

Entrepreneurs are often excited when a large company expresses interest in their technology or company. As a result, they behave tentatively, may be intimidated, and accept any offer. Sometimes a large company enters into discussions on a potential deal to take your product or technology off the market or to delay its entry because the company's products would be adversely affected.

Small Company Value to a Strategic Alliance

The value of an entrepreneurial company in an alliance lies in the skills and talents of its employees, its intellectual property and proprietary know-how (sometimes called its technology), and in its ability to make quick decisions and move projects quickly through its development pipeline.

A large company may need the proprietary technology for a new product, want to market the small company's product because it rounds out a product line, or be looking to diversify its own product base, using the small company's technology as a springboard.

Here we'll assume that any strategic alliance is being entered into by one large corporate partner and a small, entrepreneurial company. It is important for both parties in such an alliance to be clear about their motivations, the benefits they receive, and the other party's benefits.

Once you understand the reasons behind the alliance, it is essential to learn the proper steps necessary to put it together in such a way that it does not unravel. Dissolving an alliance is more costly and time-consuming than putting one together.

Why Small Companies Enter Strategic Alliances

Small companies enter strategic alliances with larger companies for one of many reasons. Two of the most important are to develop product without building infrastructure and to market and sell product without building a marketing and sales staff.

First, a larger company can provide a smaller company with facilities and personnel to take a new technology from the laboratory bench to the manufacturing floor without having to build the infrastructure.

> Dissolving an alliance is more costly and time-consuming than putting one together.

Second is access into markets. A large company can offer a small company entry into specific markets it has established over time. Such a relationship can give a start-up or young company credibility that is costly and time-consuming to develop from a standing start. The large company's access to markets also enables the small company to book sales and possibly even profits earlier than it otherwise might, making it a better candidate to receive further rounds of funding.

Preparing to Get into an Alliance

There are three major steps to take before entering into serious negotiations over the terms and structure of the alliance:

1. Understand the proposed partner's organization chart.
2. Determine the value of your proposed product or technology to your prospective partner.
3. Understand the proposed partner's corporate bureaucracy and how a decision whether or not to partner will be made.

FIGURE 18-1 Key Questions to Ask of Any Potential Strategic Alliance

There are eight key elements to consider in forming a strategic alliance.

1. *Strategic fit.* Does the proposed alliance help both partners to implement their respective strategies?

   ____

2. *Advantage and benefit.* What are the benefits each partner will receive from the alliance? Will these benefit increase each partner's strategic advantage within its own competitive universe?

   ____

3. *Partner competence.* Does each partner have the competences and capabilities needed to achieve the alliance's objectives?

   ____

4. *Resource demands.* Do the parties have the funds, personnel, and other resources the project requires? Are these resources sufficient to carry the project to the end? If either party does not have the resources today, will they be able to get them in a timely basis?

   ____

5. *Risks.* What are the risks involved in attempting to achieve the objective? What is the likelihood that any of these risks will occur? What would its impact be?

   ____

6. *Corporate dominance.* Will one partner in the alliance try to dominate the other?

   ____

7. *Profit and loss impact.* Will focusing on satisfying the commitments to any alliance mean diverting resources from other efforts? This is more often a concern for the small company partner. Small companies looking for resources and a quick route to achieving certain goals may enter into an alliance without thinking through what it will ultimately cost in resources and impact on other projects.

   ____

8. *Image.* How would the relationship, if known to the outside world, reflect on the partners? Again, this is of prime concern to the small company partner. Most entrepreneurs expect people to think their company and products must be worthwhile if a large corporation has teamed up with it. Unfortunately, there is some sensitivity, especially in the investment community, about small companies that are tightly interlinked with larger companies in alliances, and such an effort can hinder any future search for capital.

   ____

Understand the Organizational Chart

As soon as you begin discussions with a larger company about creating an alliance, you need to get a copy of the company's organization chart. Understanding the company's structure will give you a feel for the level of the people you are dealing with. Where in the organizational structure these people sit will, in turn, tell you something about how important this prospective alliance is to the larger company. If a mid-level manager is in charge of the alliance, it may not be as important a relationship as if a vice president is in charge of it.

A large corporation may keep you on the hook with meetings and ongoing discussions of your technology. The result is that you and your associates disclose too many details of your technology and spend your time talking instead of developing your business.

For example, one biotech company was excited by a large corporation's interest. The small company's top management was called in for meetings with three different departments over six months. But one of the small company's business advisors was not so impressed and asked the leadership to investigate how the three departments related to one another and how far along the corporation was in developing the alliance. Only then did the small company's management find out that the large company's leadership simply couldn't make up its mind which of the three departments should take responsibility for the partnership.

Nomenclature is not always helpful. It is sometimes difficult to ascertain the organizational level of the group you are talking to, regardless of whether it is called a department, branch, or division. Some companies call groups of more than two a department, while others may call a small group a branch.

Determine Your Value

Remember, large companies don't seek out small companies and strike up alliances because they are nice guys. They want something from you. That means you have some leverage.

Closely assess the importance of your product or technology to the prospective alliance partner. Is it a nice add-on to the company's current product line? Or does it fill out a strategic niche? Is it cornerstone technology for what could be a new product line needed to expand or even re-establish the larger partner's business base?

You want to get as much information about where your product or technology fits in without giving away too much sensitive or proprietary information. The more important your product or technology is to the prospective partner, the more negotiating leverage you have.

Understand the Decision-Making Process

Corporate bureaucracy can cause negotiations to be long and drawn out. Decisions that you and your top managers make in hours or days can take weeks or even months in a larger corporation. It is important in your early discussions about a potential alliance that you get a clear understanding of who makes decisions, what is needed from you to help that person reach a decision, and the time line for the decision being made.

> Corporate bureaucracy can cause negotiations to be long and drawn out.

Be candid about any other opportunities you may have to exploit the technology or market the product. But don't bully or establish ultimatums; let it be known that you can't sit and wait forever. After all, your company continues to exist and spend your financial resources.

Initial Conditions

Once you have received a positive response to creating an alliance from the larger company, begin negotiating the three basic conditions for the arrangement:

1. Project plan
2. Project budget
3. Relationship managers from each company

Plan

The long-term project plan, complete with major activities, tasks, time lines, and milestones for both parties must be a part of the alliance agreement even if the other lawyer says it can be worked out later. You need to make sure your activities mesh with your partner's in order to manage your company's resources and so everyone knows who will do what work and when.

Budget

A budget for implementing the project plan must be developed. Do not let your large corporation partner say it cannot tell how much money it is committing or that it wants to wait until everything else is funded. If they really want the alliance to work, they will commit to a dollar amount up front.

> It's important that the right person in the larger organization be assigned to manage your alliance relationship.

Relationship Managers

It's important that the right person in the larger organization be assigned to manage your alliance relationship. If the person is too low down in the organization, he or she may not be able to get attention from the corporation's top executives. This may also be true of someone who is part of the technical organization. And that person may be able to communicate the technical but not the business aspects of the alliance.

If you don't determine these factors, you could end up stuck in a situation where the larger company is slow making decisions and you are locked into the relationship.

For instance, one small company had an agreement with a large multinational corporation that called for a market launch of the smaller company's product within two years. But the corporation in the alliance for the start-up's medical technology argued that it couldn't plan the launch because it still needed to perform its own in-house tests, then take the product to clinical trials, despite the fact that the smaller company had already obtained patents and FDA approval for the substance.

After a year the smaller company began asking the corporation to set a timetable for market launch. This was important to the smaller company, because its payments from the larger company were tied to various milestones leading up to the product launch. Every time the larger company postponed an activity or slipped a milestone, it meant that payments were delayed. In addition, the longer it took to get the product to market, the longer it would be before royalty income started flowing.

After two and a half years the clinical testing was completed in Europe, and the multinational company said it wanted to do further clinical testing in the United States. The smaller company asked why this was necessary, and it soon became apparent that the multinational company simply had not prepared a comprehensive product plan. The alliance eventually collapsed.

> Most relationships don't falter at the organizing stage; they fall during implementation.

The Partnership Deal

Establishing a relationship between two companies that will work toward a common goal takes more than simply describing the legal form of the relationship, the financial terms and conditions, and issues such as liability and property ownership. Most relationships don't falter at the organizing stage; they fall during implementation.

Many people entering alliances believe that "once we get the agreements signed, it's all downhill." Unfortunately, downhill may mean rocky times rather than easy sledding.

The key to doing a deal is for each party to go beyond defining the purpose and nature of the relationship. Both partners must be willing to state in concrete terms what they want to get out of the arrangement, and each must

FIGURE 18-2 Partner Negotiating Checklist

Negotiating an agreement with a business partner can be emotional and traumatic for a number of reasons. Here is a list of negotiating points to help smooth the way:

1. **Planning and Preparation**
   - ❑ Use people inside your company as well as outside specialists to create a team with the necessary skills.
   - ❑ Do not change team members midcourse unless absolutely necessary.
   - ❑ Include marketing, financial, and technical people, as well as an attorney, on the team.
   - ❑ Know what you want out of the negotiations. Go in with a list of goals and objectives for the relationship.
2. **Negotiating Behaviors**
   - ❑ Don't talk too much. Everything you say provides clues to the other party about your motivations.
   - ❑ Don't fear silence. All negotiations need some "cooling off" time.
   - ❑ Don't accept a deadline without thinking it through. Don't let artificial deadlines limit negotiating, force a quick deal, or cause a "rush to close."
   - ❑ Don't negotiate when tired. Get enough rest and start negotiations after noon on Monday and end before noon on Friday.
   - ❑ Use anger constructively. Getting angry at the right moment is great, as it can force the other party out of complacency. But don't get angry too often; this becomes an emotional button the other party can press to achieve its aims.
   - ❑ Don't be critical without being reasonable. Constant criticism or ridicule of the other party's position can undermine yours.
   - ❑ Everybody reads upside down. Don't think the other party's negotiating team isn't full of grade-A upside-down readers. Be careful not to expose documents you don't want them to see. Let them see things you want them to see.
3. **Negotiating Tactics**
   - ❑ Forgetting, bypassing, or neglecting your strategy and objectives means you have lost the focus of the negotiation
   - ❑ Don't give "free" concessions.
   - ❑ Don't withdraw concessions.
   - ❑ Calculate how you will respond "spontaneously" to a new term introduced in negotiations.
4. **Negotiating "Musts"**
   - ❑ Always calculate the economic value of each term or condition.
   - ❑ Always get it in writing.

agree that the other's objectives are important and realistic. They must also define tasks and achievements each partner organization will undertake, and agree to a dispute-resolution mechanism.

Since the two organizations will be working closely together, they must understand each other's corporate culture and operating dynamics. Otherwise, they could be setting themselves up for the oft-repeated experience of one alliance.

An established East Coast corporation entered into an alliance with a growing West Coast technology company. The large corporation had a mature organization, and a bound management handbook, and tended to operate by the numbers. The West Coast company was growing fast and, in real terms, becoming large, but still operated in a fairly loose, highly flexible manner—like a start-up.

It took six months to put the arrangement together, and within a year the two companies wanted to break it up. Although they had negotiated all of the fine points of who would do and contribute what, the companies failed to define HOW they would operate together. The clashes of the two cultures were simply too much, and they found they could not work together.

The corporate executives who negotiate with you probably have negotiated fewer deals than you have. Your ideas and considerations are as important as theirs. They believe that, with the large company behind them, they have more clout. However, remember that they want your technology as much or more than you want an association with them.

Using Business Advisors

Owners and executives of small and growing businesses who are thinking of forming an alliance with another company often turn to their attorney for help. Some, however, fear that their long-time attorney is too "small time" for such a task and seek out specialists at a larger law firm.

Neither of these options is the right path. Unfortunately, most attorneys don't think like businesspeople. They are trained to think in terms of contingencies—what if's—and the documents they produce assume

FIGURE 18-3 Checklist of Business Terms and Conditions for Partnering Agreements

The partnering agreement is an important business document and a sensitive legal document. The following checklist will help you work through the process of creating a partnership agreement with another company. All but the final elements should be completed by business executives; the final section is to be performed by legal counsel.

- ❑ **1. Statement of Purpose (Legal term: "Recitals")**
- ❑ **2. Roles of the Partners**
- ❑ **3. Scope of Work:**

  Partners' and participants responsibilities for:
  - ❑ development
  - ❑ manufacturing
  - ❑ testing
  - ❑ marketing
  - ❑ milestone schedule

  Activities
  - ❑ time lines
  - ❑ milestone schedule
  - ❑ completion and acceptable criteria
- ❑ **3. Financial**

  Amount(s) paid by whom, to whom, distribution ratios, and purpose:
  - ❑ investment and form
  - ❑ services
  - ❑ advance payments and royalties

  Payees—commitment
  - ❑ extent
  - ❑ duration
  - ❑ consequences of defaults

  Proceeds
  - ❑ payments
  - ❑ royalties
  - ❑ allocation
- ❑ **5. Organization and Structure**
- ❑ **6. Rights to Intellectual Property**
  - ❑ ownership
  - ❑ reversions
  - ❑ licensing
  - ❑ exclusivity
  - ❑ assignment
  - ❑ extent of use
  - ❑ right of first refusal regarding other developments
  - ❑ escrow requirements
- ❑ **7. Equity**
  - ❑ earning basis and amounts
  - ❑ basis for changes—financial and other milestones
  - ❑ public stock issues (e.g., price, registration)
  - ❑ incentives
  - ❑ warrants
- ❑ **8. Indemnification**
  - ❑ patent infringement
  - ❑ allocation
- ❑ **9. Confidentiality and disclosure conditions**
- ❑ **10. Major exposures and consequences**

FIGURE 18-3 Checklist, continued

- ❑ **11. Conflict resolution formula**
- ❑ **12. Termination and exit**
  - ❑ during development phase
  - ❑ during full-scale operation
  - ❑ penalties
  - ❑ dissolution formula
- ❑ **13. Requirements (agreement contingent on completion of)**
  - ❑ delivery of "know-how"
  - ❑ examination of invention disclosures, papers, and patent disclosures
  - ❑ definition of "know-how" (This is sometimes referred to as application technology and intellectual property, refers to all information and anything that represents or describes the invention or innovation.)

  Included in know-how, without limitation:

  - ❑ all inventions covered by the patent
  - ❑ designs
  - ❑ drawings
  - ❑ photographs
  - ❑ instructions
  - ❑ prototypes and models
  - ❑ technical information
  - ❑ specifications for materials and production
  - ❑ special tools and equipment
  - ❑ data concerning development
  - ❑ testing and evaluation of inventions covered by patent
  - ❑ laboratory records and reports
  - ❑ Other data that have been developed, acquired, owned, controlled by the developer and are useful in the manufacturing and installation of inventions and/or maintaining and inspecting the same.
- ❑ **14. Legal Aspects (performed by legal counsel)**
  - ❑ compliance with laws of all jurisdictions
  - ❑ legal due diligence
  - ❑ contract enforcement
  - ❑ equipment patents and trademarks
  - ❑ patent infringement
  - ❑ contract/agreement drafting and review
  - ❑ key personnel agreements
  - ❑ tax planning
  - ❑ entity structure and plan (if separate entity formed)
  - ❑ examination of records:
    - ❑ articles of incorporation
    - ❑ financial statements
    - ❑ by-laws
    - ❑ review of existing contracts and lawsuits
    - ❑ lien search
    - ❑ draft and review opinion of counsel

a worst-case scenario. Agreements negotiated and written by attorneys are based on a simple business model: company A works "for" company B, and company B pays company A so much for its work. Such agreements are written so they can be enforced in court, assuming that one party will fail to perform its end of the bargain.

When two companies leave it to their attorneys to work out a deal, it often takes too long to negotiate, costs too much in attorney's fees, and comes out tying the hands of both parties into performing their roles in narrowly defined, often ritualistic ways. The contracts themselves create an adversarial relationship between the two parties.

An alliance is by nature not adversarial. Rather, it is a relationship based on trust.

But an alliance is by nature not adversarial. Rather, it is a relationship based on trust. You, as opposed to your lawyer, go into negotiations to set up an alliance in an optimistic frame of mind. You realize that in order to achieve your goals, you need to allow your alliance partner to achieve its goals as well. Sometimes this means you need to back off on reaching all of your goals in a particular area and agree to reach all of your goals in another area where your partner is willing to back off a little.

You also understand that businesses are organic and dynamic. You want to reach an agreement that allows both you and your partner some flexibility in how you reach the goals, if not in the goals themselves. You want it to bend with changes in business conditions, and not have to be constantly amended.

Large companies understand this. When they begin talking to another company about a relationship, be it obtaining rights to a patent, a license to market a product, or even a merger or acquisition, their business people take the lead in the negotiations and their attorneys are present as part of the team. Depending on the type of relationship, a particular businessperson will take the lead in negotiations. For a product license, a marketing executive will take the lead, with a finance person crunching the numbers to see if the basic parameters of a deal work financially to the company's benefit.

Once the business and operational conditions of the relationship have been defined and agreed to, the lawyers can step in to take the structured relationship and write it up in language that conforms to the etiquette of a legal agreement.

In a small company, you may not have the depth of expertise on staff to conduct such negotiations. That's the time to call in a business consultant, especially one who helps companies establish strategic alliances, joint ventures, and other partnering arrangements. Such a person understands the *gestalt* of business partnering, not merely the formalities of a legal agreement.

A specialist in business partnering agreements brings a number of special skills to the negotiating table:

- A business rather than a legal mindset.
- Business knowledge born of involvement in business operations.
- Technical familiarity with the particulars of the specific products or technologies under discussion.
- A working familiarity with a range of financial alternatives for structuring a partnering relationship.
- Negotiating skills that focus on formulating "win-win" arrangements rather than contingency planning for nonperformance.

> A business consultant will focus on sections of the agreement that explain the scope of the work.

A business consultant focuses on sections of the agreement that explain the scope of the work. Items discussed include: Which party will perform what portion of the work; timetables and milestone schedules; resources each party will contribute to the partnership; rights of each party to the intellectual property developed through the partnership; and how the organizations will work together to reach their common goals.

Chapter Key Points

- A strategic alliance is an agreement between two or more companies to join together to pursue a common and specific purpose, with each using its own resources to support its scope of work.
- A joint venture is an agreement between two or more companies to contribute tangible assets to a separate legal entity, with its own facilities and administration, and to share the proceeds from that separate entity.
- Start-up and young companies are far more likely to engage in a strategic alliance than in a joint venture.
- A strategic alliance benefits from a small company's skills and talents, intellectual property and proprietary know-how, and an ability to make quick decisions and move projects forward (often referred to as nimble management).
- Small companies benefit from strategic alliances in that they most often gain facilities and personnel to take a new technology from the laboratory bench to the manufacturing floor without having to build an infrastructure. They also gain access to markets.

CHAPTER

19

LICENSING YOUR TECHNOLOGY, PRODUCT, OR PROCESS

LET ANOTHER COMPANY MAKE AND/OR SELL YOUR PRODUCT

For a start-up or growing business, licensing is a viable approach for raising capital without giving away equity or incurring debt that has to be repaid with interest. The difficulty is finding a company willing to license your technology, product, or process that also has the ability to take it to market.

Licensing is conventionally thought of in connection with a sports or entertainment celebrity who licenses his or her image or name to be used in connection with a branded good. You may also be familiar with the use of licensing in art, collegiate activities, or designer clothing.

But licensing is a way to take a large variety of technologies, products, or processes to market. In fact, it has long been used by game designers and inventors who are purely creative individuals with no desire to become involved in the business aspects of their activities. (In fact, the publishing of a book is essentially a license granted by the author(s) to the publisher to conduct the business elements involved in bringing such a creative process to market.)

What Is Licensing?

Licensing, simply put, is the act of giving someone permission to use your intellectual property in exchange for a fee. Intellectual property is something that, according to law, the developer of has a right to claim as his or hers alone, the fruits of his or her creativity. In order to have a valid claim that a particular technology, product, process, or creative work is yours and yours alone, you must have registered it and acquired intellectual property protection. (For the rest of this discussion, we are going to talk about intellectual property licensing, rather than licensing name or likeness, as celebrities do.)

Licensing is complex. You'll need a qualified professional to help you develop a licensing plan and/or agreement.

Intellectual property is protected in the United States by patent, trademark, servicemark, or copyright. Once you have obtained protection for your intellectual property, whenever it is used, the user by law must pay you a fee.

Once you agree to let someone exploit the value of your intellectual property, the licensee can use it in a product or make it if it is a stand-alone product, or the licensee can contract with someone else to make it or a product that uses it.

This permission is defined in an agreement, called "rights," which describes the extent to which the other part can use your intellectual property. Anything you own you can use yourself, lease (rent), or sell. Granting a license for intellectual property is analogous to owning a physical asset (such as a building or machinery) and leasing it to another party. However, while only one party can lease a physical asset, many different parties can obtain licenses to intellectual property.

Within the agreement that spells out rights, you define limitations and constraints on how the intellectual property can be used. You (the licensor) and the user (the licensee) negotiate the terms and conditions under which the licensee can use the property. Issues to be negotiated include:

- how long the license is for or how many units of the product the licensee may produce;
- what geographic area the licensee has the right to sell in (i.e., you may license a product for sale in the Americas to one company, and in Asia to another company);

- in which of the licensee's products is it permitted to implant your technology (if you are licensing something that is not a stand-alone product);
- in how many facilities the licensee may implement your process (if you are licensing a process);
- whether the licensee may "assign" the rights it is licensing to another party.

The second part of the negotiation is around the method and payment you will receive for the license. Will payment be based on the period of time the licensee uses the technology, product, or process? Or on the level of usage (i.e., volume of units produced)?

If payment is volume based, will there be points at which the payment per unit increases or declines (i.e., $2 per unit for the first 500,000, $1.50 for the next 1,000,000 units, and $1 for any unit above 1,500,000)? If the license is granted for more than one year, will staged payments be cumulative over the life of the license, or will they begin anew each year?

Licensing can be a viable way for you to raise capital.

Using Licensing to Raise Capital

Licensing can be a viable way for you to raise capital. For instance:

- You are operating in a leading-edge industry and have developed technology that takes a particular device to the next stage of effectiveness.

  One entrepreneur started a company on the basis of a new communications development he had invented and patented. He did not have a facility, staff, or production capacity to build these subassemblies and sell them to communications equipment manufacturers for use in their devices.

  Yet he found a customer willing to pay in advance for exclusive rights to buy the subassemblies. On the strength of that customer contract, he found another company willing to license the development and build it.

- You might have a design or process that can help companies make a product less expensively.

  For instance, one company patented the design of a new type of cardboard box. Box manufacturers (corrugators) then negotiated licenses to use that design. It reduces their manufacturing costs, so they are willing to pay for it.

- It could be a process that allows another process to be carried out faster, such as the computer algorithm for testing chemical compounds used by pharmaceutical companies to fast-track drug development.
- It could simply be something that consumers would find useful, such as a small computer program (i.e., a calendar developer) that a maker of a larger software package licenses and imbeds into its program as a bonus.
- You may even be willing to license your product knowing that it won't be used.

  For instance, perhaps it would address a niche market. Another company operating in the industry in which this niche exists may have a product similar to yours. That company already has access to the market but knows that your product's features are superior. Rather than create competition in a small market, the company wishes to license your product, incorporate some of its features into its product, and eliminate you as a competitor; and is willing to pay you for doing so.

  For "appropriate consideration" (a legal term that means what you get out of the deal) you may be willing to license your product, knowing that it will be cannibalized and never reach the market.

Why License?

This all leads to the question of why you would want to license instead of exploiting the technology, product, or process yourself.

First, if you have a technology or process, licensing works well because the technology or process is, in effect, your product. You are producing a behind-the-scenes element that fosters production of goods for industrial or consumer use. While you don't make outright sales of the technology or process, licensing it has two advantages:

1. By creating a stream of license-fee payments (royalties) you are in effect, setting up an annuity for yourself or your business.
2. You do not transfer ownership of the technology or process to the licensee, so that party cannot turn around and sell it. You are protected against your process or technology being used by people or for purposes you do not agree to (assuming no one transfers the technology illegally).

If you have developed a product, licensing also has a number of advantages, especially for a small business.

- By licensing a product that is in demand, a large producer can get it to the marketplace far faster than if you had to ramp up production on your own.
- Suppose you are in an industry with short product lifecycle, such as fashion or software, and therefore have a small window within which to produce and sell goods before they fall out of favor. Licensing allows you to pass off some of the risk to a goods producer while exploiting the opportunity.
- If the product is something you created by serendipity and is not along your company's core product line, you may not want to produce it.

Licensing it allows you to use your production facilities for more important products.

- You may decide you want to be a product design company. Rather than ramping up production for each new product and establishing a marketing effort, licensing allows you to maintain a lean operation. And each license provides you with income to continue designing more products. In essence, each new product is a new venture, and the licensing fees from old products are used to capitalize each successive venture.

Marketing a license means determining who will benefit if they have rights to your intellectual property.

Financial Issues in Licensing

So where does the money come from in a licensing deal?

The "consideration" you as the licensor get in return for licensing your product is usually financial. There are other considerations you can get, such as access to the licensee's established markets for your other products, or cross licensing, in which case the parties exchange licenses that help each of them.

If you receive a fee or an advance payment against royalties, you can use that as you would any other capital infusion. Some companies are started and operated strictly for the purpose of developing and licensing intellectual property, with no intention of ever manufacturing any product. Other companies are established to manufacture, but license out all product marketing and selling.

Reverse Licensing

One innovative company that needed cash but wished to exploit its technology chose to sell the technology then license it back from the new owner.

Paying for Licensing

Payment schemes for licensing are usually determined by historical business practices in the industry in which it occurs. There are five basic license fee payment models.

1. A one-time payment when the agreement is signed for use of the technology, product, or process for a specified period of time. This method is far more common in process or technology licensing than for product licensing.
2. Royalty payments. This is the method most frequently used for product licensing. The licensee pays a certain percentage of either the gross or net sales price (gross minus expenses) of the product. In high technology, for instance, royalties run anywhere from 2 to 7 percent of gross sales.

   The royalty rate and the basis for calculation is determined by the nature of the product. For instance, if the licensed product is a component, the royalty could be based on the percentage of the price represented by that component.
3. An annual license fee, either fixed or based on sales volume. This can take the place of a royalty when it is difficult to compute what the royalty should be based on, or when the licensor does not want the burden of auditing the licensee's books.
4. A royalty with an advance payment against future royalties. The advance is credited against future royalties. This method has two advantages for the licensor.
   - First, it provides a capital infusion up front, although it is smaller than a one-time payment. This capital can be used to take the company forward.
   - Second, when the licensee pays an advance against royalties, it puts itself at some degree of risk, and motivates it to push the product hard in order to recoup the advance. Many licensors have found that with a straight royalty deal, the licensee

> A royalty payment is the method most frequently used for product licensing.

may put the product on the back burner and does not market it aggressively or use the technology to its fullest. Consequently, the licensor may not see any royalty income for a long time.

Sometimes licensors also put clauses into the agreement that force the licensee to begin utilizing the technology or process, or take the product to market, within a certain time; if it does not, it can either lose the license or pay a penalty fee.

5. A hybrid one-time fee plus royalties. The fee is not an advance and is not credited against future royalties.

Licensing fees and royalties are determined based on the value of the intellectual property that is being licensed.

Valuation of Intellectual Property

Licensing fees and royalties are determined based on the value of the intellectual property that is being licensed. You should therefore not set a particular fee or royalty rate just because it has been used for another product. Royalty rates for different kinds of products, processes, or technology generally fall within certain ranges, and the royalty for a particular piece of intellectual property or likeness generally falls somewhere within that range.

For instance, while 75 percent of all royalties are for less than 5 percent, rates for art generally fall between 5 and 8 percent; for entertainment property they are between 8 and 12 percent; and for events they run between 10 and 15 percent.

Valuing intellectual property can be difficult. Although many different methods have been identified, not all of them may be usable in any given situation. In addition, there are many intangible considerations in the marketing and technical areas.

In marketing, intangibles include corporate name and logo, promotion activities, and advertising. For instance, the name Stephen King automatically sells one million copies of a book while the names Ralph Alterowitz and Jon Zonderman do not; hence the authors of this book have far less leverage in negotiating a royalty deal with their publisher than does Stephen King.

Most of the time, a start-up or young business does not have much brand recognition and thus cannot command a high relative royalty rate for its product.

In the technical area, intangibles include packaging technology or process, technology updates, and production techniques. There is no limit to the number of such enhancements that can be added to the license. The technological intangibles that go along with one license will not necessarily be the same as those for another granted by the same licensor.

As a licensor, you should be cautious not to demand compensation for intangibles that can't be supported. However, you should consider if supporting the licensed technology, product, or process through technological intangibles adds value to the license without draining efforts from your core business. This might mean creating new intellectual property for license or products for your company to actually produce and sell.

You need to determine the value to users of your licensed technology or product in order to decide on the right compensation plan. Unless your intellectual property is completely new or in an industry that does not routinely use licensing, there are standard payment ranges.

Negotiating the Licensing Agreement

Every negotiation starts the same way (see chapter 31). You as the licensor should have established guidelines for licensing the technology, product, or process.

Have an intellectual property attorney prepare a standard licensing agreement for you to present to the prospective licensee. Guidelines for use of the intellectual property, such as what industries the licensee may market to, should be submitted in draft form for the other party to review.

Several conditions affect the negotiating protocol. For instance, as a start-up or young company, you may have been identified by a larger company as one that is developing innovative and potentially useful technology, products, or processes. The opportunity to license may have therefore come about because of another company's interest in your intellectual property, rather than by a determined effort on your part to license that intellectual property.

Having a potential licensee come to you puts you in a stronger negotiating position than if you were scrambling for funding and decided to use some intellectual-property ballast as a revenue source in order to quickly obtain cash and right your sinking ship.

FIGURE 19-1 Components of a Licensing Agreement

The following 11 sections must be included in any licensing agreement:

1. Definition and description of the intellectual property being licensed.
2. Type of rights granted (exclusive or nonexclusive).
3. Description of the geographic territory in which the licensee is allowed to use or sell the intellectual property.
4. Applications for which the intellectual property may be used.
5. Financial (sometimes referred to as compensation) specifying the applicable payments: fees and/or royalties.
6. Representations and warranties, in which the licensor states things such as that he or she is the owner of the intellectual property and has the right to execute the license.
7. Confidentiality agreement stating that the licensee must not divulge any proprietary information that it obtains while working with the licensor.
8. Proprietary rights, including who maintains the intellectual property rights, etc.
9. Infringement describing what happens if someone copies the product or uses the technology or process without a license.
10. Term or period during which the license is in force.
11. Termination describes what happens at the end of the agreement period, and under what conditions the agreement can be terminated early.

A number of other issues, such as accounting, auditing, and taxation, need to be laid out in the agreement. The best person to write the agreement is an attorney familiar with both intellectual property and licensing arrangements. Not every patent attorney is competent to write a licensing agreement or to pursue an infringement action.

Sometimes a licensing agreement is preceded by a letter of intent, which lays out the proposal in broad terms. Most, if not all, of the elements in the letter are then formalized in the final agreement. See figure 19-1 for the components of a licensing agreement.

Chapter Key Points

- Licensing is a viable option for raising capital without giving away equity or incurring debt.
- Licensing is a way to take a technology, product, or process to market without incurring the costs of producing or marketing it yourself.
- Licensing involves allowing someone else to use your intellectual property (in the form of a product, process, or know-how) in exchange for compensation.
- You, as the licensor, grant to a licensee certain "rights" to use your intellectual property in particular ways, in exchange for payment in the form of fees and/or royalties.
- A licensing agreement should be drawn up by an attorney with familiarity in both intellectual property and its protection, as well as commercial licensing agreements.

Chapter Key Points

SECTION III

▲ ▲ ▲

GOVERNMENT FUNDING

CHAPTER

20

SMALL BUSINESS ADMINISTRATION PROGRAMS

UNCLE SAM HAS SERVICES TARGETED FOR SMALL BUSINESSES 

The federal Small Business Administration (SBA) can be a key participant in your search for capital for a start-up or growing business through:

- Guarantees for loans made by banks and other lenders
- Equity investments made by Small Business Investment Companies (SBICs) or Specialized Small Business Investment Companies (SSBICs)
- Consulting and technical assistance provided by Small Business Development Centers (SBDCs)

SBA Loan Programs

In 1999 (the last year for which statistics are available), the SBA guaranteed about 49,000 loans totaling $12.5 billion. The SBA's total portfolio for that year was over $40.5 billion in loans to 486,000 small and growing businesses.

The SBA maintains two major loan programs, the Certified Development Company Loan Program, known as 504 loans; and the 7A loan guarantee program. It also has a number of smaller (in some cases pilot) loan programs.

Over 800 lenders have been designated SBA Certified Lenders. These lenders have extensive experience with SBA guaranteed loans and have

The magic of SBA programs is that almost any type of business can apply.

agreed to take on many of the responsibilities for analysis, structuring, servicing, and liquidation of loans that normally fall to the SBA. This strong relationship allows the SBA to respond to loan applications approved by a certified lender within three days, as opposed to the weeks it takes with a noncertified lender. Certified lenders account for about 10 percent of SBA guaranteed loans.

About 500 lenders have been designated SBA Preferred Lenders. They have full lending authority, and the SBA responds to their approved loan applications in one day. Preferred lenders account for an additional 30 percent of SBA guaranteed loans.

The SBA Web site has lists of certified and preferred lenders in its "listings and directories" section. It also has detailed explanations of the loan programs described briefly here.

504 Loan Guarantees

The 504 Certified Development Company (CDC) program is designed to help small and growing businesses buy facilities and major equipment. The program provides funding for companies that will expand employment or meet one of a number of public policy objectives, including business district revitalization, job creation in rural areas, expansion of exports, or small business ownership by minorities, women, and military veterans.

Loans are written for terms of ten to 20 years at a fixed below-market rate. They are jointly underwritten by a CDC, a nonprofit corporation established to contribute to the economic development of its region, and a private-sector lender. There are approximately 270 CDCs in the United States, each of which covers a specific geographic region.

You can put together a 504 loan either by working with a CDC that in turn brings a bank into the project or a bank that brings a CDC into the project. These loans are appropriate for projects with a total cost up to $2.5 to $3.0 million.

The typical project covered by a 504 loan is the purchase of a building or land for building, construction of a building, or the fitting of the building with machinery. The total package includes a loan of up to 50 percent of the project cost from a private-sector lender, covered by a senior lien, and a loan of up to 40 percent by the CDC, covered by a junior lien. The CDC loan is backed by a 100 percent SBA-guaranteed debenture.

The CDC's 40 percent can be up to $1 million for projects that create jobs and up to $1.3 million for projects that meet other public policy objectives. Technically, the bank's contribution can be unlimited.

Your contribution to the project is expected to be 10 percent of the cost. Project assets being financed are used as the collateral. You are also expected to personally guarantee the loan. You are eligible for a 504 loan if your company has a net worth of less than $6 million and average net income of more than $2 million in each of the previous two years.

Having three parties involved in making the loan, and the myriad federal regulations, can make this a complex transaction. Expect to pay a fee of 3 percent of the amount of the loan, which can be written in.

The SBA has increased the number of programs available and made it easier to apply for them. Review the conditions of each program.

7A Loan Guarantees

Under the 7A loan guarantee program, you apply for a loan through a bank or other lending institution. This program provides an SBA guarantee for a portion of the loan, helping the lender make a loan to a small business that otherwise would not be able to secure a loan on reasonable terms.

For loans of under $150,000, the SBA will guarantee 85 percent. From $150,000 to $1 million, it will guarantee 75 percent.

Most types of businesses are eligible. Eligibility is determined by the size of the business, calculated either as a number of employees or net worth, depending on the industry.

Loan maturities of up to 25 years are available for purchase of real estate and capital equipment, and up to seven years for working capital. The 7A program has some advantages over the 504 program for real estate purchases, including the longer maturity and no need to show public policy or job creation benefits.

You may apply for SBA programs while concurrently exploring other sources of capital.

Loans are also available for purchasing a business, buying a franchise, agricultural and fishing businesses, medical facilities, recreational facilities, and clubs. Loans cannot be used for speculative real estate, lending, or multilevel marketing (pyramid sales) companies.

Interest rates may be fixed or variable, and the SBA sets maximum rates in relation to the prime rate that lenders can charge. Lenders are not allowed to charge many of the typical fees associated with borrowing, although there is a onetime guarantee fee.

Other SBA Loan Programs

The SBA offers a host of other loan programs, including:

- SBALowDoc Loan Program
- SBAExpress
- Community Express
- CAPLines
- Prequal Pilot
- Microloans

SBALowDoc Loans

The SBALowDoc program is a pilot established to speed processing of loans of less than $150,000. Using a streamlined loan application, the lender and borrower agree on terms (within the parameters of the 7A program). Then the borrower fills out the front of the application form and the lender, the back. The lender submits the application and receives a response from the SBA within 36 hours.

Lack of available collateral or personal assets to guarantee the loan cannot be the only reason for denial. There is a onetime 2 percent fee for the guarantee. SBA guarantees up to 85 percent of the loan.

To be eligible, you must be a start-up or young business, employ fewer than 100 people, and have average annual sales of less than $5 million for each of the previous three years. You must have good credit and guarantee the principal personally.

Revolving credit loans may not be made under the LowDoc program.

> Lack of available collateral or personal assets to guarantee the loan cannot be the only reason for denial.

SBAExpress

SBAExpress loans are similar to LowDoc loans in that they are for less than $150,000 and are provided at rates consistent with 7A program guidelines. Borrowers must also meet SBA 7A size criteria for eligibility. Maturities of between 5 and 10 years are standard for working capital loans, and loans up to 25 years for the purchase of real estate and/or equipment.

However, there are some differences between the SBAExpress and other loans.

First, with SBAExpress the lender may use its own forms and processes, rather than the SBALowDoc form. The lender may also take advantage of electronic loan processing.

Second, the SBA provides only a 50 percent guarantee of loans made under the SBAExpress program.

Third, and most important, under SBAExpress, the SBA will provide a 50 percent guarantee for lender-approved unsecured credit lines of up to $25,000.

Community Express

Community Express is a pilot program of the SBA and the National Community Reinvestment Coalition (NCRC). The program is available only to selected lenders and is targeted at low and moderate income areas and SBA new-market regions.

Under Community Express, loans of up to $250,000 may be made, using the lender's own documents and procedures. The SBA guarantee decisions within 36 hours, and the guarantee is up to 85 percent for loans of under $150,000 and 75 percent for loans of $150,000 to $250,000.

As with the SBAExpress program, lenders can approve unsecured lines of credit of up to $25,000. Rates, loan terms, fees, and conditions parallel the 7A program.

In addition to its targeted nature, the Community Express program also adds technical and management assistance, provided by the lender in an effort to make borrowers more successful in both their applications and their use of the proceeds.

CAPLine is an umbrella program under which the SBA offers loan guarantees for five different kinds of short-term working-capital needs.

CAPLine

CAPLine is an umbrella program under which the SBA offers loan guarantees for five different kinds of short-term working-capital needs. The guarantee is 80 percent on loans of under $100,000 and 75 percent on loans from $100,000 to $1 million for all of the lines. The five loans are:

1. *Seasonal line.* A revolving or nonrevolving line to advance funds against anticipated inventory or accounts receivable during peak season sales fluctuations.
2. *Contract line.* A revolving or nonrevolving line available to finance the material and direct labor costs of performing a particular assignable contract or contracts.

3. *Builder's line.* A revolving or nonrevolving line available to small general contractors or builders to finance materials and direct labor costs associated with constructing or renovating commercial or residential buildings.
4. *Standard asset-based line.* A revolving line of credit for cyclical growth, recurring needs, or short-term working capital, designed for businesses unable to meet credit standards associated with long-term lending. It is asset based, and repayment comes from converting short-term assets into cash, which is remitted to the lender to pay down the line. Asset-based lines of credit require continual servicing and monitoring, and may be subject to additional fees.
5. *Small asset-based line.* A revolving line of credit similar to the standard asset-based line but with a maximum loan amount of $200,000. Some servicing requirements may be waived if the company consistently shows repayment ability from cash flow.

CAPLines are available to businesses that meet type and size criteria for the 7A program. Maturity for a CAPLine loan can be up to five years, although most lenders will establish shorter maturities for the first such loan. The guarantee fee is the same as for any 7A loan. The SBA places no fee restrictions on lenders who write asset-based loans and imposes a 2 percent annual fee based on the outstanding balance on other CAPLine loans.

CAPLines are available to businesses that meet type and size criteria for the 7A program.

Prequal Pilot

The Prequalification Pilot Loan Program (Prequal Pilot) utilizes the services of SBDCs, discussed later in this chapter, and other intermediaries to help prospective borrowers develop a viable loan application package and secure a loan.

Prequal Pilot loans are available to borrowers who meet size, type, and other eligibility standards under the 7A program. Loans can be for working capital or real estate and asset acquisition. Typical loan maturities are for up to seven years for working capital and up to 25 years for purchases of real estate and hard assets.

SBA programs can provide funding of up to $1,000,000. This means that over 90 percent of start-ups can benefit from SBA programs.

Prequal is targeted at low- and moderate-income, new-market customers, the disabled, new and emerging businesses, exporters, rural companies, and specialized industries.

This program has a $250,000 maximum loan amount, and the SBA guarantees 80 percent of loans up to $100,000 and 75 percent of loans from $100,000 to $250,000.

Once the applicant and intermediary have assembled the loan application package, they submit it to the SBA, where decisions are made within three business days. If the application is approved, the SBA issues a letter of prequalification that states the agency's intent to guarantee the loan. The intermediary then works with the borrower to find a lender that offers the most competitive rate and fees for the loan.

Microloans

Microloans are loans of up to $35,000 made by nonprofit community-based lenders to start-up, newly established, or growing small businesses. The funding comes directly from the SBA, not in the form of a guarantee.

Each community-based lender establishes its own credit and collateral requirements. Personal guarantees are expected and the maximum term of a microloan is six years.

In addition to funding, community-based intermediaries are required to provide business-based training and technical assistance to microloan recipients. They may require a prospective borrower to complete training and/or planning requirements before considering a microloan application.

Microloans are generally used for working capital, inventory, supplies, furniture, fixtures, machinery and equipment.

SBICs and SSBICs

Small business investment companies (SBICs) and specialized small business investment companies (SSBICs) were established in 1958 to help bridge the gap between venture capital and start-up businesses.

SBICs are privately owned, profit-making companies that are regulated and licensed by the SBA. They invest their own capital and have the ability to borrow from an SBA trust fund at low interest to leverage that capital. SBICs provide long-term lending, equity investments, debt-to-equity conversion funding, and management and technical assistance to companies that may not have access to nonregulated venture capital pools.

SBICs are privately owned, profit-making companies that are regulated and licensed by the SBA.

SSBICs are SBICs that provide loans and investment opportunities primarily to companies owned by economically disadvantaged entrepreneurs, such as women and minorities, and to businesses in economically depressed neighborhoods in inner cities and rural areas.

There are over 300 SBICs and SSBICs operating in the United States today. They have $6 billion under management. Most funds are smaller than private VC companies, and usually have less than $100 million available at any time.

In 1999, SBICs and SSBICs invested $4.2 billion in 4,100 deals and provided 53 percent of all institutional VC investments in the United States. Forty-four percent of these investments were made in businesses less than two years old, and 93 percent of funding was provided in equity-type investments.

Companies receiving investments from SBICs or SSBICs must meet the criteria for 7A loans in terms of business type and size. Typically, SBICs invest between $150,000 and $5 million in a company. Part may be as a loan and part as an equity purchase or a debt-to-equity conversion.

Many SBICs specialize in making investments in a small group of industries, and almost all focus within a particular region.

To convince an SBIC to become involved, a company must show ability to repay a loan. Early-stage companies must exhibit good sales and earnings, and start-ups must have a dynamic idea that can get off the ground quickly.

SBDCs provide assistance to small businesses in the areas of financing, marketing, production, organization, engineering and technical problems, and feasibility studies.

SBDCs

Small Business Development Centers (SBDCs) provide assistance to small businesses in the areas of financing, marketing, production, organization, engineering and technical problems, and feasibility studies. There are over 1,000 SBDCs throughout the 50 states, District of Columbia, Puerto Rico, the U.S. Virgin Islands, American Samoa, and Guam. In each state, a lead organization, such as a state government office or a university sponsors the SBDC and manages the programs at all locations. (A listing of sponsors is available at www.sba.gov/opc/pubs/fs43.)

SBDCs have full- and part-time staff, and also can put a small business person in touch with volunteers from professional and trade associations, attorneys, lenders, academics, and members of the Service Corps of Retired Executives (SCORE), a group that works with entrepreneurs. SBDCs also provide paid consultants to help clients with special needs.

In 1999, SBDCs provided management and technical assistance to more than 900,000 small businesses.

SBDCs are intimately involved in the SBA's Prequal loan program. They help small businesspeople to assemble a loan application package that will be approved for an SBA guarantee, then help locate an appropriate bank to underwrite the loan.

SBIRs

In addition to the loan, investment, and technical assistance opportunities provided through SBA guaranteed loans, SBICs, SSBICs, and SBDCs, the SBA also provides Small Business Innovation Research grants (SBIRs) for researching and developing technical innovations.

SBIRs provide $20,000 to $50,000 in Phase I funding for six months of basic research into a technical innovation and up to $500,000 in Phase II funding for further development of the innovation. Private sector investment funds must follow the two rounds of SBIR funding.

The SBA's sole mission is to help small businesses. For information about the many SBA programs, you can surf the agency's Web site, www.sba.gov. You can also call the SBA Answer Desk at 1-800-U-ASK-SBA for answers to specific quesitons. Local SBA offices are listed in the telephone book blue pages.

Chapter Key Points

- The SBA can be a key participant in an entrepreneur's search for capital.
- The SBA does not make loans directly to businesses, but offers a number of loan guarantees so commercial lenders will lend to small businesses who otherwise would not be considered credit worthy.
- The SBA provides funding to nonprofit community-based lenders who then make "microloans" of up to $35,000 to start-ups and growing small businesses.
- SBICs and SSBICs are privately owned profit-making VC companies that are licensed by the SBA. In addition to their own capital, they have access to low-interest loans from the SBA with which to make long-term loams, debt-to-equity

conversions, or equity investments in qualified small businesses.

The SBA also provides Small Business Innovation Research grants (SBIRs) of $20,000 to $50,000 for basic research and up to $500,000 for development of innovative technologies. These grants provide seed capital for start-up and early-stage companies with innovative technology.

CHAPTER

21

OTHER FEDERAL FINANCING PROGRAMS

MANY FEDERAL AGENCIES CAN BE YOUR RESEARCH PARTNER

In addition to the Small Business Administration (SBA), a number of federal agencies and departments provide funds for starting or operating small businesses. The three federal departments through which most of these funds are distributed are the Department of Housing and Urban Development (HUD), the Department of Commerce (DOC), and the Department of Agriculture (DOA).

Some of these funds are available in the form of loans, while others are outright grants. Much of the money available from the federal government is "passed through" state or local governments in the form of block grants, with the decision on who to fund being made at the local level. Examples of such pass-through programs are Urban Development Action Grant (UDAG) funds and Community Development Block Grant (CDBG) funds.

The best way to determine what federal programs you might be eligible for is to check with your state's economic development office, which has a good handle on what funds are available throughout the state.

HUD

Loans and grants available through HUD are targeted mainly at urban areas. Many are aimed at businesses that employ people who live in HUD-financed public housing. UDAG and CDBG are both HUD-sponsored programs.

HUD has also been charged with administering most economic development programs under federal Enterprise Zone legislation. Through this legislation, local governments are provided with funds to help businesses locate in enterprise zones, or urban neighborhoods and rural/exurban communities in the most immediate need of economic development.

Enterprise zone funding includes direct loans, interest-rate subsidies, and loan guarantees for businesses that start in or move into the zone. Locating a business in an enterprise zone also makes it eligible for loans made by banks to help them comply with the Community Reinvestment Act.

Many federal enterprise zones overlap with areas that already had been designated state enterprise zones (see the next chapter).

Locating a business in an enterprise zone also makes it eligible for loans made by banks to help them comply with the Community Reinvestment Act.

DOC

One of the responsibilities of the DOC is to promote American products overseas. It makes available loans, loan guarantees, grants, and other subsidies to American companies marketing or actively selling their products abroad.

The DOC houses an agency called the Economic Development Administration (EDA), which was created in 1965 to promote industrial development. The EDA makes money available through grants to state and local governments to help create the infrastructure that businesses need to grow and flourish.

If your business is one that helps other businesses or is starting or growing in an economically depressed area, or if you are a member of an economically disadvantaged class (i.e., African American, Latino, American Indian, Asian, Pacific Islander, or a woman) you may be eligible for money from one of these grants. You may also qualify for free technical assistance from an organization that gets money from the EDA.

DOA

It may be surprising but even those who are not farmers can receive assistance from DOA programs. The Farmers Home Administration (FmHA) is an agency within the DOA that makes direct loans and provides loan guarantees to all kinds of businesses that operate in rural areas. Priority for FmHA business programs is given to projects in rural communities and cities with fewer than 25,000 people. Even in states that are considered highly urbanized, some areas are eligible for FmHA programs.

In addition to providing loans and loan guarantees for rural housing development and public facilities, and agricultural loans for family farms and family-farm cooperatives, FmHA also provides loan guarantees through commercial lenders for the creation or expansion of industry in less populous areas.

Loan guarantees are available for acquisition of land, acquisition and renovation or construction of buildings, acquisition of machinery and equipment, and working capital for inventory and cash flow. Terms are up to 30 years for real estate, 15 years for machinery, and seven years for working capital loans. For loans of more than $1 million, FmHA requires a feasibility study. Your commitment must be at least 10 percent of the project cost, and can be as high as 25 percent.

FmHA does not require that you be turned down for a conventional loan before applying for a loan guarantee, but it does require your personal guarantee on the loan. In many rural communities, FmHA has been a major player in economic development.

Government agencies have less well-known programs in areas such as environmental and energy resources, rural development, and technology. See if your business objectives are consistent with any program charter. Your local Small Business Development Center can usually help.

Small Business Innovation Research Program

The Small Business Innovation Research (SBIR) program, mentioned briefly in chapter 19, is administered by the

SBA. The money for the research grants, however, comes from agencies and departments that participate in the program.

Part of the Small Business Innovation Development Act of 1982, the SBIR program is designed to include small businesses in federally supported research and development efforts by providing both grants and an opportunity for them to participate in government procurement of research services.

Each agency or department that participates in the SBIR program is responsible for committing a particular amount of its research and development funds to small businesses. Agencies establish their own criteria for obtaining grants or contracts. Some of the departments and agencies that participate include:

> To be eligible for participation in the SBIR program, you must be a profit-making company with fewer than 500 employees.

- Department of Health and Human Resources (HHS)
- Department of Defense (DOD)
- Environmental Protection Agency (EPA)
- Department of Transportation (DOT)
- National Aeronautics and Space Administration (NASA)

A full list of participating agencies and departments is available on the SBA Web site, www.sba.gov, or through the SBA's Office of Innovation, Research, and Technology (IR&T) in Washington.

To be eligible for participation in the SBIR program, you must be a profit-making company with fewer than 500 employees. In addition to applying for an SBIR grant, you can have the SBA's office of IR&T place you on the list for its presolicitation announcements. These let you know which agencies and departments are issuing requests for proposals (RFPs) for procurement of research services or for distribution of grants to conduct research.

CRADAs

Another opportunity for small research and development-oriented businesses to obtain government assistance is through a Cooperative Research and Development Agreement (CRADA). A CRADA is a partnership between a government laboratory and an academic or industrial research organization.

Funding and staffing commitments are shared between the parties to the CRADA (just as in a strategic alliance), with the specifics of who performs what research detailed in the agreement. Any patents or inventions that come out of the joint work of the CRADA are owned by both parties.

The government then licenses its share of the ownership interest to the industrial company for the purpose of taking the fruits of the CRADA to market. If a small business is involved in the CRADA, both parties can license the product to another company to market and sell.

Federal government laboratories are constantly looking for partners to develop technology jointly and take the lab's work public, which brings in revenue and reduces the lab's dependence on taxes for its budget.

Chapter Key Points

- In addition to the Small Business Administration, a number of federal departments and agencies provide funding for small and growing businesses.
- If your company is operating within a federally designated enterprise zone or you employ people who live in public housing, you may be eligible to receive a grant from the Department of Housing and Urban Development (HUD).
- The Economic Development Administration (EDA) within the Department of Commerce (DOC) also makes money available through grants to states and local governments, which pass them on to companies starting up or growing in economically disadvantaged communities.

- If you are starting a business in a rural community or city with less than 25,000 people, you may be eligible for direct loans or loan guarantees from the Farmers Home Loan Administration (FmHA), part of the Department of Agriculture.
- A cooperative research and development agreement (CRADA) with a federal agency can provide you with access to the innovation program of a federal research laboratory. You and the government agency share the obligations for the research, as well as rights to any intellectual property developed. You then take the product to market, and pay royalties to the government agency.

CHAPTER

22

STATE AND LOCAL FUNDING SOURCES

WHERE YOU LOCATE YOUR BUSINESS CAN PAY OFF BIG

If you sign the guest book at a local or regional VC fair, chances are within a few weeks your phone will be ringing with state and municipal officials trying to get you to locate your business in their city or state.

States and cities are all looking to attract new businesses. Not only does a business provide state corporate income, sales, and local property taxes, but the employees of the business add to the local economy by living in the area and buying goods and services from other businesses near their own place of work.

State Funding

States are increasingly rolling out the red carpet for businesses, through a combination of tax incentives, loans and loan guarantees, and other programs. Some are even sponsoring venture capital funds.

Tax Incentives

States don't usually create special tax rates for new or growing businesses. They do provide tax credits for particular activities that have public policy purposes. These credits offset corporate taxes owed by the company. Many credits are aimed at luring and keeping clean industries and technology-oriented companies.

For instance:

- North Dakota has more tax credits and incentives for high-tech businesses than any other state in the country.
- In California, the sale of advertising space is not subject to sales tax.
- Texas offers tax credits in a number of manufacturing areas, most notably for the purchase of semiconductor fabrication equipment and clean-room facilities. In addition, items purchased for joint research and development (R&D) ventures are tax-exempt.
- In New York, utilities and personal property used or consumed directly in R&D are tax-exempt, as are fees from advertising agencies and ads on the Internet.
- Illinois offers tax credits for investments of more than $12 million that will create at least 500 jobs and for large job-creation projects in manufacturing.
- In Massachusetts, manufacturing and R&D companies can get credits for construction and renovation, and tangible property. R&D expenditures made since 1991 are eligible for credits, and sales of materials, machinery, and tooling for exclusive use in R&D are tax-exempt.

Each state government has at least one office that can give you as much time as you need to figure out which programs are best for you and help you apply for them. Your business provides future tax dollars that pay their salaries.

States also often subsidize municipalities that provide property-tax phase-ins by underwriting the lost revenue to the city or town. In many states, the proportion of the lost revenue the state assumes differs depending on the city or town's relative wealth.

Loans, Loan Guarantees, and Interest Subsidies

Many states provide loans and loan guarantees similar to those provided by federal agencies. The state department of economic development is the best place to check for availability of such funds. State financing is often provided as direct loans for fixed-asset purchases, construction or renovation, and infrastructure development. There are also some funds available for working capital loans. State agencies usually co-lend with a private-sector lender.

Loan guarantees are provided by state agencies in much the same way as the Small Business Administration (SBA), for a portion of a loan made by the private lender.

States also sometimes provide interest subsidies on loans. Under an interest-subsidy program, the state may pay for 30 to 50 percent of a loan's interest. For instance, if you borrow $250,000 at 12 percent interest ($30,000 interest) and the state subsidizes 30 percent of the interest ($9,000), your interest payment is really $21,000 and your effective interest rate is 8.4 percent.

As with the federal government, state and local agencies can help you in many ways, such as getting financial assistance, dealing with international trade issues, and addressing particular markets.

Grants

State grants can be made directly to businesses, to municipalities to assist businesses in locating there, or to companies that help other companies. For instance, in some states, regulated electric companies have guaranteed that in exchange for being allowed to earn a particular rate of return on their assets, they will provide a certain amount of money (say $250,000) to small businesses for market research and energy audits.

State departments of transportation sometimes provide grants directly to companies in which a certain percentage of employees take mass transit to work, or participate in van pools.

Many states provide grants to businesses to locate daycare facilities within their walls, provided that a percentage of openings are made available to local residents.

States are increasingly piggybacking many of their grants (as well as loans) on federal enterprise zone legislation, providing businesses with additional reasons to locate or expand in these economically depressed areas.

Some states provide matching grants to businesses that win federal grants.

In addition to loans and tax incentives, many states have annual competitive grant programs.

Industrial Revenue Bonds (IRBs)

Industrial Revenue Bonds (IRBs) are issued by a state through a quasi-public agency to provide funding for acquisition and renovation or construction of industrial buildings, and the equipment needed for those facilities.

The bond is issued in the name of the corporation that will be buying and using the facility and machinery. However, the state and quasi-public agency are underwriting the bond issue, and the interest paid to the bond investors is free of federal income taxes (and state income tax for state residents). Because investors will pay less tax on interest from the bonds, they are willing to buy bonds that pay a lower interest rate, which means the cost of borrowing the funds is lower than if the company had issued the debt on its own.

Venture Capital Funding

Some states are becoming venture capitalists. Usually, these efforts are aimed at providing seed- and early-stage capital to companies within the state. The goals are to add jobs and tax revenue, and attract or keep innovative companies in the state.

Each state operates its program on a slightly different model. Some:

- Focus on funding and promoting industries that are traditional in that state; others attempt to create opportunities for a critical mass of technology-based entrepreneurial businesses to locate in the state.
- Are concerned with making a traditional venture-capital rate of return on their investments, while for others, profit is secondary to supporting local businesses.

- Have funded these operations with cash, while others have provided tax credits that the venturing operation uses as leverage to borrow funds to invest.
- Are going it alone, while others are joint-venturing their efforts with private venture capitalists.

Noncash Assistance Programs

States often provide educational, job training and placement services, as well as market research, for companies locating in the state. Some also provide free or subsidized management consulting services to companies that are new or expanding, exporters, or operating in distressed industries.

Local Funding

In addition to being the funding mechanism for Urban Development Action Grant (UDAG), and Community Development Block Grant (CDBG) funds from the federal Department of Housing and Urban Development (HUD), cities and towns can provide companies with their own incentives to locate there.

Each state has an economic development Web site that lists a range of resources available for businesses in that state.

The most popular municipal incentive is a phase-in of local property taxes on real estate, machinery, fixtures, and other business equipment. Municipalities love business taxpayers; they provide a lot of tax income without utilizing a lot of services (most of a municipal budget goes to pay for education).

Cities and towns are often willing to allow businesses to phase in property taxes over five to ten years. As part of the deal, the municipality may require the business to remain in the town for five or more years after the tax phase-in has run its course or to repay the taxes that were foregone. In addition, some cities require companies that get property tax phase-ins to create a particular number

Check out the SBA publication: "The State and Small Business: A Directory of Programs and Activities" *(Government Publication Office stock number 045-000-00266-7)*

of jobs, and they sometimes even demand that a set portion of those jobs be held by city residents.

Municipalities may also add their own money into the federal and state pot for companies that locate or expand in federal enterprise zones.

Chapter Key Points

- State funding for start-up and growing businesses includes reductions or exemptions from state corporate income and sales taxes, or tax credits for activities such as buying from local vendors and employing local residents.
- Local governments sometimes provide start-up or relocating businesses with a phase-in of the property tax due on the company's facility and equipment.
- Some states provide loan guarantees for lenders similar to those of the SBA, or interest rate subsidies directly to the borrower, which effectively lowers the interest rate on the loan.
- State grants can be made directly to a business or to a municipality to assist businesses in locating there. States also underwrite industrial revenue bonds (IRBs), which reduce a business's cost of borrowing for building or renovating a facility.
- Some states are starting VC funds, aimed mostly at providing seed- and early-stage funding for entrepreneurial companies who locate in and agree to stay in the state.

SECTION IV

▲ ▲ ▲

BOOTSTRAP FINANCING

CHAPTER

23

PERSONAL SAVINGS

INVEST IN YOURSELF, AND IN YOUR BUSINESS

The best piece of advice for any aspiring entrepreneur might be, "Don't give up your day job."

At least until you have something tangible with which to approach those who might be interested in providing you with equity financing, you should work on your idea or concept nights and weekends. Unless, of course, you have substantial personal savings.

Putting your own cash into your start-up or young business is the simplest way to go. You stay away from credit, keep your business affairs to yourself, and steer clear of any legal entanglements that come with either borrowing or selling an equity stake.

Show Yourself the Money

Many of us have personal savings we can tap into in places we might not think to look. Sometimes you have to borrow these assets, but you are in effect borrowing from yourself. In addition to your checking and savings accounts, the other places you can tap for cash include:

- Taxable investment accounts
- Tax-advantaged retirement accounts
- Cash value in life insurance policies
- Lump-sum payout on leaving a job

- Trust fund
- Hard goods

Taxable Investment Accounts

Taxable investment accounts are those you hold with brokerage houses or mutual fund companies where you must pay annual taxes for any capital gains and dividends you receive from them.

When buying equipment, tools, or other physical assets, stretch your money by buying from companies that are going out of business, secondhand stores, and distressed merchandise sales and auctions.

Remember, if you liquidate such an account, or cash out some of the investments, come April 15 of the next year you may have capital gain tax to pay on some of the proceeds. The best thing to do is to determine your capital gain liability when you cash out the funds and put that money aside to pay taxes (or leave enough in the account to remove next April 15th).

Timing the removal of such funds is important. Since you owe no taxes on funds removed until April 15 of the year following the one in which you take the proceeds, the earlier in the calendar year you remove the funds, the longer you have before a tax payment is due.

If you tell your broker you are liquidating your account in order to start a business, he or she may suggest that you not do so and instead borrow against your assets by shifting your account to a "margin" account. **DON'T DO IT.**

While it may seem tempting, margin accounts are dangerous tools. They allow you to borrow 40 to 50 percent of the value of the assets in your account. But the interest rate on a margin account is very high.

Also, if the value of the assets in your account falls (i.e., the stocks, bonds, or funds you hold go down in price), your broker may be forced to sell some of those proceeds, then use them to pay off part of your loan in order to maintain the ratio of your account value to your loan. If the assets are sold for more than you bought them for, you will still have a capital gain tax to pay, and you won't necessarily be able to time the disposal of assets and payment of taxes (i.e., the broker may have to sell out your position in December).

It's better to take the cash, put your tax liability in an account you won't be tempted to raid, and be done with it.

Tax-Advantaged Retirement Accounts

There are two options for removing funds from a tax-advantaged retirement fund.

First, you can liquidate assets the way you would from a taxable investment account. Second, you can borrow against the proceeds in some types of tax-advantaged funds. There are, however, problems with both options.

Remember, these plans were set up to encourage savings for retirement. They allow you to earn interest and dividends, and obtain capital gains on investments that gain in value, without incurring any current tax liability. When you retire and begin taking distributions, they are taxed as ordinary income, at your effective tax rate. The theory is that the majority of Americans spend their prime earning years in moderately high tax brackets but drop to a lower bracket in their retirement years. They then pay taxes at the lower rate on the distributions they take from their tax-advantaged accounts.

So, if you take money out to capitalize your start-up or growing business, you will pay income taxes at your regular rate for the amount you withdraw from a tax-advantaged retirement plan. Timing is therefore important. For instance, if you are starting a business in October, and you need $150,000 for the first year of operations, you want to calculate your current year income tax liability (based on what you and your spouse have already earned) and determine what tax bracket you are in. This helps you decide how much to withdraw this year, and how much next year (when you will have earned income from a different job and may be in a lower bracket).

There's one more catch. There is a 10 percent penalty tax on all distributions from tax-advantaged retirement

It's better to take the cash, put your tax liability in an account you won't be tempted to raid, and be done with it.

plans made by individuals younger than 55 who are not permanently disabled. Again, when you determine how much you need to take out of a tax-advantaged retirement plan to capitalize your business, you need to calculate your tax liability and take out enough to pay the liability, or leave enough in the account to remove it next April 15th to pay the taxes.

In terms of borrowing, many employer-sponsored 401(k) plans for for-profit businesses allow borrowing. You are limited to 50 percent of the amount in your plan account, to a maximum of $50,000. And the loan must be repaid within five years.

Loans from a 401(k) have a low interest rate, but you are foregoing the tax-free compounding on the amount of money you borrow for the time you borrow it. If you have other borrowing options, pass on this one.

Also, you cannot borrow against 403(b) retirement annuities, IRAs, or Keogh or SEP plans if you are already self-employed.

Whole life, universal life, and variable-life annuity life insurance policies all have a cash value you can get by canceling or borrowing against the policy.

Cash Value in Life Insurance

Whole life, universal life, and variable-life insurance policies all have a cash value you can get by canceling or borrowing against the policy.

Most entrepreneurs should not cancel any cash value life insurance; if anything, you should be increasing its death benefit when you strike out on your own.

Borrowing against the cash-value in a policy is a viable option. Loans against cash value in life insurance come at a low interest rate (usually 4 to 6 percent). However, should you die while the loan is outstanding, its value will be deducted from the death benefit paid to your beneficiary or beneficiaries.

Here's a way to have your cake and eat it too. Use the built-up cash value to pay for the premium on the policy. This allows you to use the cash you would have paid for the premium for your new business and maintain your life insurance at the same time.

Lump-Sum Payout from a Job

If you are currently working and thinking about starting your own company, you may be able to take advantage of a company buyout program and walk away with a chunk of cash to fund your start-up.

Many companies routinely offer buyout programs or are amenable to negotiating a separation package. These are usually aimed at middle-aged employees (45 to 60) as an early-retirement incentive program. Companies often offer from one to four weeks' pay for every year of service with the company, with a maximum of one or even two full years of pay. They will sometimes make these payments as a lump sum rather than weekly or biweekly.

Again, if you are able to maneuver into such a position, timing is critical. You want to accept a lump sum buyout as early in the calendar year as possible, to maximize the time until you have to pay taxes.

> If you are currently working and thinking about starting your own company, you may be able to take advantage of a company buyout program and walk away with a chunk of cash to fund your start-up.

Trust Fund

We should all be so lucky!

Some people are beneficiaries of trust funds. Some of them receive funds when they reach a certain age. For others, distribution of funds is at the trustees' discretion.

If you are the beneficiary of a trust with trustee discretion, make a pitch for your share just as you would to any other angel or venture capitalist. The trustee(s) have a fiduciary responsibility not only to you but to all the other beneficiaries.

By placing money in your business, they are reducing the trust's assets and therefore its growth potential. You may have to waive some or all of its posible future benefits if you receive a large amount of funding.

Large companies that use the same kind of equipment you need may have old equipment taking up space. They may be willing to sell it to you cheap, or provide it as part of a strategic alliance.

You may also see if the trust documents allow for an investment in a private venture, and if the trust wishes to become an equity investor.

Hard Goods

Most people don't pawn the family jewelry to start a business, but it does happen. There are "high-end" pawn shops in some communities that cater to loaning sizable amounts of money to well-off people against quite substantial hard goods. That gold Rolex you got as a gift from your employer for the multi-million-dollar deal you made five years ago might have some real value after all.

Art work, musical instruments, artistic rugs and carpets, and antique furniture all have a market and can sometimes be liquidated quickly to raise cash. Loans are usually given at a fraction of the price that would be paid in an outright sale.

Chapter Key Points

- Most entrepreneurs start their businesses by putting up their own cash. Many people have cash they can tap in places they don't often think about.
- You can use money from your stock or other investments; after all, starting your own company is an investment.
- You can borrow against some tax-advantaged retirement accounts (401k) but not others (IRA, Keogh).
- Cash value from whole, universal, or variable-life insurance policies can be tapped in three ways: cash out the policy, borrow against the cash value, or use the cash value to pay the policy's premiums.
- High-end pawn shops specialize in making loans to the wealthy on expensive hard goods such as jewelry, art, or antiques.

CHAPTER

24

HOME EQUITY

YOUR HOME CAN BE YOUR MOST VALUABLE ASSET

For many Americans, their house is their largest and greatest asset. This is as true for entrepreneurs as for anyone else.

You may have enough equity in your house to get your business off the ground. This is especially true if you have been living in it for a few years and are in a part of the country where real estate prices have been booming rather than crawling upwards. Remember, equity is the difference between the market value of the house and the amount of your current loan.

If you bought a house seven years ago for $150,000 and took out a 30-year fixed-rate mortgage for 80 percent of the price ($120,000), you have paid down a few thousand dollars of the debt by now. Perhaps you owe $110,000.

At the same time, if your house has appreciated about 5 percent a year (compounded of course), today it is worth over $200,000—let's say $210,000. That means you have $100,000 of equity in it.

There are two ways to get equity out of the house you own. One is to refinance with a new mortgage. The other is to take out a home equity loan or home equity line of credit against your available equity. There are a few variables to consider before deciding which route is better for you.

Among these are the interest rate of your current mortgage and the interest rates currently being offered in the marketplace; how long you expect to live in your house; how much equity you would like to take out; and your ability to qualify for a new mortgage.

Refinancing

If current interest rates are lower than when you obtained your current mortgage, take a look at refinancing with a new mortgage first. In our hypothetical, you could borrow 80 percent of your $210,000 house value, or $168,000. After paying off your $110,000 old mortgage, you would have $58,000 in cash.

With many banks and finance companies looking for business in a slow economy, some may offer exceptionally good terms for a creditworthy borrower.

Here's the rule of thumb for when to refinance: if the current market interest rate is more than 1 percent lower than your present rate, and you expect to live in your home at least another five to seven years, the lower interest payment (based on your current loan balance) will allow you to recoup your up-front fees for the refinancing. Use this as a first-step to guiding your decision; if these conditions prevail it's a point in favor of a new mortgage.

Given the fact that most home equity loans and lines of credit peg their interest rate to the prime rate banks charge their best corporate customers, mortgage interest rates are sometimes lower. If mortgage rates are lower than home equity rates, that's a point in their favor.

There is, of course, one big problem with applying for a new mortgage. If you didn't plan well and waited until you left your job and started your business to apply for the new mortgage, unless your spouse's income can swing the payments, the bank may not look favorably on you as a risk.

To counter this, you can apply for a mortgage for 70 percent of the house's value instead of the traditional 80 percent. This will allow you to get a "no-income verification" mortgage from many banks. The downside, of course, is that you've left equity in the house that you could have used for the business. (A 70 percent mortgage would mean you'd only borrow $147,000 and only have $37,000 after paying off your old loan.)

The lesson in this, of course, is that if you are thinking of refinancing your house in order to start a business, begin the process early while you can still show the bank a steady income stream.

The other downside of a new mortgage is the extra fees involved. Banks usually charge an application fee, as well as a mortgage-origination fee called "points." One point is one percent of the amount of the loan. For instance, if you are taking out a $200,000 mortgage, with a charge of two points origination, the fee comes to $4,000. Some banks will allow you to add the points to the loan but that raises the monthly cost and may reduce the actual amount of equity you can take out if you are borrowing the maximum that your income will allow you to qualify for.

The other downside of a new mortgage is the extra fees involved.

Other fees include a new title search and title insurance (even though you own the house, and demonstrated clear title the last time your borrowed), and the attorney's fees for closing on the loan. Points, fees, and other closing costs can run 5 to 6 percent of the loan value, and reduce the cash available for your business by that much.

Tap the Equity

If you want to get at the equity without going through the hassle or expense of a new mortgage, banks and nonbank financial institutions offer home equity loans written for a fixed term (usually 10 to 15 years) or home equity lines of credit.

Most home equity loans (either fixed-term or lines of credit) have minimal fees. They do not require a new title search or title insurance. They do not have origination points attached to them. The documentation is less complicated, and the attorney's fees for closing on the loan are less.

Whether you take a term loan or a line of credit, you should be able to take out the full difference between your current loan balance and 80 percent of your home's value (in this case $58,000). In either case, the bank or other institution would take a second mortgage on your home.

In the case of a term loan, the bank would write you a check for the same amount, and you would begin making monthly payments on the note. With an equity line of credit, you would get a checkbook on which you could write checks up to the amount of your credit line. You would receive monthly statements showing your balance available, and your monthly payment would depend on how much of your credit line you have used. As long as you pay the monthly interest, you can pay all or part of the credit line as you are able.

Chapter Key Points

- For many Americans, the equity they have in their house is their largest asset.
- If you have owned your home for more than three years and home prices have appreciated, you have enough equity to make it worthwhile to try to pull some of it out to help start your new business.
- You can tap the equity in your house either by refinancing the mortgage or by taking an equity loan.
- Refinancing is usually the better option if mortgage rates are 1 percentage point lower than on your current mortgage and you plan to remain in your house for at least another five years.
- You can borrow against your equity either by taking a fixed-term loan or opening a floating-rate line of credit.

CHAPTER

25

EQUIPMENT LEASING

LEASING ASSETS FREE UP CASH FOR INTELLECTUAL CAPITAL

Equipment leasing has long been used by entrepreneurs to reduce their cash outlays for many of the high-cost items necessary to run a business, such as real estate and equipment. The lease is a simple transaction; a party that owns a good such as a building or piece of equipment (a lessor) offers to rent the use of that good to a party that needs it (a lessee) for a specific period of time.

Despite the simplicity of the transaction itself, the decision on whether to lease or purchase (either outright with cash or financed via a commercial loan) is complex. Imaginative people in the last 50 years have constructed many variations on simple leases that offer financial and tax advantages to the lessor, the lessee, and third parties.

Your decision about whether to lease or buy is one you should discuss with your financial and tax advisors. You should also have representation in negotiating such a transaction. This chapter will deal with leasing equipment rather than real estate. Although the basic concepts are the same, real estate leases are usually entered into for a longer period of time, and there are important extra advantages often attached to equipment leasing.

Leasing Advantages

There are four major advantages to you as an entrepreneur in leasing equipment rather than purchasing it.

A lease can be created for used equipment.

1. *Leases can be entered into quickly.* Leasing arrangements are constructed so that lessors don't need to perform the same kind of analysis of your financial condition or subject you to the restrictions and covenants that banks and other lenders do when making an equipment loan.
2. *You avoid the risk of technological obsolescence.* Because you do not own the property being leased, you avoid the problem of holding obsolete systems. You can write leases for varying periods of time, depending on how quickly the technology involved becomes obsolete.
3. *You can lease goods as you need them, without incurring large capital investments.* As your needs for space and equipment increase, you can lease more. You can also time new leases so they expire with old leases, allowing you to acquire an entire new generation of equipment at the same time.
4. *Traditional leases are recorded as regular monthly expenses on your income statement, rather than as assets and consequent loan liabilities on your balance sheet.* This "off-balance-sheet financing" shows a more favorable view of your financial condition when looked at by other potential lenders or investors.

The Operating Lease

The operating lease, sometimes referred to as a "true lease," gives the lessee the advantages of use without ownership and gives the lessor the advantages (and risks) of ownership. The lease can be written in such a way that the lessor and lessee share responsibility for some elements of the item's upkeep, reducing the risk of ownership to the lessor.

An operating lease provides a lessee with a single monthly payment that covers the cost of the rental plus that portion of the risk of ownership it is covering. For instance, the lease may include payment by the lessee of some portion of property taxes and general maintenance, or this may be covered completely by the lessor.

As owner of the property, the lessor benefits from tax deductions for property taxes paid on the leased item, as well as depreciation deductions, and reaps any actual appreciation in market value. In the case of real estate, the lessor may also receive tax credits available for rehabilitation of property.

The Finance Lease

Over the years, sophisticated lessors have created a number of modifications of traditional leases that benefit lessees and lessors alike. For example, there are now leases that look more like collateralized loans, with the item being leased acting as collateral for the loan.

These modified leases are called finance or capital leases. Some of the modifications were driven by tax-law changes enacted in 1986, which reduced deductions available for "passive investors" of real estate and equipment. Others were driven by the increasingly short lifecycles of typically leased equipment, such as computer and telecommunications equipment.

A large corporation with old equipment may lease it to you for a fraction of a regular lease in order to provide some income from an otherwise idle piece of equipment.

The major modifications that create a capital or finance lease include:

- Writing leases for the economic life of the item instead of a fixed amount of time, or for a fixed time with an option or series of options to extend the lease through the item's economic life.
- Lease-to-purchase provisions. These can be options to purchase at the end of the lease term, or a requirement to purchase the property at the end of the lease period for a fixed amount, or for fair market value, or to pay the difference between the fair market value and the stipulated purchase price determined at the beginning of the lease term.

With a "use" lease, available for some equipment (e.g., photocopiers), your lease fee is dependent on how much you use the equipment each month. If you lease old equipment from another company, see if they will write a use lease.

- Monthly rental payments may be variable. They can be gauged to volume factors such as use (number of copies for a photocopier) or sales of goods produced with the machine. They can have an interest rate that floats in relation to some index, like any other variable-rate business loan. They can increase over the term of the loan to provide you with lower payments while your company is younger and account for inflation. Or they can be reduced later to provide you with a future cash-flow increase.

Capital leases make it easier for the lessor to repossess the property if you default.

But capital leases with options to renew allow you to use a piece of equipment for its true useful life, not just for the life of the original lease. If the property becomes obsolete quickly, you don't have to renew; if it has a longer useful life, you can exercise options.

Some capital leases are written so the lessor maintains equipment and provides automatic upgrades when items become obsolete. Telecommunications and computer equipment companies have become masters at writing leases that provide growth opportunities for entrepreneurs while protecting the equipment manufacturers.

Venture Leasing

Since the 1980s, a few companies have offered an additional way to use leasing as a financing tool for start-up and early-stage companies. As part of their leases, they write a provision to take part of the payment in the form of stock or warrants in the company instead of cash. This is called venture leasing. (Estimates are that fewer than 20 of the 800 or more leasing companies in America today engage in venture leasing.)

Venture leasing companies are also sometimes referred to as subprime leasing companies, since they often lease to new and emerging businesses that wouldn't meet credit requirements from traditional leasing companies. In exchange for taking part of the payment over the life of the lease in the form of equity, they mark up the effective interest rate on the finance lease to 15 to 18 percent. Depending on how much equity they take, the total cash cost of the lease can be substantially less than with traditional leasing.

Venture leasing works best for companies in emerging technology that burn through cash rapidly and need to put as many dollars as possible into research and development. These companies, which often don't have any salable products, are not considered creditworthy enough to get a bank to give them an equipment loan.

Venture capitalists often suggest that their high-tech portfolio clients enter into leasing arrangements early on after acquiring capital. Leasing extends the leverage of the venture capitalist's cash investment since it is not being used to purchase equipment.

While it may take six months or more for an early-stage company to raise a round of venture capital, a venture lease deal can be closed in three to six weeks. Venture leasing companies are often willing to write lease lines for millions of dollars. They consolidate equipment purchased from a number of different vendors, including soft costs like cabling and installation services, into one umbrella lease. Leases can be written with automatic equipment "refreshing" at regular intervals.

In addition to saving money, the single-source venture lease can save entrepreneurs a lot of time, since they don't have to go from one funding source to another or work out lease arrangements with each individual equipment vendor. Neither do they have to engage in pitching their company to angels and venture capitalists.

If you already own equipment, you can create a sale/lease-back, in which you sell the equipment to another party, then lease it back for a period of time. This provides the new owner with the tax benefits of ownership and you with increased cash. Check out www.equipment-sale-lease-back.com for over 3,000 capital sources for a potential sale/lease-back arrangement.

Chapter Key Points

- Equipment leasing reduces the cash outlay for high-cost items necessary to run a business.
- Leasing rather than buying equipment allows you to plan when to upgrade and avoid owning obsolete equipment.
- An operating lease, or "true lease," provides you with a single monthly payment for the cost of equipment rental and can be written so it includes maintenance and taxes.
- A finance lease, or "capital lease," is written for the economic life of the item or for a fixed time with options to renew. It can also include lease-to-purchase provisions and may have variable monthly payments.
- A few leasing companies offer "venture leasing," in which they will accept part of the payment for the lease in the form of equity in your company.

CHAPTER

26

PERSONAL LOANS

SHOW THE LENDER WHO YOU ARE AND WHAT YOU ARE MADE OF

Getting a personal loan to start a business is very difficult. Here personal means a loan to your business (whether it's incorporated or not) based on an idea, concept, or business plan without any track record.

In a way, every loan to a small business is a personal one, since you will be asked to personally sign a guarantee for the loan's repayment, even if the company is incorporated and the loan is being guaranteed by the SBA or another entity.

Despite the fact that banks are in the money business, they are leery about lending to unproven businesses. However, they are becoming less tight fisted. In fact, some banks are setting up special small business lending centers and training bankers to be small business lenders.

They are also working more closely with the SBA and state and local economic development agencies to leverage their loans to start-up or growing small businesses in enterprise zones or other disadvantaged areas.

Banks can work with you to apply for an SBA guaranteed loan. The SBA is constantly coming up with new ways to reduce the paperwork and hurdles for small businesses to acquire loans. The LowDoc and Microloan programs allow bankers to loosen some of their restrictions against lending to companies with little or no track record.

More than 30 percent of all loans to small and start-up businesses come not from banks but from commercial lenders such as Allied Capital or GE Credit. These companies are often willing to assume more risk than banks (consequently they charge a higher interest rate) and may allow intangible factors like your personal integrity to override the lack of an operating history for your business.

The Five C's of Credit

Lenders look at five major factors—often called the five C's of credit—when evaluating whether to loan you money. They are:

- character
- capacity
- collateral
- capital
- contribution

Lenders take into account who a potential borrower is, whether you are a longtime resident or transient, and whether you are active in the community.

Character

Character is considered a "soft" or subjective criteria. Lenders take into account who a potential borrower is, whether you are a longtime resident or transient, and whether you are active in the community.

One element of character—your credit history—is objective. Credit history is a one-way street: Good credit might get you a gold star, all things being equal; bad credit knocks you right out of the box.

Before you apply for a loan, be sure to obtain a copy of your credit history and do whatever you can to buff it up. Make sure it is correct (it isn't always), and contact any individuals or companies that have entered negative information.

One banker commented that any small business loan application that shows the applicant making child-support payments (court mandated or not) automatically gets rejected.

Capacity (Cash Flow)

Capacity is a measure of your ability to repay a loan. For a start-up business, a lender will look at your business plan and projections for revenue and cash flow.

For a business with a history, the lender will look at your previous two year's cash flow. It should be sufficient to meet the terms of the loan, pay all operating expenses, and provide a cushion for emergencies.

Projecting cash flow is tricky. Try to adhere to industry norms and provide sound reasoning if you project departs from these norms.

Capacity is a measure of your ability to repay a loan.

Collateral

No lender writes loans based on collateral alone. But lack of collateral is a real problem. You will be asked to personally guarantee any loan you take for your business, and by doing so you put your assets at risk. Even if the lender does not formally take a lien on your home (through an equity loan and second mortgage) to obtain repayment of the loan principal, they can go after your house if you pledge it as collateral on your loan.

The only way to protect assets from your personal guarantee is to put them in the name of a spouse or child. Assets jointly held can only be taken by the creditor to pay a loan if both parties have signed the loan documents; however, the creditor may be able to force the sale of jointly held assets to pay off the loan.

Capital

Lenders will scrutinize your net worth before making a loan. Your net worth is the amount by which your assets exceed your liabilities.

Contribution

Lenders want entrepreneurs to have a significant amount of equity in the business. This "skin in the game" on the part of the entrepreneur aligns his or her interests with those of the lender. Lenders don't like to see people trying to start businesses using only other people's money.

The SBA uses a 4 to 1 ratio. In order to guarantee a loan, it wants the business owner to have put in equity equal to 20 percent of the total assets of the loan plus equity (e.g., if you are seeking a $100,000 loan, the SBA wants you to have put about $20,000 in equity into the business).

Friends and family may find it difficult to invest in your company but might give you a loan on better terms than a traditional lender.

Loan Guarantees

In addition to federal agencies like the SBA and some state economic development agencies, individuals also sometimes provide loan guarantees for an entrepreneur.

A loan guarantee can be provided by a friend or family member, or by an arms-length third-party angel. In theory, anyone willing to make an equity investment in your company should also be willing to guarantee a loan. If the company fails, it doesn't matter whether his loan guarantee is exercised or his stock ends up worthless.

The advantage for a potential angel investor to guarantee a loan is that he or she does not actually have to provide you with the funds; rather the money just has to be put away as collateral against the loan guarantee (where it is still maintaining or increasing its value). The angel only loses the money if your company can't pay back the loan. Some guarantors will also ask for a small percentage of the company's revenues going forward for the time the guaranteed loan is outstanding.

The downside for the individual guaranteeing your loan is that there is no potential that the investment will turn to gold. However, the investor does usually get warrants to buy company stock at a deep discount as part of the guarantee deal.

Expenses of Privately Guaranteed Loans

There are a host of fees that come along with a privately guaranteed loan. Your bank will charge a loan origination fee. The bank providing the letter of credit for the guarantor to your bank will also charge a fee. If you work through a broker who finds wealthy people willing to guarantee loans for entrepreneurs, there is another fee (you can make your own deal with an angel you know or with a friend or family member).

Given the fact that most banks that write such loans will demand that the interest payment for the first year be taken out of the proceeds of the loan, a $1 million loan may only yield between $800,000 and $850,000 in usable proceeds (an effective interest rate that can hit close to 20 percent).

The bank providing the letter of credit for the guarantor to your bank will also charge a fee.

Guarantees as Bridge Financing

A privately guaranteed loan is usually taken out as a short-term bridge financing mechanism to provide the company with a quick infusion of capital for immediate needs. At the end of the term (usually one to two years), the company pays off the guaranteed loan with a new loan. It doesn't need a guarantor because the company has demonstrated ability through cash flow or the proceeds of an equity sale to pay off the new loan.

If the guaranteed loan has been put to good use and the company is now producing steady revenue and has measurable assets, a capital investment by an angel or venture capitalist will not cost the company as much equity as it would have before the guaranteed loan was established.

Chapter Key Points

- Getting a personal loan to start a business is very difficult.
- More than 30 percent of loans to small and start-up businesses are made by nonbank lenders, most by commercial finance companies.
- Lenders look at the five C's of credit—character, capacity, collateral, capital, and contribution—when determining whether to loan you money.
- Every lender wants to know that you are putting some of your own money at risk (skin in the game) before letting you start a business using other people's money.
- Sometimes an angel investor will guarantee a loan for you.

CHAPTER

27

CREDIT CARDS

CAREFUL FUNDS MANAGEMENT KEEPS YOU FROM "KITING"

Starting a business by using credit cards can be easy and enticing. But it can also be also extremely expensive and risky.

Credit cards are an easy, convenient way to buy the furniture and business equipment needed to start a business. For operating expenses, you can always get a cash advance.

If you think you can get a business up and running and earning income within a couple of months, "putting it on plastic" can save you the time and trouble that goes along with acquiring other kinds of financing.

But with most cards charging 15 to 20 percent annual interest, unless your company is able to rack up sales quickly and get rid of the debt, credit card financing is not the way to go over the long haul.

That's not to say it hasn't been done. There are entrepreneurs that have put a quarter of a million dollars and more on credit cards to bootstrap a business.

But if you are going to use credit cards to that extent, you need a plan. The only way to beat the finance charges is to create a self-funding pyramid by acquiring new credit cards and using the account-balance transfer provisions (usually offered at a discounted rate) to pay off the balances on the old cards in full, thereby negating interest charges.

The following seven steps outline a plan for a credit-card pyramid.

Set Up a Spread Sheet

The first step to financing a business start-up with credit cards is to set up a spread sheet and list every card you have (or acquire); the day of the month the account closes; the grace period; the date when the discount rate on balance transfers ends; and your current balance on the card. This will be extremely important as you build your credit card pyramid.

Using credit cards as well as checks enables you to track expenses.

Acquire Two to Three New Cards Every Month

Never turn down an offer of a new credit card. If the application you receive have not been presorted with your name, fill in your middle initial on some and not on others. Many credit data bases track the different names as two separate accounts, which can give you added leverage (higher maximum balances or more cards).

Apply for every kind of card that offers credit: Visa, Mastercard, Discover, and American Express Blue, Optima, or AmEx Small Business Open.

Don't start using a new card as soon as you get it. Hold onto it for when other cards become old and stale.

Use Courtesy Checks

Courtesy checks can be used for things you can't do with a credit card, like paying employees or professional advisors and consultants.

Use Some Cards for Purchases, Others for Cash Advances

Remember, when you transfer a balance from one card to another, the interest starts ticking on the new account immediately. This is also true when you write a courtesy check, which is considered a cash advance.

You should therefore use some cards for purchases only and others for paying off the monthly balances on those cards by transferring the card balances. Use the cards with the lowest courtesy rates as the ones from which you will pay off other balances and write courtesy checks.

Many cards offer low-interest time-limited rates, often referred to as "teasers," for a period of time after you acquire the card. Whenever possible, shift higher-interest balances to the cards with the teasers.

As long as you zero out the balance for the billing period shown on your card, there is no interest for any purchases made using the card after the account closed. But if you write a cash advance check or transfer a balance using that account, all of the purchases made with the card also incur interest charges.

Start Moving the Money Around

Now that you've set up your card accounts for purchases, as well as the accounts for courtesy checks to pay other expenses and the card-purchase account balances, you need to keep track of when the discounted rate ends on each of the accounts to which you are transferring balances or from which you are issuing courtesy checks.

When a discounted rate is about to expire, pay off the balance with one or more new cards that you have acquired and held onto. Move the card with the expired discount rate into the group of cards you use for credit-card only purchases and keep it there until another low-rate transfer offer comes along.

Most credit card companies will provide a quarterly management report that categorizes expenses by type and employee and provides a tax organization form.

Get Rid of High-Interest Stale Cards

Credit cards stop being useful after a time. Once you have many cards that you are using for only credit-card purchases, you can start culling out the ones that charge the highest interest rate or annual fee, or that have not issued an offer for low-interest balance transfer checks in the previous six months.

Getting rid of credit cards frees up space on your credit report for you to acquire more cards.

Prompt payment will give you a good credit history that can be used in the future to support a loan application at a bank or finance company.

Find Another Source of Funding

Unless you are a fan of Charles Ponzi and three-card monte dealers, you will probably only be able to stay sane and run a credit-card operation for nine months or a year before it becomes enormously cumbersome.

If in that time your business isn't generating revenue to allow you to get bank or commercial financing, or some buzz that makes you a candidate for angel or VC funding, you might want to close up and get a job.

Finally, during all this credit card wheeling and dealing, you should have been able to wrack up some serious frequent flier miles. After you've recapitalized your business, treat yourself and your significant other to a vacation.

Chapter Key Points

- Using credit cards to pay for start-up costs seems easy, but it can be risky.
- In order to use credit cards for more than small immediate financing needs, you must have a plan.
- Credit card financing involves many credit cards: some for purchases and some for balance transfers and courtesy-check writing.
- Always use the cards with the lower interest rates for paying off higher-rate balances and writing courtesy checks.
- Take maximum advantage of low-interest time-limited "teaser" rates for new cards.

CHAPTER

28

ACCOUNTS RECEIVABLE AND FACTORING

BORROWING AGAINST WHAT YOU'RE OWED KEEPS CASH COMING

New and growing companies don't always get the best credit terms from their suppliers, and therefore have to pay suppliers before their customers pay them. This can create cash-flow problems. In order to maintain cash flow, companies pledge their accounts receivable as collateral on a loan, or "sell" those receivables to a company known as a factor.

Using Receivables as Collateral

Many banks and finance companies that would be unwilling to provide you with an unsecured working capital loan will lend to a business using accounts receivable as collateral for the loan. They usually use a monthly borrowing-base calculation, which is based on historical averages. A lender will typically finance 80 percent of good-quality receivables (those that are not too old and deemed collectable).

As receivables are paid, you pay the bank, which lowers the borrowing basis until you make the next round of sales.

This is a labor-intensive type of loan. Both you and the bank must keep voluminous records, and banks usually charge higher interest rates than for other loans, as well as more service fees.

Factoring

In a factoring arrangement, rather than simply supplying a loan against accounts receivable collateral, a finance company actually buys the accounts receivable from the business (banks don't factor). Keep in mind the following points about factoring.

Factoring is used by companies large and small to cope with short-term cash-flow problems or long-term cash needs.

- Factoring is expensive.
- The factor does not pay the company 100 cents on the dollar. There are also charges and commissions for their collection services.
- There are advantages to using a factor. Money is paid almost immediately after the sale, and the company gets to limit its credit, collection, and bookkeeping expenses to a fixed percentage of its credit sales (the commission it pays to the factor). Many companies use factoring to avoid setting up a credit and collection department in-house.
- Most factors also work with companies ahead of time to help do credit checks on customers who wish to open and establish proper credit lines for those customers.

There are two types of factoring: old-line factoring and maturity factoring.

Old-Line Factoring

In an old-line factoring arrangement, the factor pays a certain percentage of each account receivable, known as an advance payment. It may trade receivables for advances on a monthly, weekly, or even daily basis. The advance rate, which can vary from 70 to 90 percent of total receivables, is determined by subtracting historic bad debt, slow paying, etc., from a base of 100, then adding back somewhere between 10 and 15 percent (or points); and then subtracting this number from 100 again. This final calculation is called the dilution. A "spread" is then added to the dilution to determine the final amount the factor will advance.

For instance, if your company's dilution rate is 7 percent and the factor takes a 13 percent spread, it will advance you 80 percent against each receivable.

The factor is actually lending the company the advance payment at a rate of 1 to 3 percent over the prime rate. When the factor collects against the account receivable, the first 80 percent expunges the advance the factor has paid against the receivable. If more than the 80 you have been advanced gets paid, the factor pays you cash, minus a "discount fee" of 2 to 6 percent, plus the interest you owe against the advance.

Some old-line factors also hold reserves against uncollectable accounts.

If the factor works without recourse, it gets stuck with any deadbeat receivables or deficiencies below what it has advanced. (It will, however, use these deficiencies and no-pays to recalculate your dilution rate.) If the factor works with recourse, you are responsible for picking up deficiencies of receivables that age out.

The factor is actually lending the company the advance payment at a rate of 1 to 3 percent over the prime rate.

Maturity Factoring

In maturity factoring, you and the factor determine the amount of credit that will be paid against each credit customer and the average collection period for all your accounts receivable. At the end of that period, the factor pays you the entire value of each customer's receivable up to the credit limit the factor will cover (less its commission for collections), regardless of whether the entire receivable has been paid off.

For instance, if your average collection period is 45 days and XYZ's credit limit is $25,000, 45 days after a sale to XYZ the factor will pay you the entire $25,000 (minus a commission of 2 to 6 percent for handling the collection), even if it has only collected $10,000. Many factors that work with maturity factoring will charge you interest on the difference between what they have collected and what they pay you, again at 1 to 3 percent over the prime rate.

While maturity factoring provides some protection against deadbeat customers, you do end up paying interest on uncollectable bills the factor has advanced against.

Check out www.thefactoringnetwork.com for an evaluation of whether factoring will work for you and to access to over 150 factors.

Using Factoring Wisely

It's important when establishing a relationship with a factor to understand the full extent of that relationship and create a strategy to use it to your advantage.

Factors have a stake in your customers' creditworthiness. Use their knowledge and expertise to perform credit checks, and let them work with you to establish realistic credit terms for your customers.

Some factors specialize in working with companies in a particular industry. Try to find one that specializes in your industry.

There are also factors that specialize in working with companies of different sizes. Many require you to have minimum monthly accounts receivable before they will work with you (this can be as low as $10,000 or as high as $250,000). Many also reduce their fees as the dollar volume of accounts receivables increases and increase their fees for smaller dollar-amount receivables. Try to find a factor that works with a lot of companies of your general size.

Take the factoring relationship into account when you establish prices and credit terms. Think of factoring the same way you think of credit-card selling (where you have to pay a processing commission to the credit card company).

Use the proceeds from factoring to get the best terms possible from your own suppliers. The savings you receive from timely payment discounts can offset some of the costs of factoring.

Six Questions to Ask a Potential Factor

Remember, factoring is a service being provided to you. As with any other professional service provider, the agreement you sign with a factor should define the level of service being provided for you and the payments you will make for those services. Before you sign an agreement, find out the answers to the following important questions.

1. Do you require a minimum monthly dollar volume of receivables? If so, what is it?
2. What is your basic discount fee? Does it depend on the dollar volume or number of receivables? What other fees and charges are there?
3. What is your advance rate (dilution plus how many points)? How quickly is the advance on new receivables paid (daily, weekly, monthly)? How frequently do you recalculate the dilution rate? Do you increase the advance rate for larger dollar volumes?
4. Do I have to sell you all of my receivables or a certain percentage or dollar volume?
5. What level of service do you guarantee? Do you perform credit checks on my accounts? If so, how frequently do you monitor my accounts' credit rating? How aggressively will you pursue a collection? What other services do you provide?
6. How long is the agreement for? What are the terms under which I can get out of the agreement?

As with any other professional service provider, the agreement you sign with a factor should define the level of service being provided for you and the payments you will make for those services.

Chapter Key Points

- New and growing companies often have to pay suppliers before their customers pay them.

- Many banks and finance companies that will not provide an unsecured working-capital loan will lend against your accounts receivable.
- Loans to banks collateralized by receivables are labor intensive and expensive.
- In a factoring arrangement, rather than simply supplying a loan collateralized by accounts receivable, a finance company buys your accounts receivable, then takes the responsibility for debt collection.
- Factoring has become increasingly specialized. There are factors who work with particular industries, factors who work with client companies of a particular size, and factors who work with accounts receivable of a particular dollar value.

SECTION V

▲ ▲ ▲

DOING THE FINANCING DEAL

CHAPTER 29

INVESTMENT AGREEMENT: BOILERPLATE CLAUSES

GET IT IN WRITING, AND GET IT RIGHT

The first rule of investment agreements is that you must insist on a written agreement with every investor and professional who performs services for your company. Some people say they only need written agreements for big deals or deals involving strangers.

Nothing could be further from the truth. Handshake deals can breed misunderstandings because you or the other person may not have thought of certain details, you may forget some points involved in the deal, or you and the other party may have different interpretations of a particular element of the deal.

A written agreement is a formal recognition of an arrangement that acts as a reference point for all parties and an enforceable instrument if one party or another does not perform as expected. It clearly describes the complete terms agreed to, and states that additional terms can be enforced if necessary.

Standard practice dictates that attorneys be involved in the final drafting of all agreements and transactions needed to bring a company forward. Entrepreneurs too often try to save money by picking up appropriate forms from office supply stores or using agreement forms that come in small-business legal kits. They say they will get a lawyer involved only when "really important agreements" come up.

Saving money by postponing the use of lawyers to draft agreements is a false economy. By saying that you do not need to know about the clauses in the documents you will execute, you are entrusting your future to your own legal judgment or that of other businesspeople.

Investment Agreements

There are three types of equity investment offerings that can be made by a start-up or growing business:

1. Private placements, using either a term sheet or a private placement memorandum (PPM)
2. Direct public offering of common stock (DPO)
3. Initial public offering of common stock (IPO)

> All investment offerings are regulated by the Securities and Exchange Commission (SEC) and/or state securities regulators.

These various investment vehicles are described in chapter 11.

All investment offerings are regulated by the Securities and Exchange Commission (SEC) and/or state securities regulators. In order to produce the documentation necessary for these types of offerings, you need to hire an attorney competent in securities law and such securities offerings.

A private placement of equity securities may be documented with a term sheet or a more detailed private placement memorandum. A term sheet is simply an agreement between you and an individual investor. It is typically used in transactions involving professional VC investors.

The rest of this chapter describes the standard clauses of a term sheet.

Term Sheet

A term sheet is, in effect, a proposal; it summarizes the key investment terms (e.g., how much the investor will be paying for your company's equity securities). The venture capitalist or sophisticated angel investor will draft a term sheet that outlines what you need to provide to them if you want the money.

A term sheet is merely a starting point for negotiations. You will have an opportunity to review it with your counsel, decide which terms you would like to have changed, and begin negotiations. However, the reality is that most venture capitalists are fairly adamant about the terms of their agreements, and your negotiating leverage depends on how attractive your business opportunity is.

In many respects, a term sheet is like a letter of intent. It lays out the general parameters around which the deal is to be constructed.

A term sheet should be nonbinding, meaning that the party to whom it is presented does not have to accept it. It is not binding until both parties—the entrepreneur and the investor—sign it.

All investors have different ways of making a commitment or beginning the commitment process. Some produce a commitment letter. In his book on venture capital investing (written for venture capitalists), David Gladstone discusses his preference for detailed commitment letters instead of term sheets. He suggests this as "an intermediate step between the oral understanding and the legal documents." He believes that a commitment letter allows people to state in business language what they believe the parameters of the deal to be.

All investors have different ways of making a commitment or beginning the commitment process.

Whether you (or a venture capitalist you work with) use a term sheet or a commitment letter, either document has five specific items it needs to cover:

1. Terms of the investment
2. Conditions of the loan (if there is one), including collateral
3. A preferred stock arrangement in the case of an equity investment
4. Representations you make about the company
5. Conditions under which the deal will be completed

Here, any document drawn up preliminary to final legal closing documents that lay out the parameters of the relationship will be called a "term sheet."

Get It in Writing

The assumption is that you only seriously discuss an investment in your company with people you already have a relationship with. You may therefore be tempted to create an agreement based on trust. When discussing the terms and parameters of the deal, someone may say "that's straightforward, it doesn't need to be written down."

Write it down. Recollection varies with time, events, and emotions.

It is much harder to enforce an agreement that is not in writing. Even if both parties agree to something, and even if writing it down will cause the entire document to be redrafted, put it in.

Defining the parties means stating whom the parties to the agreement are.

Major Sections of the Term Sheet

The subject of legal agreements is obviously complex and cannot be adequately described in a few pages. The descriptions given here of major sections of term sheets are informational only. To draw up a complete term sheet, you should always work with an attorney (see chapter 32).

The five major sections of the term sheet discuss:

1. Defining parties
2. Recitals
3. Business content
4. Financial considerations
5. Boilerplate clauses

Defining Parties

Defining the parties means stating whom the parties to the agreement are. For instance, the agreement is between your company and Uncle Mort, or you and the ABC Venture Partners.

Recitals

Recitals are the "whereas" and "wherefore" clauses that state the purpose of the agreement, as generally understood by both parties. Typically the recitals will indicate that the agreement provides for a cash investment in the company in exchange for certain considerations.

Business Content

The business content section concerns itself with operations of the business. This includes the role each party will play as it relates to the effort they are jointly undertaking. Any board representation, consulting, or other role the VC will play, is spelled out in this section.

Business content and financial considerations are the portions of the agreement that are most often negotiated.

Financial Considerations

The financial consideration section describes what the investor gets in return for the money being put into the business. Business content and financial considerations are the portions of the agreement that are most often negotiated; they are discussed in greater detail in the next chapter on clauses specific to the deal.

Boilerplate Clauses

"Boilerplate" refers to standard clauses in every agreement that ensure parties understand the mechanics of doing what they have agreed to. Within these clauses, there is room to describe the specific circumstances under which the agreement is being put into effect.

Boilerplate clauses, though standard, affect conduct or interaction between the parties. For this reason, they are important and should be understood. The details of these clauses tie them to the specific situation covered by the agreement.

Though the details are usually straightforward, some of them could be the basis for negotiation due to the preference of either party. Also, some lawyers differ on which clauses are boilerplate and which should be written with more specificity.

A few of the important boilerplate clauses, around which there may be some discussion, are:

Certain clauses are in every agreement, but their content varies depending on the nature of the agreement. You need to pay attention to these.

Integration/Entire Agreement

This clause states that the agreement being entered into supersedes any previous agreement, written or oral, between the parties regarding any of the included subjects.

Dispute Resolution, Jurisdiction, and Governing Law

In the event that a dispute cannot be resolved amicably by the parties, the agreement may have an approach, formula, or process they have agreed to in advance for resolving the dispute.

Lawyers argue long and hard over this clause. Especially when companies are incorporated in different states, they each want disputes to be litigated in court in their home state under their state's rules and procedures.

The reality when dealing with a VC or sophisticated angel is that he who has the cash gets to pick where any dispute will be settled.

More companies are therefore turning to so-called alternative dispute resolution (ADR) means of settling disputes, such as mediation and/or arbitration.

Mediation is conducted by a neutral third party who facilitates discussions between the parties in dispute in an effort to find a workable solution.

Arbitration is conducted by a single arbitrator or panel of arbitrators that listens to presentations by each party and rules in favor of one or the other. Arbitration can be binding or nonbinding.

In cases of mediation or nonbinding arbitration, a party who does not feel a proposed extra-judicial solution is appropriate can still take the case to court. This means the issue of where and under what state's applicable laws the suit will be heard is not necessarily dead.

Binding on the Parties, Successors, and Assignees

Under this clause, anyone who inherits or obtains your interest in the property that is the subject of the agreement is bound by the terms of the agreement unless there is a statement exempting or relieving the person or persons of their obligations.

During the term of the agreement, notices may be sent from one party to the other.

Severability

This says that if one clause in the agreement is found to be invalid, it is not applicable; however, the rest of the agreement may still be valid and enforceable.

Confidential Information

This clause describes how the parties will handle confidential information. Each party must keep confidential any information it learns about the other party in the course of the agreement and their work together.

Notices

During the term of the agreement, notices may be sent from one party to the other. In investor agreements, such notices may be about stockholder meetings, successful sales, personnel changes, or possible defaults on covenants in other agreement.

The parties should note in the agreement the addresses to which such notices should be sent. The address should be one at which someone is always available to receive notices and correspondence that may come via special mail service.

Term

The term is the length of time the agreement—and therefore the arrangement between the parties—remains in force. The reference date is usually in the paragraph where the parties are named (i.e., "This agreement is made between X and Y on ABC date").

Chapter Key Points

- You should have a written agreement with every investor.
- There are three kinds of investment agreements used for a sale of equity securities: a private placement (term sheet or private placement memorandum), a direct public offering, or an initial public offering.
- A term sheet is used with venture capitalists and sophisticated angels; a private placement memorandum is used for a friends and family offering, or an offering to less-sophisticated angels.
- The VC firm or angel will present you with a term sheet; there may be little room for negotiating if you need the investment.
- A term sheet covers the terms of the investment, conditions of and collateral for any loan, the representations you make about the company, and the conditions under which the investment will close.

CHAPTER

30

THE INVESTMENT AGREEMENT: SPECIFIC CLAUSES

KNOW ALL THE INS AND OUTS OF YOUR RIGHTS AND RESPONSIBILITIES

After the term sheet is negotiated and accepted, the complete agreement is prepared. Remember, the term sheet is primarily concerned with the "business content" and "financial and associated business terms" of the basic agreement, as discussed in chapter 29.

This chapter discusses the terms and conditions that encompass the final investor agreement. Not all clauses will be in every agreement, and there may be others not covered here (either because they are rarely used, or because they haven't been fully thought out and structured yet).

Knowing what these terms entail, and what effect they can have on your company, can help you design your game plan for dealing with investors who ask for these specific clauses and for your capital-raising strategy in general.

At the time you execute a major investment agreement, there may also be other agreements that must be put together. These often include an agreement regarding the transfer and voting of the securities being divided up; agreements creating a company stock purchase plan for employees; an agreement outlining the stock-option program for key employees; and employment agreements for key personnel.

As you move from raising capital from friends and family to angels and venture capitalists, investment agreements become more complex.

Private placement memoranda drawn up for friends and family investors are simple for two reasons. First, no single investor at this point will be a major equity holder in the company. Therefore, there is little likelihood they will make substantive demands. Second, they don't tend to be sophisticated angel investors and are usually not knowledgeable regarding the nuances of these investments.

This is not to say that you should take advantage of your friends and family. On the contrary, treating them fairly can create important allies down the road. You should create a basic set of arrangements for all friends and family equity stake holders who make their investments during a particular "round" of financing, and treat them all equally.

Agreement on a term sheet means that the parties agree to go forward and ultimately "close" on the agreement.

A round is defined by the pricing of the securities being offered. Everyone who is offered the opportunity to buy equity securities at a particular time must be offered the same terms. Sometimes the round will also be defined by a total amount of money that needs to be raised; if that amount is not raised, the financing round may be cancelled. In such an instance, all funds are held in escrow until the total amount of funding is secured.

Most term sheets are not binding. Agreement on a term sheet means the parties agree to go forward and ultimately "close" on the agreement. By definition, if the parties can't come to an agreement on the term sheet, there will be no closing. The final agreement usually is binding and may include some kind of a penalty clause if for some reason closing cannot occur.

The closing occurs when funds pass from the investor to the company and a security (stock, convertible stock, or debentures) passes from the company to the investor. Although it is expected the closing will occur, there are occasions when a term sheet is signed and closing never occurs. Closing is always contingent on satisfactory outcome of the investor's due diligence of the company.

Again, it's important to stress that when you deal with professional venture capitalists, they will present you with the term sheet. The professional venture capitalist is almost always investing funds raised from passive investors and has a fiduciary responsibility to those investors to negotiate vigorously for the most favorable terms.

Investment Agreement Structure

The agreement has three main purposes:

1. Summarize the key financial terms.
2. State major legal conditions.
3. Provide information about the company's status.

A typical investment agreement contains more than two dozen various terms. We have organized them into six categories, although in an agreement they are not necessarily placed together. These categories are:

- Initial capitalization
- Capital structure (rights)
- Capital structure (restrictions)
- Management control
- Information
- Legal issues

A typical investment agreement contains more than two dozen various terms.

Under each of these categories, there are two to ten or more specific terms. Many of these items will not be necessary for simple agreements between entrepreneurs and angels.

For each of the categories, you will find a matrix that lists the specific terms down the side and indicates in which agreements (friends and family, angel, and venture capitalist) they are usually incorporate.

Initial Capitalization

There are four clauses under capitalization, as shown in figure 30-1.

Amount of Financing

This clause states simply the amount of money the investor(s) is/are investing.

The price per share determines how many shares of stock will be issued in exchange for the investment being made.

Price Per Share

The price per share determines how many shares of stock will be issued in exchange for the investment being made. The price per share is determined as a part of defining the company's valuation both pre-closing (before the investment is made) and post-closing (after the investment is made).

Remember, the percentage of a company an investor is buying is determined by the post-closing value. For instance, if the pre-closing value is $4 million and an investor invests $1 million, the investor is not buying 25 percent of the company ($1 million = 25 percent of $4 million) but rather 20 percent ($1 million = 20 percent of $4 million pre-closing valuation plus $1 million new money invested = $5 million post-closing valuation).

If the investor is a venture capitalist, it may act as "lead firm" in a "syndicate" of investors. Many venture capitalists do not want to take the entire risk of backing

FIGURE 30-1 Initial Capitalization

	Friends/Family	Angel	Venture Capitalist
Amount of financing	✓	✓	✓
Price per share	✓	✓	✓
Type of security	✓	✓	✓
Use of funds		✓	✓

an entrepreneurial company. In addition, especially with highly technical new companies, a VC firm may want to bring in a firm with specific experience in a certain technological area.

Type of Security

As we've pointed out, venture capitalists and most angels do not like to invest in a straight common stock deal. The exact type of security needs to be spelled out in the agreement. Venture capitalists and sophisticated angels usually take preferred stock that is convertible to common stock.

The stock sold in each financing round is designated as a "series." For instance, the first round of stock is called Series A preferred stock. Preferred stock purchased by VC firms and sophisticated angels usually has all the features of a corporate bond (i.e., a regular dividend). However, preferred stock looks better than debt on the entrepreneurial company's balance sheet when it comes time to raise further capital. Usually the dividend payments are accrued rather than paid out and are paid out at conversion in the form of extra common stock, or when the investment is redeemed.

Parties to an investor agreement have relationships at several levels: finance, legal, and management. It is too easy to focus on one relationship and its issues, and neglect the others.

Each successive round of equity financing needs to negotiate concessions with the owners of the previous round's equity in terms of each series of stock's value and where each round's investors are situated in case of bankruptcy proceedings.

Use of Funds

Investors are concerned about how funds will be used. Venture capitalists are particularly concerned that company founders not use the proceeds of any future round of financing to buy out some of their stock, partially cashing out their equity interest in the company, and that they not pay themselves fat salaries with the proceeds of each successive round of financing.

Accordingly, in the term sheet, use of funds will be limited usually to working capital (ongoing operations), acquisitions of other companies, or plant and equipment. Sometimes other restrictions are placed on the use of funds.

Capital Structure (Rights)

This is the category where the most clauses fall. Here "rights" refers to those granted to the investor (which often result in restrictions on the entrepreneur). The clauses that come under capital structure, or rights, are shown in figure 30-2.

FIGURE 30-2 Capital Structure: Rights

	Friends/Family	Angel	Venture Capitalist
Antidilution		✓	✓
Conversion	✓	✓	✓
Dividends	✓	✓	✓
Future stock purchases		✓	✓
Liquidation preference		✓	✓
Participation protection		✓	✓
Redemption ("put" provision)		✓	✓
Registration rights			
• Demand registration		✓	✓
• "Piggyback" rights		✓	✓
"Tag-along" rights		✓	✓
Unlocking provisions		✓	✓

Antidilution

An antidilution clause is common to angels and venture capitalists, and can even be provided to friends and family and other "seed-stage" investors.

This clause provides protection for early investors against later investors being given a larger percentage of the company. Remember, at the time each successive round of financing is organized, the company is revalued. This means that an investor who purchases 500,000 shares in the third round will be buying a different percentage of the company than an investor who purchased 500,000 shares in the first or second round.

In an antidilution clause, when the next round of financing is obtained, if the company's value is increased and it costs more for a new investor to purchase a share of stock, the early investor is provided with additional shares so his or her investment retains the same relative value in terms of the percentage of the company he or she owns. This means the entrepreneur's equity in the company is usually reduced when new financing is brought it, but early investor's equity is not.

> An antidilution clause is common to angels and venture capitalists, and can even be provided to friends and family and other "seed-stage" investors.

Conversion

Conversion rights offer the investor the option to exchange his initial preferred stock for common stock at a fixed price during an agreed-upon time frame.

Conversion rights may be triggered if there is an IPO or if control of the company changes (i.e., a sale).

The conversion may be adjusted for dividends, changes in the capitalization of the company, or stock splits.

Dividends and Interest

Dividend and interest payments are called for in some types of securities. Both dividends and interest may be deferred. Most VCs do defer interest and dividends until there is a conversion or sale. Also, an investor may, as a concession to investors in later rounds of financing, waive the interest if he or she converts to common stock.

Future Stock Purchases

Investors often want the right of first refusal on any future sales of stock by the company in order to increase their share in a promising company. Exercising this right also prevents or minimizes dilution. Venture capitalists often require that original investors invest in successive rounds of financing in proportion to their original pro-rata share in the company. This is sometimes referred to as participation protection.

Investors often want the right of first refusal on any future sales of stock by the company in order to increase their share in a promising company.

Liquidation Preference

This right takes into account the contingency that the company suddenly loses value or closes. Holders of the preferred shares are entitled to be "first out" before holders of common stock. In other words, if the company goes into a liquidation or bankruptcy, the preferred-stock investors get anything left over after the lawyers, creditors, and debt holders, and ahead of the entrepreneur, who always holds common stock.

Venture capitalists usually set a time when they will at least calculate a liquidation value for their investment, even if they do not actually liquidate their position. The investor sets a target for receiving its original investment plus some gain (often stated as a multiple of the investment). A merger or acquisition, or any change in control of the company, is usually "deemed to be a liquidation" and the liquidation guidelines apply. This is often referred to in the agreement as a "liquidity event."

Participation Protection

This clause requires the original investor to invest with each successive round of financing. The early investors must invest proportionately to his or her original pro-rata share of the company. The clause benefits the entrepreneur, because it raises more money when he might need it. It also works against diluting the early investors' equity and forces the entrepreneur to give up equity in order to bring in new investors. Very few, if any, sophisticated investors agree to such a clause.

Redemption ("Put" Provision)

A so-called "put" provision is commonly used to force the company to buy back a specified portion of the investor's stock at a given time and for a predetermined price.

Registration Rights

There are a number of different types of registration rights. The two most common are so-called demand rights, and a "piggyback" provision.

In order for a company to conduct any public offering of capital stock, it must register the stock with the SEC and comply with the securities laws of any state in which the offering will be made. In addition, many owners of large blocks (i.e., founders and equity investors) can also register their stock, which becomes part of the sale to the public.

In order for a company to conduct any public offering of capital stock, it must register the stock with the SEC and comply with the securities laws of any state in which the offering will be made.

In the case of initial public offerings (IPOs), pre-IPO owners of stock who do not sell at the time of the IPO are often restricted from selling for months or even more than a year after the IPO is carried out.

Registering pre-IPO stock and selling at the IPO is how venture capitalists, angels, and other passive investors cash out of their investments that actually engage in an IPO. Very rarely do they hold stock after the

IPO. Many friends and family, and some angels, continue to hold part or all of their position after an IPO.

Demand Registration

Under a demand registration, investors can force the company to register the investor's shares regardless of whether any other shares are being registered.

"Piggyback" Rights

In order to be guaranteed the right to have the company register the investor's stock at the time it registers its own, the investor must have "piggyback" rights, which allow the investor to have his or her stock registered with the SEC.

Some VCs also insist on "drag-along" rights, in which they drag the company's founders into the sale as well.

"Tag-Along" Rights

Under this clause, also called co-sale rights, if an entrepreneur decides to sell all or part of his or her shares to a third party, investors are allowed to "tag along" on the sale. It may be written in such a way that an entrepreneur may not sell his or her stock unless the buyer agrees to purchase an equal proportion from the investors who have tag-along rights.

Some VCs also insist on "drag-along" rights, in which they drag the company's founders into the sale as well.

Unlocking Provisions

Early investors, especially angels, are most likely to ask for an "unlocking" provision that calls for the company to buy out their position in the event that a valid offer to buy the company is made and subsequently rejected. This clause gives angels some control, even though they may not have board influence, over possible sale of the company.

It also unlocks them later on when venture capitalists do have control, and the venture capitalists' interests may not totally coincide with the angels'. For instance, if two years after venture capitalists have made an investment an offer is made that the venture capitalist doesn't deem "good enough," an angel may feel that he or she, having sat on the investment for five or six years, has earned enough and should get out.

Capital Structure (Restrictions)

Venture capitalists and some angels impose restrictions and limitations on the entrepreneur in order to protect their investments. The capital structure (restriction) clauses are shown in figure 30-3.

Venture capitalists and some angels impose restrictions and limitations on the entrepreneur in order to protect their investments.

Founder Stock Restrictions

This clause is concerned with transfers of the entrepreneur's stock to third parties. It may include prohibitions against or special treatment of the founder's stock for estate planning or gifts. It usually contains the investor's right of first refusal and co-sale issues, if they are not explicitly stated in a section by that name.

Founder Vesting

An investor may insist that a founder give up some of his or her stock to the investor if particular milestones are not met or if the founder leaves the company.

FIGURE 30-3 Capital Structure: Restrictions

	Friends/Family	Angel	Venture Capitalist
Founder stock restricition		✓	✓
Founder vesting		✓	✓
Right of first refusal		✓	✓

By taking control of more stock if milestones are not met, the investor is, in effect, revaluing the company because of lost opportunity.

At the time of the investment, a key factor in any venture capitalist's decision to invest is the quality of management and of the founder or founders. The investor usually wants to retain the founder(s) for as long as possible and does this by allowing the founder(s) to have access to blocks of stock according to a preset schedule.

At the time of the investment, a key factor in any venture capitalist's decision to invest is the quality of management and of the founder or founders.

Forcing the founder to remain with the company for a predetermined period of time in order to be able to retain stock is often referred to as "golden handcuffs." Since investors invest in entrepreneurs as much or more than in their ideas, the company's value is inextricably bound up in the founder's remaining.

Right of First Refusal

For the venture capitalist, this clause usually refers to having the first chance to buy any stock that another investor wishes to sell. This allows the VC firm to increase its holding in the company without having to go through an entire recapitalization process. This also prevents stock from falling into the hands of others who might challenge the VC firm for control of the company.

Management Control

One of the major issues concerning the investor is management control. Especially for venture capitalists, having some degree of control over management's decision making is absolutely essential in order to protect its interest. These clauses are shown in figure 30-4.

Board of Directors

The issue around the board of directors is how many directors each investor or investor group will be allowed to name. The condition usually sets out the total number

FIGURE 30-4 Management Control

	Friends/Family	Angel	Venture Capitalist
Board of directors		✓	✓
Veto rights		✓	✓

of directors on the board and the number of directors that each stock class can elect.

Usually the clause dictates that the bylaws authorize an odd number of directors (often no more than five). On a board of five seats, usually two would be representatives of the major-investor VC firm, which holds preferred stock and has the right to name two directors (thereby holding 40 percent of the board control). Two other directors would be named by the common-stock owners (founders) as a group, and one board member would be an independent mutually agreed upon individual.

Directors make fundamental decisions that guide the company's activities on behalf of their various constituencies. There is usually a provision that a given percentage of the board members (usually less than a majority) can call a special meeting.

Directors make fundamental decisions that guide the company's activities on behalf of their various constituencies.

Veto Rights

This is the other means of control a major investor can obtain. It is very typical in deals with VC firms. Such a clause specifies the kinds of issues over which the investor will have a veto without having to have a vote of the board. The kinds of things venture capitalists usually want veto over are change in the capital stock structure, merger or sale, change in control of the company, declaration of dividends, major capital expenses, taking on debt, and even the "burn rate" (the rate at which the company uses cash).

Information

Interaction between the entrepreneur and an investor always begins with the entrepreneur providing the (potential) investor with a business plan and associated back-up materials. The negotiation phase is likely to generate more requests for information.

After the deal closes, the investor wants to make sure he or she is kept abreast of developments that affect the company and the investment.

The major information-related clauses are shown in figure 30-5.

Sophisticated investors insist that the company report to them on all significant matters.

Disclosure of Other Stockholder Terms

Information about investors in prior rounds (amount invested, price per share, and equity stake) is always provided in the documentation for a subsequent financing round.

Reporting (Information Rights)

Sophisticated investors insist that the company report to them on all significant matters. They want information on monthly financial statements, budgets, agreements executed by the company (some of which may need their concurrence) and any changes in the company's business plan.

Although this clause is not always insisted on by friends and family, you should provide these investors with some reporting.

FIGURE 30-5 Information

	Friends/Family	Angel	Venture Capitalist
Disclosure of other stockholder terms	✓	✓	✓
Reporting (information rights)	✓	✓	✓
Representations and warranties	✓	✓	✓

Representations and Warranties

There are usually from five to 25 clauses in this section. They state that you are fully disclosing all matters concerning the company to your investors and potential investors. They state that the investor is investing on the basis of the information you are providing.

While there may be exceptions or qualifications noted to aspects of the information provided, the key is that the investor must have all the information he or she needs.

This includes information regarding insurance coverage and corporate assets, as well as about litigation pending and compliance with laws and regulations.

Legal issues cover a broad spectrum and deal with interactions between you and the investor.

Legal Issues

Legal issues cover a broad spectrum and deal with interactions between you and the investor. An investor is normally in for the long haul and wants the best possible working relationship with an entrepreneur. Investors also want a relationship that protects their investment.

The clauses that often appear are shown in figure 30-6.

Assignment

This clause deals with the conditions under which an investor may transfer securities to other parties.

FIGURE 30-6 Legal Issues

	Friends/Family	Angel	Venture Capitalist
Assignment	✓	✓	✓
Confidentiality	✓	✓	✓
Indemnification	✓	✓	✓
Legal fees and expenses		✓	✓
Purchase agreement		✓	✓

Confidentiality

Some investors, especially venture capitalists, may require an entrepreneur to keep negotiations and the potential investment confidential, at least until the deal closes.

Indemnification

The indemnification clause is directly tied to the representations and warranties you make.

The indemnification clause is directly tied to the representations and warranties you make. The clause makes you responsible for settling any legal dispute between you and another party that you did not disclose in your representations, or that you lied about in your warranties.

In addition, indemnification requires that the company obtain directors' and officers' (D&O) insurance to cover board members in their deliberations (i.e., that you indemnify any venture capitalist or angel who sits on your board). It may also require the company to act as a responsible party when incurring liabilities, such as those associated with stock registration, and compensate investors for any expenses they incur in this regard.

Legal Fees and Expenses

Under this clause, the investor is able to recover reasonable costs associated with the closing, including fees for legal counsel as well as expenses for documentation, review of closing documents, and other matters.

Definitive Agreements

A closing requires that separate definitive agreements be drawn up before the investment is made. These include a purchase agreement, an investor rights agreement, a stockholder agreement, a preferred stock registration, and can include other separate agreements.

Chapter Key Points

- The term sheet is only an agreement to agree. The full investment agreement is much more comprehensive.
- A typical investment agreement includes descriptions of the initial capitalization, the capital structure, rights and restrictions, management control, information, and legal issues.
- Venture capitalists and sophisticated angels almost never invest in common stock; they invest in preferred stock with a host of special preferences and the right to convert to common stock in the event of a successful public offering.
- Venture capitalists and angels are very concerned about protecting their rights and the percentage of the company they own in the event of either subsequent rounds of financing or liquidation of the company.
- Investment agreements limit founders in what they can do with the proceeds of the funding, and bind them in other ways to align the interests of the investor(s), the founder(s), and the company going forward.

CHAPTER

31

NEGOTIATING

KNOW WHERE YOU WANT THE DISCUSSION TO END

During the course of raising capital, you will be operating in two different modes.

In the first, with family and friends and with smaller angel investors, you will provide a private placement memorandum with the terms and conditions of the investment agreement. Individual investors will not be able to negotiate these terms.

In the second, with more sophisticated angels and venture capitalists, you will be the recipient of a term sheet from a professional investor. In this mode, there will be some negotiations, although you may be at a disadvantage.

Negotiating occurs when the parties intending to enter into a prospective business arrangement discuss the terms that will be in their agreement. It is a complex process, involving strategy, tactics, and psychology.

The intent here is to present basic outlines of negotiating strategy and tactics. We've already touched on negotiating in the chapter on creating strategic alliances (chapter 18).

Win-Win, Win-Lose, or Give a Little and Get a Little

Many people think that negotiations are zero-sum; if one party wins the other party must, of necessity, lose. But that is usually not the case.

Others argue that every negotiation should look for the "win-win," where both parties come away having gained. Again, in many instances that is unrealistic. While the world may not be zero-sum, each undertaking that is subject to negotiation does have finite limits to how far each party can go.

In reality, negotiations are discussions in which both parties must continually reassess the various trade-offs associated with the undertaking they are discussing. When negotiating, you must always be thinking, "If I give this, what must I get in return to maintain my same relative position vis-à-vis the other party?"

In reality, negotiations are discussions in which both parties must continually reassess the various trade-offs associated with the undertaking they are discussing.

A Negotiating Strategy

There are two ways you can cause a deal to fail.

One is by not understanding why you want to do the deal and not determining what you are willing to "pay" in order for the deal to be done.

The other is by not having a plan for how to implement the arrangement.

Even if you have done your prework, if the other party fails in either of these regards, he or she can cause the deal to fail.

When considering what you are willing to give up—to pay—for the deal to come together, you need to think about whether you are negotiating as the party who has put the terms of the deal together (from a position of strength) or are responding to a proposed deal put together by someone else (from a position of weakness).

If you have put the terms of the deal together, your preplanning should involve creating responses to objections that could be raised about any particular term and "fall-back" positions you can take that might cut down your advantage but not negate it totally. When dealing from this perspective, you should never have to accept a term to the deal that ties your hands and reduces your flexibility.

For instance, if you are presenting a PPM to a relative for a $50,000 investment, what will your position be if Uncle Mort says during the meeting, "You know, I've been thinking, not that I don't trust you, but if I'm going to give you this kind of money, I want to be a cosigner on all checks."

Seven Negotiating No-Nos

Since negotiating is a ballet, you have to know how to dance. This means knowing where you want to move and where your negotiating counterpart will be moving as well.

Any one of the following slipups can cause you to fall and bring the entire performance to a halt:

1. Not knowing what you want at the conclusion of the negotiations.
2. Not knowing what the other guy wants.
3. Not knowing who is "coming to whom" and thus who has the advantage of being able to sit back and see what happens.
4. Accepting a deadline. Negotiating against the clock gives the other party an advantage.
5. Not considering contingencies; where do you go if the deal falls apart?
6. Reacting spontaneously to new terms. Any new term introduced during negotiations needs time out for analysis.
7. Responding spontaneously to intimidation.

If you are responding to terms outlined by the other party, your preplanning should involve defining firm positions behind which you will not allow yourself to be pushed.

Or, what would you say if he said, "I was talking to my friend Tom the other day, who invests in start-up companies—I never knew he did that until I told him about this deal—and he said every angel—that's what he called me, an angel—should have a seat on the board of directors."

Finally, what would you say if Mort said, "Tom told me I should have an antidilution provision. I don't understand exactly what he means, but I know we didn't talk about it."

If you are responding to terms outlined by the other party, your preplanning should involve defining firm positions behind which you will not allow yourself to be pushed.

For example, if a VC firm is offering a $2 million investment in exchange for 22 percent of the company, it is going to want representation on the board of directors. Your board is currently nine members, with you sitting as the chair. The VC firm's term sheet says that it will have three seats and a veto over the chair. How would you respond?

Would your response depend on the financial condition your company was in at the time the offer was made (i.e., the terms are terrible, but you REALLY NEED the money)?

Thinking through all of these possible scenarios and questions you might be asked about your terms and defining your response is what we call creating your negotiating strategy.

Negotiating tactics are the way you undertake the actual negotiation.

Defining the End Point

The end point of your negotiating strategy is what you see as the eventual outcome.

Let's use a simple example: You see a car dealership advertisement that says: "Pull, drag, or tow your car to us and we'll give you $3,000 for it in trade." You know that your 12-year-old car is worth about $200 in a legitimate trade (essentially the dealer will pay what it would cost you to have it towed to a junkyard).

You have researched new cars, and the one you want has a sticker price of $23,500 and a "dealer invoice" of $18,200. You know the dealer invoice gives the dealer a profit of about $3,000, which is OK because he has real estate, inventory, support people to pay, etc. You're willing to pay $200 over invoice, which will be the commission to the salesman.

You don't care how you get there, as long as your net number ends up at $18,400 plus sales tax. You go in there knowing $18,400 plus tax is what you will pay, and the sales guy can talk himself in all kinds of circles, but you will not pay one penny over $18,400.

Negotiating Tactics

Negotiating tactics are the way you undertake the actual negotiation. To some degree, negotiations are a ballet, intricately choreographed to get to an ultimate conclusion everyone knows will occur.

In the car example above, you know that the salesman is going to come at you with all kinds of feints, jabs, and sucker punches to try to get you to pay closer to $23,500. "Look, I'm giving you $3,000 for your tin, so I can't start anywhere below sticker; $20,500 is a great deal for this. Of course, I gotta charge you $300 for the registration, $900 for 'dealer prep' and $500 for 'destination charges' but these are things I can't waive. That's $22,100. Five percent under sticker, how can you beat it?"

"Sorry, $18,400."

"Okay, I'll waive the destination charge. Maybe I can throw in the options package, that's $1,400 off the sticker. Let me go talk to the business manager and see if I can put you in this thing for $20,200."

"Sorry, $18,400. I did my research. The dealer is making a profit at the $18,200 dealer invoice."

"Well, let me see if I can get this down a little more for you..."

If he would just shut up and take his $200, he could go deal with another customer who hadn't done his homework.

If you are willing to walk out the door if you don't get the car for $18,400, you have the upper hand. That's because you have a strategy and a defined end point, and are implementing good tactics to get there.

Car salesmen have no strategy. Their modus operandi is to obfuscate and talk at you until you either cave in or walk. They know that anything over $18,400 they can get out of you, they get 30 or 40 or 50 percent.

In serious business negotiations, if both sides have created a strategy, they should be able to spend a couple of hours feeling around to see if there is a nook or cranny they can exploit that the other guy hasn't thought of, then "put their cards on the table" and hash out an agreement in a short time.

They will each give a little. They will each get a little. No one will win, and no one will feel bitter that the other guy ripped him off.

Common Negotiating Mistakes

There are a number of negotiating mistakes you can make that can lead to failure to reach an agreement. They include:

- Having a negotiating team that is too narrow.
- Using "gut" numbers.
- Treating negotiations too casually.

A Too-Narrow Team

Too often, a company's CEO negotiates a deal personally. In start-up or small companies with small staffs, the founder or CEO is almost always the one to negotiate deals.

This can be a disaster. When only a company's leader—or the company's leader and his or her trusted advisor (often the small company's lawyer)—is involved, the agreement can become more an exercise in ego than in moving the company forward.

First, CEOs do not always know all the details of their company's operations and how the proposed deal will affect those operations.

Second, the CEO is often using the negotiations as a means to stake a claim to a certain position of prestige, or maintaining a certain relationship vis-à-vis the other party.

In negotiating with potential investors, the small-company founder or CEO often has his or her entire ego wrapped up in the business, and issues of giving up control or needing to change operating models to adhere to covenants and terms of the agreement can be very difficult.

Small negotiating teams are good. They are able to remain focused, and the head of the team does not lose control. Make sure all those in senior positions who will be affected have some input into the negotiating strategy.

Quick concessions are only good if you have thought about them, the content of the situation has not changed, and making the concession allows you to focus the negotiations on your objectives.

But there should be a single spokesperson for the negotiating team.

It's best to hire a business consultant to help you negotiate investment agreements. Allow this person time to get to know you and your company. This person can often be a dispassionate analyst of proposed agreements and can tell you whether you are getting enough to outweigh what you have to give up.

Using "Gut" Numbers

You should never negotiate on the basis of "gut" feelings, "guestimates," or "ballpark" figures when it comes to numbers.

Negotiating is like being Alice in Wonderland: If you don't know where you want to go, it does not matter how you get there.

Before entering serious negotiations about an investment, you need to have a realistic evaluation of your business to determine its value.

For example, in a meeting with a prospective angel considering a substantial investment, a start-up CEO told the angel that she would receive 1 percent of equity for each $100,000 of investment. The angel suggested such a valuation (approximately $10 million) seemed quite high.

The CEO did not have the numbers at hand. Previously, his attorney and financial advisors had prepared an analysis and valued the company at substantially more, such that the $100,000 investment would command 0.6 percent of equity. The angel willing to invest $500,000 was taken aback to hear that her investment would only purchase 3 percent of the company rather than 5 percent. Negotiations collapsed. Later, when the company was unable to find other financing, it was forced to go back to this angel and give her 5 percent for her $500,000 investment.

Treating Negotiations Too Casually

Negotiations are serious business. They should be conducted as you would a diplomatic mission. And your discretion should extend beyond the actual negotiating discussions to any "off-line" comments.

Never do what one CEO did: During intense negotiations between the lawyer for a large corporation and the representative of a small growth company, the corporate CEO came by, took his attorney into the hall, and asked in a voice loud enough so all in the conference room could hear, "Are we f—-ing them good?"

Patience

Remember, negotiations require patience. Take as much time as you need to consider offers and counteroffers. And allow your counterparts to take as much time as they need.

Don't give away concessions too soon or concessions that are too big. The deal is a package of trade-offs. Making a concession demands getting something of equal value back. While it is not necessary to give everything to the other guy, the deal as a package must work for him if in the long run it is to work for you.

Finally, rehearse your position. Know the arguments you are going to make and have supporting materials to bolster those arguments. Alternatives and fall-back positions should be known and ranked.

Remember, negotiations require patience. Take as much time as you need to consider offers and counteroffers.

Chapter Key Points

- Negotiation is not a zero-sum game; it is possible for both parties to get what they want.
- Good negotiations begin with a negotiating strategy.
- Know what you want and what you need before starting a negotiation.
- Make sure your negotiating team is broad enough and understands all aspects of your company.
- Negotiations require patience. Take as much time as you need to get it right.

CHAPTER 32

FINDING QUALIFIED LEGAL ASSISTANCE

MANY ATTORNEYS ARE COMPETENT, FEW ARE GREAT

Entrepreneurs usually obtain their first legal assistance from a friend, a family attorney, an attorney referred by a friend or business associate, or an attorney they have become acquainted with through some unrelated legal matter. This attorney probably undertook as a first assignment for you the incorporation of your business.

The lawyer may have helped you with the arrangement for leasing office, laboratory, or production space. He or she may have helped you create employment contracts for key employees and establish terms with suppliers and/or customers. These are all relatively mundane legal tasks that any competent attorney can handle.

But when you move from these basic legal tasks associated with starting and operating a business to the detailed and specific tasks involved in raising capital, or from determining a company's value to drawing up complex investor agreements necessary to exchange capital for equity with angels and venture capitalists, you are entering a specialized legal terrain known as securities law. This calls for expert legal assistance.

Attorneys who specialize in working with securities (both equity and debt) have a thorough and deep knowledge of the SEC regulations as well as the laws under which those regulations are promulgated. They know how to work both effectively and efficiently in doing such things as registering securities and applying for exemptions from registration.

At an early stage of your capital-raising endeavors, selling equity to friends and family may not be complex. But even here, thinking through the distribution of equity for you and your passive investors, providing ownership opportunity for key employees (or all employees), and thinking through the equity allocation for future financing rounds requires someone who understands investment matters, their implications, and the dynamics of securities law.

It is possible to find law firms that have expertise in these areas. If your first-level business attorney is part of a firm, such expertise may even be there, and he or she may become your "relationship manager" or corporate counsel, while much of the technical work is handled by other attorneys at the firm. If you have been working on a technical application for which you have sought intellectual property protection, your intellectual property or patent attorney may be able to put you in touch with a specialist in securities law, since the two often work hand in hand with entrepreneurs.

If your corporate legal needs are being handled by an individual attorney or one with a small firm that does not have a securities practice, your securities attorney does not have to displace this person, but rather should be hired as a legal consultant who reports to your corporate attorney.

When looking for an attorney to do your securities work, the right fit is as important as the fit between you and your employees, you and your board of directors, and you and your major investors.

Finding the Right Fit

Many places in this book have highlighted the concept of "fit," or how you work with counterparts in one business relationship or another. When looking for an attorney to do your securities work, the right fit is as important as the fit between you and your employees, you and your board of directors, and you and your major investors. In fact, it might be more important.

Your securities attorney will be the person you entrust to help you get the "best deal" when structuring major capital investments in your company.

For that reason, we do not think it is impolite or improper to interview potential securities lawyers, interview them thoroughly, and perform some level of due diligence (not simply taking their work at face value but considering their presentation to you as a marketing effort). If you are going outside the firm in which your corporate attorney practices, it is not even improper for that attorney to come with you and participate in these interviews; after all, the securities attorney will be a contracting consultant working with the corporate attorney.

During an interview with a prospective securities counsel, be conscious of whom you meet with in the firm. Is it a senior partner, a younger or junior partner, or an associate? Is it an individual or a team? If a team, how long does the most senior member stay in the meeting? Are you being treated warmly or brusquely? Do you get a sense that the firm really wants your business or that the meeting is being conducted as a favor to someone?

Competence and compatibility are both important when selecting legal representation.

Questions to Ask

When interviewing a prospective attorney (by extension a firm) to conduct your securities work, you should ask straightforward, pointed questions about the amount of such work the firm does and whether your assignment will be undertaken by seasoned securities professionals. You may want to set up a spreadsheet to rank the various firms you meet with (such a form is seen in Appendix C).

Among the most important questions to ask are:

- What securities services do you offer?
- How is your firm's client base divided between large corporations and start-up or growth companies?
- What services do you think a law firm should offer to a start-up or small company?
- What types of start-up and small companies do you work with most? What kind are you most skilled at handling? What kind do you find most enjoyable to work with?

- What are the practice areas in your firm that you consider "specialty areas?" Do you consider securities work one of your firm's strongest practice areas?
- How do you work with start-up and growth companies? Secondary questions under this heading include:
  - What role do partners play in working with start-up and growth companies? What role do securities experts play?
  - Who will be the "relationship manager"? Will it be a securites expert?
  - What is your pricing structure when working with smaller companies?
  - Do you ever take an equity stake in exchange for services? (This was common in the late 1990s, much less so today.)
- How well connected is your firm with the local and regional angel community?
- How well connected is your firm with the local and regional venture capital community?
- How well connected is your firm with the venture capital community that specializes in my type of company?
- How much work do you do on initial public offerings (IPOs) of common stock? What is your track record of successful IPOs?
- When you work on an IPO, which investment banks do you usually deal with? How much input do you have in choosing an investment bank?
- Do you have experience in direct public offerings (DPOs)?
- Do you ever weigh in on the decision of if or when a company should go public?

During an interview with a prospective securities counsel, be conscious of whom you meet with in the firm.

- What post-IPO services do you provide?
- Why do you want to work with me, and why should I want to work with you?

Chapter Key Points

- You need to be very honest in determining if your current attorney—be he or she a long time friend, family member, or old college buddy—is the right person to help you raise capital.
- To successfully raise capital for an entrepreneurial venture, you need an attorney well versed in SEC and state securities regulations.
- When looking for an attorney, "fit" is as important as legal skill.
- As you meet with prospective attorneys and/or firms, ask questions, listen to answers, and take note of body language and etiquette to get a sense of how important your business is to them.
- Set up a spreadsheet with all of your important criteria, then immediately after you return from your meeting rank each prospective firm against those criteria.

CHAPTER

33

BUSINESS FINANCING SCAMS

WORK ONLY WITH BROKERS WHO TREAT YOU AS A PROFESSIONAL

In the two or three years leading up to the dotcom bust, more money than ever before was available to entrepreneurs. The CEO of one successful company making devices for dotcom companies said that his venture capitalist told him to spend the third round of funding as quickly as possible because the VC firm wanted to show its fund investors that the money was being put to use.

Yet, while some entrepreneurs were being showered with VC funding and growing wealthy from IPOs only months after starting their companies, many others still could not raise the capital they needed. Reasons included poor business plans and presentations, and simply being in the wrong market or industry.

These people were ripe targets for losing their money either to one of the incompetent capital brokers and finders who flooded into the marketplace for these kinds of services, or to outright fraud artists. While not fraudulent, the incompetents were committing unintentional fraud, taking money from clients for services they obviously had no ability to perform.

The Scam

When operated by one of the deliberate con artists, the scam goes by one of three names: "advance-fee fraud," "prime-bank instruction fraud" or "venture capital fraud." In all cases it works about the same.

An entrepreneur pays an up-front fee, ranging from about $50,000 to over $1 million, to a broker who supposedly has close dealings with investors or investment syndicates (sometimes they even say they represent the investors). In return, the broker says he will pitch the entrepreneur's company to the investors in the hopes of acquiring a capital infusion as large as $50 million.

The con works because the purported investor or syndicate seems very creditable. He speaks well, dresses well, seems to know important people, says he is calling from exotic places where he is in discussions with wealthy individuals, and tells you he has been successful for other clients. In a business area as opaque as raising money for entrepreneurs, it is sometimes difficult to tell who is for real and who is not.

Anyone hungry for money and power is a candidate to be scammed.

An agreement is made for the supposed finder to provide "best efforts to assist you" to find financing. These best efforts are never clearly stated. Nothing is promised, because, hey, you can't promise success, only effort. Agreements usually call for a one-time fee to kick off the finder's efforts, then monthly payments for a retainer and expenses.

Once an entrepreneur is sucked into an advance-fee arrangement, losses can be substantial. In most cases, victims only lose their up-front fee and possibly some expense money that is taken in cash. However, the agreement may also contain provisions for the finder to take part of his payment in the form of stock or warrants under certain conditions, such as your defaulting on payments.

As we have said, licensed brokers and finders can accept equity as part of the fee. An unlicensed broker running a scam will get around this by having a clause in the contract that says he is not acting as a fiduciary, but only as a consultant.

You may even be asked to put stock or warrants in escrow to cover any such defaults. Often, the more fraudulent the deal, the more egregiously you are hemmed in while the other party is seemingly void of obligations.

The Inventor Variation

Another iteration is the invention consultant fraud. These scams are operated by con artists who promise to take your invention, patent it if possible, and help you create marketing, distribution, and manufacturing arrangements.

The costs of using a patent attorney to help you obtain intellectual property protection for an invention can be high, and the time line for obtaining a patent can be long. These companies advertise quick turnaround and low fees because they say, "This is our only business."

Not only do such firms rarely provide the services they say they will, they often inflate the price by adding charges for extra unnecessary services, which also are often not performed. In addition, by turning over your innovation documents to such a company, your invention can be pirated.

Protecting intellectual property is important and can be tricky. In one instance, an entrepreneur described an application and a type of device to perform the application to a technical individual who said he could help the entrepreneur bring the product to market. This product developer was then paid by the entrepreneur to develop a product prototype.

Protecting intellectual property is important, and can be tricky.

When the developer came back to demonstrate his prototype for the entrepreneur, the entrepreneur learned that the developer had filed an application for patent on the device. The developer, who claimed intellectual property rights to the device the entrepreneur had conceptualized, then pressured the entrepreneur for a one-third equity stake in the business. The entrepreneur could have contested the patent filing by claiming to the patent office that he was co-inventor and arguing that the developer had committed fraud. But given the cost involved, he decided simply to go along.

How They Find You

If you are hungry for capital, your name gets around. Con artists running advance-fee frauds and incompetent broker/finders prowl entrepreneur networking events. They shmooze, and they get business cards.

Then they start working the telephones.

The first defense against being conned is to ask for a written agreement and have it reviewed by an attorney familiar with business agreements.

If you meet ten people at an entrepreneur's networking event who say they can help you raise capital for your business, in all likelihood one or maybe two will be highly professional; another one or maybe two will be competent but not much more; and the final six to eight will be incompetent.

Con artists also run classified ads in newspapers and magazines, especially those aimed at entrepreneurs.

How They Operate

As we said earlier, when working with a legitimate broker/finder you will usually be asked to pay a small upfront fee (something on the order of $2,000 to $10,000), monthly expenses, and a sometimes sizable performance fee based on the amount of capital raised.

In a less than legitimate operation, the purported broker/finder/agent/representative will ask you for a large up-front fee (often $50,000 to $100,000). Basically, the scam involves a "you show me your money then I'll show you my money" arrangement, with the entrepreneur being asked to show the money first. Sometimes the advance is called something else, such as a "good-faith deposit." But why should you be making a good-faith deposit?

To allay your fears that a large up-front fee will simply vanish, the con artist proposes that you to put the fee in escrow, so that he knows it's available, and keep it there until the deal closes. You may be asked to deposit this money with an escrow agent suggested by the broker/finder.

DON'T DO IT!

If its a con, the escrow agent is in on it. If you are ever asked to escrow, use an escrow agent who your attorney has dealt with in the past, such as a bank.

Advance-fee frauds can involve huge amounts of money, and the deals are often set up in a complex multitiered way. The end game usually does not involve trying to take millions of dollars from you but rather anywhere from $50,000 to $250,000.

The deals are often constructed so that it looks like you are receiving $10 or $20 million from a syndicate of investors. The fee for such a deal might be 15 percent ($1.5 to $3 million) to be paid from the proceeds. But you are also supposed to pay a separate fee on the front end, sometimes called a work payment order, to cover interest from the time documents are signed until the investor's money is actually deposited in an account for your use. This can be hundreds of thousands of dollars.

Sometimes there is also a little scam within the big scam, a "back-end kicker." This might involve a letter of credit guaranteeing the broker/finder's fee. Since you don't have that kind of money (if you did, you wouldn't need to get involved in a flaky deal like this) you are asked to put up 2 to 5 percent of that amount (anywhere from $30,000 to $75,000) to a third party who will front the deal for you.

These fees, the work payment order, and the fee to the finder's finder, are due on the day of "closing" when all documents are signed. They are usually taken as wire transfers, often through overseas banks. This way you can't stop payment on a check if you get cold feet.

Financing scam networks can be large, depending on the amount of money involved and the complexity of the "deal" being set up. They can involve all sorts of people purportedly helping to facilitate the deal. Trying to find the pea under the shell can be nearly impossible.

Another defense against the con is not to disclose all of the details of your business to anyone unless you know the person or the person has been referred to you by someone you know and trust. Make believe you have signed a confidentiality agreement with yourself.

"References" are often part of the scam. You need to find a way to go outside the network to get information. The bottom line is, if it doesn't feel right to you—and more important maybe, to your attorney or other business advisor—walk away.

The traditional path might be longer and harder, but you won't be taken for a ride.

The National Fraud Information Center can be reached at 1-800-876-7060 and www.aat.com/fraud.

The Advance-Fee Smell Test

While it is easy to be taken in by a line of fast patter from a con artist, there are usually a number of hints that the deal "smells bad." If you or one of your key business advisors don't like the way a proposed deal is coming together, walk away.

The following five steps can be taken to avoid falling for an advance-fee scam. DON'T:

1. Pay an up-front fee before you have done serious due diligence on the potential broker/finder, including checking references they provide and your own sources in the venture investment community.
2. Use an unknown escrow agent. Use only one with whom your attorney has done business. If the other party insists on using only his escrow agent, say no thanks to the deal.
3. Sign any documents until you have them reviewed by your attorney. If your attorney wants to make changes and the other party refuses to negotiate, end the deal.
4. Work with "offshore" funding. Many advance-fee scams use a web of offshore bank accounts to make your wire transfer disappear within a matter of minutes, leaving a trail that dead-ends in a country where bank-secrecy laws are tight.

5. Pay fees electronically; always pay by check. Checks provide an audit trail, and payment can be stopped. If a broker/finder insists on wire or electronic fund transfers (EFTs), find another person to work with.

Chapter Key Points

- Once you begin looking for capital, your name gets around, and con artists can try to rip you off.
- Use your network to find potential investors; don't answer classified ads in newspapers or magazines.
- Don't work with any broker or finder who asks for a large up-front fee.
- If you agree with a broker or finder to escrow part of your fees, always use an escrow agent you have dealt with before, not one suggested by the broker or finder.
- Pay all fees using checks, not by electronic fund or wire transfer.

APPENDIX

A

ENTREPRENEUR PROFILE

The Entrepreneur Profile has nine questions, each of which demand some level of analysis. The answers you give to these nine questions may differ at each stage at which you are seeking capital. (Feel free to photocopy this page and use it regularly.)

1. Who are you as an entrepreneur?

2. What is the geographic area in which you want to start (operate) your venture?

3. What type of business are you in?

4. What and where is your market?

____

____

____

____

5. What round of financing are you seeking? (i.e., seed, mezzanine, third-round VC, etc.)

____

____

____

____

6. How much money do you need in this round of financing?

____

____

____

____

7. What do you need the money for at this time?

____

____

____

____

8. How quickly do you need the money?

____

____

____

____

9. Are you looking to raise capital through debt or equity sale?

____

____

____

____

APPENDIX

B

ANGEL INVESTMENT MEMORANDUM

StartUp, Inc.: Summary of Terms for Proposed Convertible Preferred-Stock Investment

Issuer:	StartUp, Inc. ("**Company**").
Investor:	VC, L.P. ("**Investor**").
Amount of Investment:	$[ ] (the "**Investment Amount**").
Ownership:	____ % (based on $________ fully diluted, post-money valuation with __________ common equivalents).
Type of Security:	Series A Convertible Preferred Stock ("**Preferred**").
Use of Proceeds:	The funds will be used to fund working capital and continued growth of the Company.
Conditions to Closing:	(1) Investor shall complete its due diligence investigation of all aspects of the Company. During the due diligence investigation, the Company agrees to provide Investor and its accountants, attorneys, and other agents and representatives complete access to the Company's facilities, employees, books, records, customers, prospective business pipeline, and suppliers. [(2) The Company shall have provided to the Investor (a) annual financial statements for the fiscal year ended December 31, 20[], and (b) financial statements for the most recent year-to-date period.] **[subject to availability]** (3) All documents required by the Investor, including without limitation a Securities Purchase

Agreement, a Shareholder Agreement, an Investor Rights Agreement, and all required agreements with management and employees.

(4) Absence of litigation or adverse proceedings against the Company.

(5) No material adverse changes shall have occurred with respect to the Company.

Investor shall be under no obligation to continue with its due diligence investigation or to extend the financing contemplated herein if, at any time, the results of its due diligence investigation are not satisfactory to the Investor for any reasons at its sole discretion. In such event, the Investor shall immediately notify the Company, in which case the "Exclusivity" paragraph shall no longer be binding on the Company. In addition, the Company acknowledges that the pre-money valuation contemplated herein is preliminary and subject to the verification of a number of factors to be confirmed in due diligence.

With the Company's complete cooperation, Investor agrees to complete its due diligence investigation on the Company on or prior to _______, 20[].

Anticipated Closing: Assuming satisfactory completion of the due diligence investigation and timely acceptance of this term sheet, the Investor expects to negotiate and complete definitive documentation with the Company by or before ______, 20[] (the date of completion of definitive documentation is the "**Closing Date**").

Rights, Preferences, Privileges,and Restrictions of Preferred:

(1) **Conversion:** Each share of Preferred will be convertible at any time, at the option of the holder, into one share of Common Stock of the Company. The conversion rate will be subject to appropriate adjustment in the event of stock splits, stock dividends, recapitalizations, etc. and as set forth in paragraph (6) below. The Preferred will be automatically converted into Common Stock, at the then applicable conversion rate, in the event of an underwritten public offering of shares in which the net proceeds to the Company are not less than $___________ and the per share issue price is at least [4X] the conversion price per share.

(2) **Mandatory Redemption:** Redeemable at the holders' option at the stated value (plus accrued or accumulated and unpaid dividends thereon) upon the death or voluntary departure of [Founder] or the [fifth] anniversary of the issuance of the Preferred or the [] **[insert other performance milestones]**.

(3) **Liquidation Preference:** In the event of any liquidation or winding up of the Company, the holders of Preferred will be entitled to receive in preference to the Common Stock an amount equal to the stated value (plus accrued or accumulated and unpaid dividends to the date of redemption, to the extent of retained earnings) and to receive a pro rata (in kind) distribution of the amount payable to the holders of Common Stock on an as if converted basis.

A consolidation or merger of the Company (in which the shareholders of the Company before the merger or consolidation do not, after such transaction, own greater than 50.1% of the voting control of the successor corporation) or sale of all or substantially all of its assets will be deemed to be a liquidation for purposes of the liquidation preference for those holders of Preferred that do not convert prior to the closing of such transaction.

(4) **Dividend Provisions:** The Preferred shall be entitled to semiannual cumulative dividends, which shall accrue at the per share annual rate of [8%] of stated value. Such dividends shall be payable, at the Company's option, either in cash or in kind, upon any conversion of the Preferred or any distribution that is calculated on an as if converted basis. The Preferred will also share pari passu on an as if converted basis in any dividends declared on the Common Stock.

(5) **Voting Rights:** Except as with respect to the election of directors and certain protective provisions for extraordinary events or significant changes in the nature of the Company's business, all matters requiring shareholder approval will be submitted to the holders of Preferred and Common, voting together as a single class. The holders of Preferred will have the right to that number of votes equal to the number of shares of Common issuable upon conversion of the Preferred.

	(6) **Antidilution Protection:** The conversion price will be subject to weighted average adjustments for certain issuances below the conversion price then in effect to persons other than officers, employees or consultants.
Information Rights:	The Company will timely furnish the Investor with annual, quarterly, and monthly (actual to budget) financial statements.
Registration Rights:	(1) **Demand Rights:** The holders of the Preferred (or Common Stock issued upon conversion of the Preferred) will have the right, on two occasions, to require the Company to file a Registration Statement covering Common Stock issuable upon conversion of the Preferred (subject to certain standard conditions). These rights shall be exercisable at any time after the earlier of six months after the Company's initial public offering and three years from the Closing Date.
	(2) **Registration on Form S-3:** In addition to the rights under paragraph (1), holders of the Preferred (or Common Stock issued upon conversion of the Preferred) will have the right to require the Company to file an unlimited number of Registration Statements on Form S-3 (subject to certain standard conditions), if such Form is available.
	(3) **Piggyback Registration:** The Investors will be entitled to unlimited "piggyback" registration rights on all registrations of the Company, subject to underwriters' cutbacks.
	(4) **Registration Expenses:** All customary registration expenses will be borne by the Company.
Shareholders Agreement:	The Company will secure a Shareholders Agreement among the Investor, the Company, and all principal shareholders, providing the Investor with the following:
	(1) **Preemptive Right:** Investor will have a right of first refusal with respect to any proposed sale of Common Stock or securities convertible into Common Stock by the Company to the extent necessary for the Investor to maintain its percentage interest in the Common Stock on an as converted basis, which right will terminate upon a public offering.
	(2) **Right of First Refusal:** The Company, and then Investor, will have a right of first refusal with respect to

any proposed resale of Common Stock by any stockholder, which right will terminate upon a public offering.

(3) **Co-Sale Provision:** The current holders of Common Stock will grant Investor a right to participate on a pro rata basis in any sales of the Company's Common Stock made by them.

(4) **Take-Along Provision:** The current holders of Common Stock will agree to enter into any sale transaction with respect to their Common Stock or the Company that is approved by the holders of a majority of the issued and outstanding capital stock of the Company.

Board Representation: The Board will consist of [7] members. Unless a default under the Purchase Agreement occurs, and is continuing, the Preferred will elect [2] directors, the Common will elect [3] directors, and together they will elect the [sixth and seventh] directors. The charter or bylaws will contain appropriate protective provisions under the laws of the Company's jurisdiction of incorporation.

Preferred Protective Provisions: The Company shall not amend its charter or bylaws or take any other corporate action without the approval by the holders of at least a [majority/super-majority] of the then outstanding Preferred, if such amendment or corporate action would:

- in any manner (a) authorize, create, amend or issue any class or series of capital stock ranking, either as to payment of dividends, distribution of assets or redemption, prior to or on parity with the Preferred or (b) authorize, create, amend or issue any shares of any class or series or any bonds, debentures, notes or other obligations convertible into or exchangeable for, or having optional rights to purchase, any shares having any such priority or on parity with the Preferred;
- in any manner alter or change the designation or the powers, preferences or rights or the qualifications, limitations or restrictions of the Preferred;
- reclassify shares of Common Stock, or any other shares of any class or series of capital stock hereinafter created junior to the Preferred into shares of any class or series of capital stock ranking, either as

to payment of dividends, distribution of assets or redemption, prior to or on parity with the Preferred;

- increase the authorized number of shares of Preferred, issue additional shares of Preferred or authorize any other class or series of capital stock of the Company or its subsidiaries;
- result in any substantial change in the nature of the business engaged in by the Company;
- create, authorize, reserve or involve the issuance of more than an aggregate of [ ] shares of Common Stock in connection with options to purchase shares of Common Stock heretofore or hereafter issued to officers, employees or directors of the Company pursuant to any plan, agreement or other arrangements, including without limitation, options granted pursuant to the [**insert names of any plan(s)**];
- result in the redemption, repurchase or other acquisition by the Company of capital stock or other securities of the Company or its subsidiaries, except for (a) contractually obligated, nondiscretionary repurchases or other acquisitions of capital stock of the Company from employees of the Company upon such employees' termination of employment from the Company pursuant to the terms and conditions of agreements which provide the Company the right to repurchase such capital stock upon such termination of employment and (b) the redemption or repurchase of the Preferred pursuant to the terms thereof;
- result in (a) any liquidation, dissolution, winding-up or similar transaction of the Company or its subsidiaries or (b) a sale of all or substantially all of the assets of the Company or its subsidiaries or a merger, consolidation, sale of capital stock or other transaction in which the holders of capital stock of the Company and its subsidiaries, in the aggregate, immediately prior to such transaction will not hold, immediately after such transaction, more than 50 percent of the aggregate voting power of outstanding capital stock of the surviving corporation;
- result in the incurrence of additional indebtedness of the Company or its subsidiaries, including, without limitation, any loan agreement, promissory note (or

other evidence of indebtedness), mortgage, security agreement or lease, or any commitment for any of the foregoing, whether in a single transaction or a series of related transactions, in an amount exceeding [$50,000];

- result in a sale, lease or assignment of any assets of, or interests in assets held by, the Company or its subsidiaries outside the ordinary course of business, or a series of related sales, leases or assignments, having an aggregate value exceeding [$50,000];
- result in a capital expenditure of the Company in excess of [$50,000];
- result in the removal or election of any corporate officer, or the termination or hiring of any employee earning annualized compensation in excess of [$100,000];
- result in the formation of a contract or any other transaction with any holder of Common Stock or any affiliate of any holder of Common Stock;
- result in the hiring or engagement, as an employee, consultant or service provider, of any member of, or entity controlled by, any holder of Common Stock's family or any other person or entity affiliated with any holder of Common Stock;
- result in additional securities of the Company's subsidiaries being issued or would in any way alter the current ownership structure of the Company's subsidiaries;
- in any way amend, alter, restate or otherwise change its charter or bylaws, or those of the Company's subsidiaries, as they are currently in effect;
- reduce the amount payable to the holders of Preferred upon (a) the voluntary or involuntary liquidation, dissolution or winding up of the Company or (b) any acquisition of all or substantially all of the assets of the Company, or an acquisition of the Company by another corporation or entity by consolidation, merger or other reorganization or combination in which the holders of the Company's outstanding voting stock immediately prior to such transaction do not own, immediately after such transaction, securities representing more than 50 percent (50%) of the voting power of the corporation or other entity surviving such transaction; or

- result in the grant of registration rights to any other class or series of capital stock of the Company or its subsidiaries more favorable than or on parity with those granted to the holders of the Preferred.

Employment Contract: The Company shall enter into an employment contract with [Founders] on mutually agreeable terms including appropriate nondisclosure and noncompetition covenants.

Noncompetition Agreements: Unless such agreements already exist in a form satisfactory to the Investor, the Company shall enter into one-year noncompetition agreements with all officers and key employees identified by Investor.

Key Man Insurance: The Company shall obtain and maintain term life insurance on [Founder] for [$_________], with proceeds payable to the Company, for the purpose of redeeming the Preferred if the Investor elects to redeem. **[tied to redemption trigger for death of Founder]**

Exclusivity: Except with respect to the Company's discussions with [________________], for a period of [30 days] from the date of acceptance of this term sheet, the Company and each principal shareholder of the Company shall (i) deal exclusively with the Investor in connection with the issuance or sale of any equity or debt securities or assets of the Company or any merger or consolidation involving the Company; (ii) shall not solicit, or engage others to solicit, offers for the purchase or acquisition of any equity or debt securities or assets of the Company or for any merger or consolidation involving the Company; (iii) shall not negotiate with or enter into any agreements or understandings with respect to such transaction; and (iv) shall inform the Investor of any such solicitation or offer. Each of the parties agrees to cooperate and negotiate in good faith during the exclusive period.

Expenses: If the Closing occurs or if the Investor does not proceed with the transaction due to material misrepresentation to Investor by the Company regarding its business, then the Company will bear the Investor's out-of-pocket, legal, consulting, and other expenses incurred with respect to the transaction, up to a maximum of [$30,000].

Other Conditions: The Company shall take any and all necessary actions with respect to amending its charter to [consolidate all existing classes of capital stock into a single class of voting Common Stock and] permit the issuance of the Preferred with its attendant rights, preferences, privileges and restrictions.

Expiration:	This proposal shall expire [_________], 20[].

Except for the terms of this Summary under the heading "Exclusivity," and "Expenses" which upon execution will be binding on the parties, this letter is not a binding agreement or an offer. This letter does not contain all material terms upon which the parties intend to agree and is only intended to provide a basis on which to begin to work on a final agreement. A binding commitment will only be made pursuant to the execution of a definitive purchase agreement mutually acceptable to the Company and the Investor and only after all of the Conditions and Conditions Precedent noted above have been satisfied.

We look forward to working with you to complete our due diligence and continuing the relationship that we have developed to date.

VC, L.P.

By: ______________________________

Title: ______________________________

StartUp, Inc.

By: ______________________________

Title: ______________________________

APPENDIX

C

LAW FIRM SELECTION CRITERIA AND EVALUATION

Item	Firm 1	Firm 2	Firm 3
Compatibility Integrity Ability to work together			
Competence/Track Record IPOs DPOs PPMs Term sheets			
Commitment Level of contact Resources Interest			
Contacts Angels Venture Capitalists Underwriters			
Costs IPO DPO PPM Term Sheet			

Item	Firm 1	Firm 2	Firm 3
Overall impression of value add			
Other comments (Scale 1 [low] to 10 [high])			

Index

Interested in downloading the tools, forms, and reference materials found in this book so you can modify them for your personal use?

Visit www.venturetechcorp.com

On this site you may also

- submit a question for online answer
- view other people's questions and the answers provided
- view additional material of interest to entrepreneurs
- link to other sites for entrepreneurs
- provide your own "war stories" about raising capital